Advance Praise

"One of the things I love about Dan T. Bloom's books is the ease at which they can be read and, more importantly, understood. And certainly, this applies to Dan's new book, The *TLS Continuum Field Guide!* Once again, Dan has clearly demonstrated his knowledge of the three components within the TLS Continuum, namely the Theory of Constraints, Lean, and Six Sigma. I am particularly impressed with Chapters 3, 4 and 5, as Dan presents the principles of each of the individual components of the TLS Continuum. Why do I especially like these three chapters? Like any methodology, understanding the basic principles of each component in any methodology forms the basis for how and why things work. And Dan does an outstanding job in presenting the basic principles of TOC, Lean, and Six Sigma. The other thing that I truly enjoy about Dan's new book is the emphasis he places on the Theory of Constraints. I have been using the Theory of Constraints (TOC) for quite a few years simply because I believe it is the most vital part of any improvement initiative. I'm not saying that Lean and Six Sigma aren't important, because they are. What I am saying is that using TOC in conjunction with Lean and Six Sigma, the improvement efforts will be focused and directed on that part of the system that will maximize profitability. Throughout Dan's new book, it's very clear that Dan has embraced the importance of TOC and delivers the TLS Continuum beautifully! It is with deep humility that I congratulate Dan for writing another incredible book and I highly recommend this book to everyone! In fact, in my opinion, the *TLS Continuum Field Guide* is Dan's best book to date! Great job Dan and please keep writing!!"

Bob Sproull, *Goldratt Jonah*
Author, Focus and Leverage

"Daniel's *TLS Continuum Field Guide,* his latest book, encompasses all the tenets of Lean Six Sigma and Continuous Improvement science practices and methodology based on empirical and theoretical foundations. From the perspective of a former public-school educator and established and successful HR professional, his experience, insight and understanding where organizations fall short in their operations, processes, and, most importantly, their leadership and cultures, is second to none! If you are seeking inspiration and motivation to move yourself and your organization forward as a professional, regardless of your sector, this field book is an excellent place to start. I highly recommend it."

Bill Horniak
HEI & K12 Education Advisor & Consultant

"Blending the Theory of Constraints and Lean Six Sigma (TLS) increases efficiency and enhances data-driven decision-making. Daniel T. Bloom provides an excellent roadmap on how to accomplish this effort."

Terra Vanzant Stern, Ph.D.
CEO of SSD Global Solutions,
Lean and Agile Project Management author

"*TLS Continuum Field Guide* is an absolute must-read for anyone who wants to acquire a masterful foundation of Lean Sigma along with various tools, techniques, and applications. Daniel has done a wonderful job blending the concepts with real hands-on examples that are applicable across all industries and functions. One of the best 'How-to Books' I've read in years."

William Mazurek
President of Maz-Tec & Associates,
Adjunct Professor/Master Black Belt

"In war, sports, and politics, we often declare one side true and virtuous and the other side foolish and evil, but there is always something that can be learned from both sides. The "war" between the supporters of Lean, Six Sigma, and the Theory of Constraints is the same. In his latest book, Daniel T. Bloom presents a TLS Continuum manifesto – a clear picture explaining how the Theory of Constraints, Lean, and Six Sigma can and should be combined into a continuum (rather than a cycle). If you enjoyed *The Goal*, but were left wondering how to combine Goldratt's ideals with the scientific rigor of Six Sigma, then this book is for you."

Jeremy Garrett, CSSBB, CQE, CRE

"In his new book *The TLS Continuum Field Guide: How Theory of Constraints, Lean and Six Sigma Will Transform Your Operations and Process Flow*, Dan Bloom captures a methodology and the necessary tool sets to identify, solve and implement solutions on any type of problem we might face. He reminds us of the power of TOC to look across our Socio-Technical systems and identify the constraints, while reviewing the core principles of both Lean and Six Sigma, plus the concepts/tools to identify system goals and scope. Being a Human Capital professional, I believe that Organizational Change management is one of Dan's "native" languages, as such he has managed to weave this process and tools throughout the TLS Continuum. If you are a technical professional and process is a native language, it would be beneficial to spend some time learning how to help an organization manage the stress of change. With the case made, Dan introduces us to the TLS Continuum Manifesto and Implementation plan. Walking through each element of the TLS framework, Dan offers effective strategies to begin implementing each Pillar.

We all know that continuous improvement is a journey. Dan's new book has inspired me to continue my personal journey become a better problem solver through learning new concepts, methodologies, and tools. My hope is that it will inspire you too!"

Jeff Summers
Senior Enterprise Lean Six Sigma Manager,
Littelfuse, Chicago, IL
Formerly with Motorola University

"This book is a one-of-a-kind business book that is a practical guide for anyone interested in a holistic approach to continuous process improvement. Dan Bloom has done an incredible job of integrating the principles of Theory of Constraints, Lean and Six Sigma into a logically cohesive and practically relevant framework for achieving operational excellence in every enterprise. It is a must-read for every practitioner in the subject."

Phil Samuel, Ph.D.
AWS Operational Excellence Leader,
Amazon

"This is a must-read for every Improvement Leader! The simplicity of the prose also makes it very palatable for novices, with abundant, exciting facts and stories. Most importantly, if you are a leader and you are not practiced in Continuous Improvement, the TLS Continuum addresses the paradigms ("Whack-a-Mole") that have prevented organizations from implementing an improvement program. We live in an ecosystem, so we must respect that deterministic Improvement Programs will run out of gas since they have a start and end. The TLS Continuum enables foraging to continue to build the momentum of excellence in your organization."

Jim DeVries
Founder, President
The Enhance International Group

The TLS Continuum
Field Guide

This book provides a roadmap for implementing a powerful technique that will reduce waste and accelerate flow within a process—the TLS Continuum methodology.

The letters TLS stand for the three components of the continuum. The letter T stands for the Theory of Constraints. Created by Dr. Eliyahu Goldratt in his book *The Goal*, it is a critically thinking-based system for determining where the obstacles lie within your organization. Through the use of various tools, it asks you to determine where the obstacles are in the process. The purpose of the Theory of Constraints (TOC) involvement in the continuum is to determine what needs to be changed, how to change it, and how to accomplish the change. TOC operates at the level of the chain looking for the weakest link. It is in essence the hypothesis of the problem-solving method overall.

The letter L stands for Lean. Most organizations are familiar with the concept of Lean. It is centered around removing waste from the organizational processes so that the customer receives their orders faster. Understand that faster may not mean cheaper or better quality; it means only that we expedite the process.

The final letter is S, and it represents the concepts of Six Sigma. The primary goal here is to remove variation from the processes.

If we combine the three letters of the acronym, what we find is that the TLS Continuum is organized around a process in itself. We use the TOC to locate and identify the obstacles within the system. What is holding up the process? Where is the weakest link in the process? With the introduction of TOC, the system asks you to elevate the obstacles and determine how to remove them.

We use Lean to do what it is meant to do, and that is to remove the obstacles. We have identified the obstacle and determined through the critical thinking tools how to remove that obstacle and then use the Lean tools to actually remove the waste.

Finally, the system utilizes the Six Sigma tools to create the standard of work and remove any variation from the process. When we do this, we have completed the improvement process by creating a progressive system for resolving the problems that occur within many organizations. It is an evidence-based effort to identify, remove, and improve the system so the problem does not recur.

The TLS Continuum Field Guide

How Theory of Constraints, Lean, and Six Sigma Will Transform Your Operations and Process Flow

Daniel T. Bloom SPHR, SSBB

Routledge
Taylor & Francis Group

A PRODUCTIVITY PRESS BOOK

First published 2024
by Routledge
605 Third Avenue, New York, NY 10158

and by Routledge
4 Park Square, Milton Park, Abingdon, Oxon, OX14 4RN

Routledge is an imprint of the Taylor & Francis Group, an informa business

ISBN: 978-0-367-13923-0 (hbk)
ISBN: 978-0-367-13915-5 (pbk)
ISBN: 978-0-429-02919-6 (ebk)

DOI: 10.4324/9780429029196

Typeset in Garamond
by Apex CoVantage, LLC

Contents

Figures

Part 1: The Foundation: The TLS Continuum

Part 2: Continuous Process Improvement Journey

Part 3: Defining the Boundaries

Part 4: Identification of the System Constraints

Part 5: Elevate the System Constraints

Part 6: TLS Continuum Implementation

Foreword

Daniel T. Bloom and I share an obsession: the conviction that there is a lot to be gained by combining the ideas of the Theory of Constraints, Lean, and Six Sigma (TLS). Most professionals choose just one, most often Lean, or sometimes two (Lean Six Sigma). Whereas most people underline the differences and emphasize the incompatibilities, Daniel T. Bloom looks for synergies and positive reinforcement. He recommends that we build and maintain a system based on the strengths of each of these three approaches to improve operations management and process flow.

It was this shared involvement with "TLS" (please forgive us proposing yet another acronym) that also led both Daniel and I to link up with Bob Sproull, another aficionado of this cocktail. And interestingly, the three of us were also drawn to William Dettmer's Logical Thinking Process, which is part of the Theory of Constraints.

This book will make you realize that the Theory of Constraints, Lean, and Six Sigma are often saying the same thing, but each with their own vocabulary. To always seek to improve flow. To be customer-centric. To better focus by not doing what we should not be doing. To always double-check whether what we are trying to improve is really necessary and truly adds value. To insist on the importance of standardized work. To incessantly hunt down waste like Taiichi Ohno recommended. To always be guided by the voice of the customer. To think scientifically. To think logically.

Daniel T. Bloom emphasizes the necessity of properly defining the purpose of the organization and the boundaries of the system you are trying to improve. He insists on the importance of standing back and defining the goal of the organization (using the goal tree) and how best to get closer to it using the TLS Continuum.

He proposes a TLS Continuum Manifesto consisting of ten basic principles to guide readers in how to implement TLS.

It is no surprise that in these ten principles the people component is significant, since Daniel has always reminded us of the importance of looking at operational excellence through the lens of human resources.

Pure Six Sigma (without Lean) is no longer used much in corporations. As a result, we threw out the baby with the bathwater, and we claim we can strive for excellence without using statistical analysis for problem solving or measuring the "voice of the customer" (VOC). This book argues that the quantified monitoring of VOC should be used more often. Indeed, the VOC is one of the three pillars of the TLS Continuum implementation plan. Daniel reminds us that we must learn to think like our customer. He argues convincingly that in today's marketplace with instant comparison of products and service offerings, that customer loyalty has become nearly nonexistent, thereby reinforcing the need for continual rigorous monitoring of customer reactions.

If you find that the silo mentality of the TOC, Lean, and Six Sigma communities are regrettable, you will enjoy this book. You will be constantly challenged to consider new, fresh combinations. What does Karou Ishikawa's fishbone diagram have in common with Eliyahu Goldratt's current reality tree? Is Lean's organizational purpose the same as the Theory of Constraints' "goal"? Why should you sometimes use Dettmer's Logical Thinking Process during your Gemba walk? Why not implement Goldratt's rules of flow using PDCA? And so on.

Daniel T. Bloom's extensive experience in human resources management is one of the strengths of this book. It transpires in many places, from the omnipresence of "people" issues in his description of Lean to his preoccupations with organizational alignment as one of his pillars of TLS. His human resources background gives weight to his arguments in favor of cross-functional teams and his recommendations for defining team roles and responsibilities.

One last quality of this book is that it is up to date with the latest development of ideas. You will find the latest thinking by Jeffrey Liker on leadership alongside the latest rules of flow by Efrat Goldratt-Ashlag.

In this *TLS Continuum Field Guide*, Dan T. Bloom's seventh book, he offers us his accumulated experience and wisdom of open-minded organizational improvement. His recipe takes nearly all of Lean, adds a great deal of Six Sigma, and sprinkles a lot of Theory of Constraints all over it. Bon appetit.

Phillip Marris
CEO, Marris Consulting
Paris, France
Experts in the Theory of Constraints consulting and training

Preface

I have a question for you, and I want you to think about it before you answer. Have you ever taken an educational opportunity or participated in a meeting that changed your life for the foreseeable future?

I have had several of these over the course of my lifetime. First was attending a meeting in which the speaker was Col. Edward L. Hubbard (USAF retired) who was a prisoner of war (POW) in the infamous prison camp dubbed the "Hanoi Hilton" for 2936 days, who discussed the wonder of human potential in his book *Escape from the Box: The Wonder of Human Potential.* In his presentation he talked about seeing the bigger picture rather than the narrow view we so often take.

The second event, if you will, came over 20 years ago when someone recommended that I pick up a business novel called *The Goal* by Eliyahu Goldratt. Reading *The Goal* led me to subsequently read his additional books which followed the story in *The Goal* (*It's Not Luck, Critical Chain, Necessary But Not Sufficient,* and *Isn't It Obvious?*). Reading Goldratt's works started me on the path of looking at the world from a different view. In fact, in 2001, I took Goldratt's Theory of Constraints and applied the concept to the corporate mobility industry in an article for *Mobility Magazine* titled "Driving the Relocation 500." This new perspective was to look at the various processes that came into my life with a logical thinking basis. Critically viewing the world from that prism changed my life both professionally and personally. I began to critically look at every process that I was presented with, whether the process made sense. I have to admit I found more that did not than ones that did.

The third event came about during a job search. I asked myself whether I had all the necessary credentials that the marketplace was seeking. It came down to a choice between earning an MBA and getting an additional certification. This one as a Six Sigma Black Belt. I ended up making the choice to go beyond the concepts from Goldratt and earning the Six Sigma certification. I reached out to the local community college, who over a time span of a little over a year and a half, offered training in Six Sigma leading to certification as a Six Sigma Black Belt. Considering the events that had transpired, I began to consider whether there was a way to combine all of this system knowledge into one concise methodology.

About this time, I found in the local bookstore a copy of Bob Sproull's *The Ultimate Improvement Cycle* which answered the question in my mind by combining the three methodologies. It allowed me to utilize a battery of tools that forced me to look even deeper into the methodology.

Reviewing this new normal methodology, I discovered a small deficiency in what I was seeing. The deficiency was a problem in viewing the continuous process improvement effort as a cycle. Here is why. The website Lana Labs tells us that

> During a process cycle, a certain path (process path) is followed through the process. Individual process cycles can be different within the same process, for example, if the process contains an OR decision. Each process cycle, but also each activity, has a cycle-time. Different process variants arise due to different cycle options.[1]

The idea of the continuous process improvement effort being viewed as a cycle with this never-ending circle, with one step leading into another seemed to miss a valuable concept as presented.

With the publication of *The Field Guide to Achieving HR Excellence through Six Sigma* in 2016, I changed the term ultimate improvement cycle to that of the TLS Continuum. The reason for the change was that I did not view the effort as a cycle, but rather a chain of events that finished one chain and began simultaneously a new chain. I utilized this new term in all my learning and development efforts going forward. In the interim since 2016, I have never fully explored the parameters of the TLS Continuum in its entirety. That is the purpose of this field guide.

Over the course of 23 chapters, I will explain what the TLS Continuum is and how the continuum can be utilized in your organization. In Part 1 (covering Chapters 1–6), we will discuss what the TLS Continuum is. Further, we will look at the various components of the TLS Continuum and how they are interrelated toward our eventual goal. In Part 2 (covering Chapters 7–9), we will look at the continuous process improvement journey and how we construct our goals or problem statements. In Part 3 (covering Chapters 10–12), we look at how our process improvement efforts must stay within certain boundaries in order for the effort to be successful. While we need to implement full thinking into our process resolution, we do not need it to go out haphazardly into the organization into areas that do not bring value to the process. In Part 4 (Chapters 13–15) we begin to lay out the process of implementing the TLS Continuum through the identification of the system constraints. Once we have identified the system constraints, it is necessary that we elevate the constraints, so they become a system priority. In Part 5 (Chapters 16–17), we look at the process of removing non-value-added steps and the use of one of the TLS Continuum tools: the drum-buffer-rope system. In Part 6 (Chapters 18–23) we discuss what to do with the process resources that do not affect the system constraints in any way. They are part of the organizational processes, but at this given moment, they are not of primary concern. However, we still need to utilize them. We also recognize that when we resolve one system constraint, a new one will appear. These chapters also look at how we go about recognizing the new constraints and how they are handled. Chapters 22–23 look at a model of a TLS Continuum implementation model that you can use to bring the whole concept together in your organizational process delivery to create a more vibrant effort to meet the needs of your customers.

Note

1 Definition of Process Cycle. *LanaLabs*. https://lanalabs.com/en/glossary/process-cycle/#:~:text=During%20a%20process%20cycle%2C%20a, activity%2C%20has%20a%20cycle%20time

Acknowledgments

As I reach the point of three-quarters of a century on this globe I call home, this book you are reading may be the swan song of my career. I have asked you to join me on a journey of transformation that I have already taken on my own. This unexpected journey has provided me with a new perspective on the processes around us, with its rewards and its challenges. While I continue to empower clients and others through virtual opportunities, this book was in some ways the culmination of my unexpected journey that I hope you decide to also join.

Prior to his death in 2011, Dr. Eliyahu Goldratt discussed the concept of standing on the shoulders of giants. By this, he meant "using the understanding gained by major thinkers who have gone before in order to make intellectual progress."

I, likewise, have had the opportunity to stand on the shoulders of giants, who have guided me along my journey to this place. It began back in 2001, when I reached out to Dr. James Holt, a Goldratt Jonah and professor emeritus of the University of Washington, Vancouver, who took me on my personal Shu Ha Ri process as he walked me through the Theory of Constraints as it applied to the corporate mobility process, which resulted in the *Mobility Magazine* article "Driving the Relocation 500." I am honored by the individuals who have contributed to my past works, including Dr. John Sullivan of the University of San Francisco, Dr. David Cohen of DS Cohen & Associates, and Phil Samuels of Lean Concepts.

Still additionally, there are those who fit Goldratt's definition of giants. Dr. Larry Miller of Management Mediations, a college classmate; Jeff Summers, formerly of Motorola University and currently with LittleFuse; Bob Sproull, another Goldratt Jonah, who has not only helped with background on the content of my books but has also become a friend; and there is my partner-in-crime, Julie McMullian who is a continuous improvement engineer with a Fortune 100 corporation and was my partner through the Black Belt training.

Last but not least, Toyota Production System advocates for individuals starting this journey to have a sensei or mentor to guide them along the path. I found such a major asset in the form of William Mazurek, who in 2008–2009 served as the instructor for my Six Sigma Black Belt certification and to this day continues to be a friend, mentor, and sounding board for ideas and concepts as I took this journey.

I also wish to thank my fellow improvement specialists who were willing to share their knowledge and experiences to make both their knowledge base and mine that much larger.

Finally, I would be remiss if I did not express my thanks and appreciation to the people at Taylor & Francis who took a chance a decade ago with essentially a first-time writer and provided me with a platform to run with my ideas that were, at the time and still are, out of the norm of the way some think about this continuous process improvement movement. Special thanks go out to Michael Sinocchi and Iris Fahrer, who took my ideas on paper and turned them into excellent final products.

I also would like to thank Phillip Marris for agreeing to write the Foreword to this work especially. We are entering new ground as to how we look at the world and how we improve it.

About the Author

 **Daniel T. Bloom** is a well-respected author, speaker, and human resources (HR) strategist who during his career has worked as a contingency executive recruiter, member of the internal HR staff of a Fortune 1000 corporation, an HR consultant, and a corporate relocation director for several real estate firms. He is an active participant within the HR social media scene, having maintained blogs since 2006, and has written over 40 articles, which have appeared online and in print, in addition to authoring six books. He is certified as a Senior Professional in Human Resources by the Human Resources Certification Institute and as a Six Sigma Black Belt through the Applied Technology Program at St. Petersburg College. He is the founder and chief executive officer of Daniel T. Bloom and Associates, Inc., an HR consulting firm dedicated to empowering organizational change in the HR community.

Other Books by Daniel T. Bloom

Achieving HR Excellence through Six Sigma
Achieving HR Excellence through Six Sigma (2nd Edition)
Employee Empowerment: The Prime Component of Sustainable Change Management
Field Guide to Achieving HR Excellence through Six Sigma
Just Get Me There: A Journey through Corporate Relocation
Reality, Perception and Your Company's Workplace Culture
The Excellent Education System: Using Six Sigma to Transform Schools

TLS Continuum Acronyms

ASQ	American Society for Quality
BIHR	Business Impact Human Resources
BMGI	Center for Strategic Problem Solving
BPMS	Business Process Management System
CAD	Computer Assisted Design
CAP	Change Acceleration Process
CEO	Chief Executive Officer
CFO	Chief Financial Officer
CHRO	Chief Human Resource Officer
COE	Center of Excellence
COPQ	Cost of Poor Quality
COR	Cost of Recruitment Worksheet
CSF	Critical Success Factor
DDC	Dow Design and Construction
DISC	Dominance-Influence-Steadiness-Conscientiousness
DMAIC	Define-Measure-Analyze-Improve-Control
DPMO	Defects Per Million Opportunities
DSS	Design for Six Sigma
EHS	Environmental, Health, and Safety
FMEA	Failure Modes and Effects Analysis
FMLA	Family Medical and Leave Act
FT	Functional Transformation (Honeywell)
FTE	Full-Time Equivalent Employee
GAAP	General Accepted Accounting Practices
GE	General Electric
GPHR	Global Professional in Human Resources
HR	Human Resources
HRM	Human Resource Management

HUE	Honeywell User Experience
INCOSE	International Council on System Engineering
IO	Intermediate Objectives Map
ISLSS	International Standard for Lean Six Sigma
ISO	International Organization for Standardization
IT	Information Technology
IVR	Interactive Voice Response
JUSE	Union of Japanese Scientists and Engineers
KPI	Key Performance Indicators
MSD	Musculoskeletal Disorder
NLRB	National Labor Relations Board
LSS	Lean Six Sigma
LTV	Lifetime Value
MAIC	Measure-Analyze-Improve-Control
MBTI	Myers-Briggs Trait Indicator
NC	Necessary Conditions
NPS	Net Promoter Score
OSHA	Occupational Safety and Health Administration
PC	Personal Computer
PDA	Personal Digital Assistant
PHR	Professional in Human Resources
QFD	Quality Function Deployment
R&R	Repeatability and Reproducibility
ROWE	Results Oriented Work Environment
RSD	Recruiting Strategy Discussion
SHRM	Society for Human Resource Management
SIPOC	Supplier-Input-Process-Output-Client
SPHR	Senior Professional in Human Resources
TLS	Theory of Constraints–Lean–Six Sigma
TOC	Theory of Constraints
TQM	Total Quality Management
TPS	Toyota Production System
VOC	Voice of the Customer
VPD	Velocity Product Development
VUCA	Volatility, Uncertainty, Chaos, Ambiguity
WIFM	What's in It for Me
WIP	Work in Process

1

THE FOUNDATION
The TLS Continuum

Take a moment out of your reading this and think about your organization. Every organization is involved in some form of continuous process improvement. Some of you may be doing it informally, but you are still doing it. So, answer a simple question. Which process improvement methodology are you using?

Some of you will respond that you are using the Toyota Production System. Others will state they are using the Shingo methodology. Still others will say they are using the Six Sigma methodology.

To resolve some inner fighting, still others will say they are using the Lean Six Sigma methodology. I attended a conference awhile back where someone told me, "We don't do Six Sigma, we only do Lean." But here is the real essence of the purpose of Part 1 of this book. Why would you only bake a third of a pie?

Now that we are coming out of this global pandemic COVID-19 somewhat, you might be considering hosting a get-together for friends and family. Part of your preparations might very well include baking cakes and pies for the celebrations that will soon follow. Many of you will follow recipes that have been handed down over generations in your families. But what if someone came to you and said, "This year why don't you only make a third of a pie?" Sound ridiculous?

I in essence ask the same question when I hear the statement that someone only does Lean or only does Six Sigma. This is like baking a third of a pie. Let me explain the argument.

In my article in *QHSE Magazine* I introduced the concept of the TLS Continuum. It is the continuum which comprises the three parts to the pie.

DOI: 10.4324/9780429029196-1

The first third of the pie is the identification of the process obstacle. The Theory of Constraints (TOC) tells us what needs to change, what to change it to, and how to make the change happen. Basically the TOC side of the pie enables us to identify through strategic thinking tools what the problem is that we are experiencing. From there, the critical thinking tools identify what the critical success factors are to reach the goal of removing the obstacle. We cannot just go out into the business world and say we have this goal to remove obstacle X without identifying what will tell us that we have reached the goal. However, these two steps are necessary, but not sufficient without a detailed look at the necessary conditions that must be present in order to create the critical success factors. The first part of the pie therefore lays the groundwork for the remainder of the system of continuous improvement. We have essentially met the first part of the TLS goal of delivering the product or service faster, better, and cheaper. We have identified how to make the end result *better* with a higher level of quality.

The second part of the pie is Lean. Productivity Press's *LeanSpeak* (2002) defines Lean as a system "that has relatively little non-value adding waste and maximum flow." It is the second part of the pie which delivers the end product or service *faster.* The primary function of Lean is to remove the obstacle and the accompanying waste. The obstacle that we identified in the TOC stage is slowing down the system due to the inability of the system to deliver the voice of the customer when they need the service delivered. This can occur because the process has added steps which to someone made sense but does not to the customer. This can occur because we have introduced into the system demands that overtax the system, causing longer delivery times.

The final third of the pie is that of Six Sigma. The intent of Six Sigma is to ensure that our processes meet three criteria. First the problem-solving method creates a standard of work. We do not remove the ability for an organization to innovate, as this is critical for organizational competitiveness in today's marketplace. It does, however, put in place a system that is the same every time we begin to complete the process. If we are going to hire a new human capital asset for the organization, the hiring process components are the same each and every time. One of the characteristics of a Six Sigma process is that it is repeatable. The second part of the process is that it is credible. This means that the data we use to implement the change is based on verifiable data from the operation.

The TLS Continuum focuses on continuously improving the *transactional process quality, getting the product or service to market faster,* and *reducing cost while improving the price to the customer.* It is the total pie that delivers the promise of the TLS Continuum to produce measurable continuous process improvement.

In Part 1, we will look at the essence of the TLS Continuum. Beginning with Chapter 1, we will look at why we choose to call it a continuum instead of a cycle. In Chapter 2, we will take an in-depth look at the TLS Continuum. In Chapters 3–6 we will look at the operating principles behind each of the components of the process improvement pie. We conclude this part with a look at the TLS Continuum framework, where the three parts come together in your organization.

Chapter 1

A Cycle vs. a Continuum

In his article "Whole System Architecture: A Model for Building the Lean Organization,"[1] my Parsons College classmate Dr. Lawrence M. Miller, president of Management Mediations, suggests that our organizations are composed of two separate but interdependent systems.

The first is a technical system which represents all of our work processes. It is important to establish at this point that no matter what the size of your organization is, everything we do is governed by a process. At the same time, each of our processes is part of a system of some sort. Further, each of the systems requires the same resources (suppliers, inputs, processes, outputs, and end users) which exist in some sort of environment.

The second system is referred to as the social system, which covers our human capital asset's skills, their motivation, and the way the organization arrives at decision-making. The two systems are equally important and must be aligned with each other. The combination of the two is called the socio-technical system.

Further understand that all of our systems (processes) have at their root four distinct strategies to implement a process improvement effort. The Explorance.com[2] blog tells us that these strategies are as follows:

1) We need to identify the need for change. Using the tools that will be discussed throughout this work, we need to discuss what is in it for the organization. We must be clear as to the challenges and the rewards for making the required changes.
2) We can't hope to improve the organizational system unless we know what is going on with the process. We need to determine why something is happening.

DOI: 10.4324/9780429029196-2

3) Change does not come by itself. The TLS Continuum is no different than the other methodologies in that their success is contingent on the corporate mantra becoming what we are all seeking to make the improvements in the process.

4) Once we have made the changes, we need to develop the path to make the improvements based on a sound strategy.

Dr. Miller further tells us that many of today's organizations are based on yesterday's assumptions about how we handle not only the problems but also its people and the processes on which those problem-solving efforts are determined. Part of the outcome of these assumptions is that we operate two separate kinds of systems. Each of them has their own ramifications for the organization as a whole.

1.1 A Closed System

Your dictionary defines a cycle as a complete set of events or phenomena recurring in the same sequence.[3] In a typical closed system, we start at the beginning and work our way to the end.

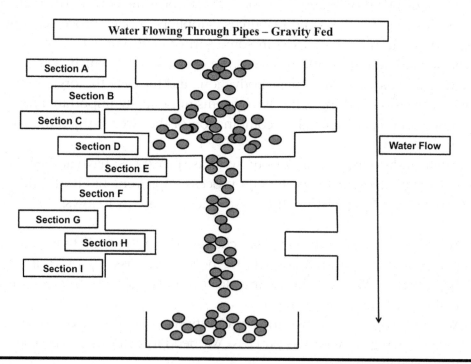

Figure 1.1   A closed system.

The website Smart Capital Mind tell us that a closed system is defined as a system "that has no interaction with any elements outside the system itself."[4]

From our perspective, the methodologies that we discussed earlier are all examples of a closed system. Each methodology has its own process designs, and the expectation is that you repeat the process as is every time. The process runs its gamut, and at the end the organization is presented with the opportunity to start over or stop the process in its entirety.

One of the characteristics of a closed system is that the improvement team tends to arrive at their decision-making efforts from a narrow perspective. We have this problem, and we have had it happen before, and we resolved it. The belief is that the solutions we used in the past will work again. It is characteristic of Dr. Richard Feynman's statement, when he tells us that "we must be careful not to believe things simply because we want them to be true."

1.2 An Open System

The other format is what is referred to as an open system. The International Council on Systems Engineering (INCOSE) suggests that an open system is one that has flows of information, energy, and/or matter between the system and its environment and that adapts to the exchange.[5] An organization that operates an open system is one that looks to expand the search for solutions to include all the benefits of full collaboration. It is one that is willing to explore the full ramifications of the Design4Growth[6] methodology and the power of full-spectrum thinking. It is the open system that brings a more vibrant solution for the problem to the table. Note that we did not say results. While results are important, it is more important for us to develop solutions rather than results. The open system provides the greater impetus to develop these solutions.

This brings us to the question presented by this chapter. With the option to choose either an open system or a closed system, which do we choose?

1.2.1 The Nature of a Cycle-Based System

Many of the current methodologies to bring about process improvement are grounded in a cycle-based system. If you look at the graphics for DMAIC, Kaizen, and PDCA, they are all shown as cycles. The intent of the cycle presentation is that it shows each step in a set order, much as we see in Figure 1.1 on page 6.

Our issue with a cycle-based system is that the assumption (and we know what happens with assumptions) is that once you have made it around the circle, you are left with only two paths forward. The first is that you can wrap up the problem-solving process and then identify the next system constraint and begin the process all over again. The second alternative is that you can determine that you have resolved the issue that was presented and falsely return to the status quo prior to the problem presenting itself. If you make that choice, you are opening yourself to the same issues you already had.

Randy Woods, a freelance writer of an article for ISixSigma.com titled "Lean Six-Sigma Remains Strong in Manufacturing,"[7] references the study done by CompData Surveys (now part of Salary.com) in 2009 and 2010. The results of those surveys can be found in Figure 1.2. For the purposes of our discussion here, the numbers are of no real importance.

The importance of these surveys is that each of the methodologies presented in the surveys when displayed graphically are examples of cycles. The intent of the cycle presentation is that it shows each step in a set order, much as we see in Figure 1.1 on page 6. Each, therefore, is an example of a closed system when they are put into operational situations.

Method/Tool	2009	2010
5S	67.6%	69.2%
Six Sigma	58.5%	58.6%
Kaizen	57.9%	55.7%
Value stream mapping	46.6%	47.3%
Kanban	43.5%	40.6%
Takt time analysis	24.6%	22.1%
Other	5.7%	6.1%

Figure 1.2 CompData survey results.

Source: CompData Surveys, 2010.

5S or Lean (Sort, Set in order, Shine, Standardize, and Sustain) takes you through the steps of the work cell construction in a logical order. Six Sigma uses the PDCA or DMAIC cycle to resolve a workplace problem; Kaizen is laid out in a series of definitive steps; value stream mapping follows a process from beginning to end with time intervals inserted; Kanban utilizes the visual management tool and follows a process from beginning to end while moving resources from one stage to another; and takt time utilizes a cycle by measuring time allotments. Each follows a natural progression, but each has an end outcome.

1.2.2 The Nature of the Continuum-Based System

In the continuum-based system we start from the perspective that we are working from the critical chain. Genius ERP defines a critical chain as "the longest path in the schedule and considers activity interdependence and resource constraints."[8]

With that definition in mind, we can understand that the flow of solutions runs during our processes and before, and it does not mean that we can choose to stop the process when we are theoretically done and go back to a status quo.

1.2.3 The Argument for a Continuum

We understand that in the normal context we follow the critical chain from the suppliers we utilize to complete our processes to the point where we send our products or services to the end user. That is well and good. But wait a minute: are there not others involved in the process?

The answer to the question is yes, there are other interested parties along the way, and they need to be considered. The present continuum runs from our suppliers, to our organization, to the end user. But what about from our end user to their end user? What about the suppliers in our process to their supplier? An occurrence of any kind along the chain has the potential to disrupt the entire continuum. If one player in the process must hold up their delivery, it means that everyone else will be delayed.

As we will see in the next chapter, the TLS Continuum takes the open system concept and applies it to resolving the problem at hand. As we take our journey forward in this work, we will optimize all the resources at our disposal.

Notes

1 Miller, Lawrence. *Whole-System Architecture: A Model for Building the Lean Organization.* www.lmmiller.com/wp-content/uploads/2011/06/Whole-System-Architecture-Article1.pdf

2 4 Steps for an Effective Business Process Improvement Cycle. October 2013. https://explorance.com/blog/8-steps-effective-business-process-improvement-cycle/

3 Definition of a Cycle. www.yourdictionary.com/cycle

4 Definition of a Closed System. www.smartcapitalmind.com/in-business-what-is-a-closed-system.htm

5 Definition of an Open System. www.incose.org/about-systems-engineering/system-and-se-definition/more-systems

6 Liedtka, Jeanne and Tim Ogilvie. *Designing for Growth: A Design Thinking Tool Kit for Managers.* New York, NY: Columbia Business School, 2011

7 Woods, Randy. *Lean Six Sigma Remains Strong in Manufacturing.* Six-Sigma Website. www.isixsigma.com/methodology/kaizen/lean-six-sigma-remains-strong-manufacturing/

8 Definition of Critical Chain. www.geniuserp.com/blog/what-you-need-to-know-about-critical-chain-project-management

Chapter 2

What Is the TLS Continuum?

2.1 Introduction

There is a constant discussion regarding the use of acronyms in the press and in our public discourse. Some contend that it makes it easier for us to communicate. Others will tell you that why use them because no one understands what they stand for in the first place outside of the scientific community. Further common protocol states that you should only use an acronym if you are going to use it more than two times in a work. We will be obviously using TLS far more than twice in this book. As a human capital asset scientist, I can understand both sides of that argument. In this case it is my belief that the use of the TLS acronym carries weight to the discussions.

What does the acronym TLS mean? The acronym represents the three integral parts of the methodology presented in this field guide.

The letter T stands for the Theory of Constraints. Created by Dr. Eliyahu Goldratt, in his book *The Goal*, the Theory of Constraints is a logic thinking–based system for determining where the system constraints lie within your organization, using various tools. The purpose of the TOC involvement in the continuum is to determine what needs to be changed, how to change it, and how to accomplish the change. Remember in the last chapter when we were discussing the nature of a continuum? This is where it comes into play. TOC operates at the level of the supply chain, looking for the weakest link. It is in essence the hypothesis of the problem-solving method overall.

The letter L stands for Lean. Most organizations are familiar with the concept of Lean. It is centered around removing waste from the organizational processes so that the customer receives their orders faster. Understand that faster

DOI: 10.4324/9780429029196-3

may not mean cheaper or better quality; it means only that we expedite the process. The final letter is S, and it represents the concepts of Six Sigma. The primary goal here is to remove variation from the processes. If we combine the three letters of the acronym, we find that the TLS Continuum is organized around a process. We use the Theory of Constraints to locate and identify the obstacles within the system. Ever watch the British TV show *The Weakest Link?* That is what we are doing here: identifying the weakest link.

We use Lean to do what it is meant to do and that is to remove the system constraints and wastes. We have identified the constraint and determined through the logical thinking tools how to remove that constraint and then use the Lean tools to remove the waste. Finally, the system utilizes the Six Sigma tools to create the standard of work and remove any variation from the process. When we do this, we have completed the improvement process by creating a progressive system for resolving the problems that occur within many organizations. It is an evidence-based effort to identify, remove, and improve the system so the problem does not recur.

The TLS Continuum provides you with a roadmap to guide you through the improvement process. It helps you explain why one organization discovered that the job requisition was reviewed and approved three times during a hire, *by the same person.* It helps explain how one organization was able to reduce the time to hire by 61% in six months. When we recognize that the improvement process is tackling a world system, as proposed by Dr. Lawrence Miller in his article, "Whole-System Architecture: A Model for Building the Lean Organization,"[1] then we understand that the TLS Continuum is a vital tool in resolving those world system problems and system obstacles. It is a dynamic system designed to provide you with new insight into how your organization operates and processes flow. The base is to not concerned with whether you are talking about a process that produces something or a process that produces a service in the long run. A widget such as a candidate for an open position or the introduction of a new mindset to the organization.

This will become clearer as we look at the remaining chapters in Part 1. Over the next four chapters, we will break down each component to look at what drives each and then how they come together in the end.

Note

1 Miller, Lawrence. *Whole-System Architecture: A Model for Building the Lean Organization.* www.lmmiller.com/wp-content/uploads/2011/06/Whole-System-Architecture-Article1.pdf

Chapter 3

The Principles of the Theory of Constraints

In 1984, an Israeli business guru was suggesting a new way to look at continuous process improvement in organizations. It is important to note here that Eliyahu Goldratt was a consultant to business but was not an engineer. He began his career as a physicist. With that scientific influence, Eliyahu Goldratt believed that you could resolve the struggles facing businesses by applying scientific principles. He brought to the forefront the strong operating philosophy that using the tools of the scientist, you could resolve business obstacles through a set of logic-based tools. To present his views in more detail, he released to the world his book *The Goal*, which has become a vital part of our business school curriculum worldwide. Written as a novel, it followed the path of an executive charged with turning around his company.

The basis of *The Goal* was the introduction of the Theory of Constraints (TOC). It works primarily at the level of a chain, driving the organizational focus to the weakest links and then to the linkages between that constraint or weakest link and other aspects of the system. TOC, with its logic-based tools, provides strength to the process using qualitative analysis, helpful for dealing with those rock-and-hard-place dilemmas that we all face.

Frank Patrick of Focused Performance (the firm is no longer in existence) provided us with the best descriptions of the basic tenets of TOC[1] when he compared TOC to Six Sigma. We will utilize the principles of Six Sigma in the appropriate chapter.

Principle #1: TOC works primarily at the level of the chain, driving focus to the weakest link and then to the linkages between that constraint and other aspects of the system.

Remember our discussion of the open system vs. the closed system in Chapter 1? It is at this point that the continuum is presented in the process. As we discussed earlier, the open system is a continuous process with no end in place. It represents the entirety of the flow of materials and services through the critical chain. As Goldratt demonstrated with his example of Herbie[2] in *The Goal*, it is inevitable that whenever you have a process-critical chain, somewhere along the chain there will be a hiccup. Something will slow down the even flow of the process. The Theory of Constraints works at that point. It is designed from the outset to see the hiccup as well as the linkage between the other parts of the system or process and the weakest link.

It is of utmost importance that we reiterate that the entire continuum must be aligned with both the needs of the organization and the customer needs. As the Herbie example shows, when on a hike if someone slows down, the whole line slows down. The result is that we need to be cognizant about the flow of the process to identify the "Herbies" within the organization.

Principle #2: TOC, with its logic-based tools, provides strength in dealing with what might be considered "qualitative" analysis, helpful for dealing with "rock-and-hard-place" dilemmas.

Dr. Mikel Harry, in his seminal work, *Six Sigma: The Breakthrough Management Strategy Revolutionizing the World's Top Corporations*,[3] laid out for us some key performance indicators which dictate how we begin the process of implementing the TLS Continuum. Dr. Harry tells us that we don't know what we don't know; we can't do what we don't know; we won't know until we measure; we don't measure what we don't value; and we don't value what we don't measure.

The Theory of Constraints achieves this understanding using a set of tools which are based on reviewing the process using logic-based tools. They are designed to get us to the root causes of the problem we are facing.

The logical toolbox begins with identifying where we are. What is the nature of the organizational environment right now and in this place? The tool that we use is the current reality tree, as will be discussed later in this chapter. Once we determine the nature of the current system, we need

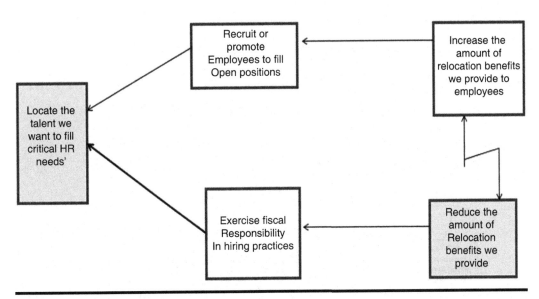

Figure 3.1   Evaporating cloud.[4]

to determine what we don't know. The Theory of Constraints utilizes the evaporating cloud to ferret out the points of conflict behind the problems we are facing.

The evaporating cloud is designed to uncover the conflict within your processes. Consider for a moment the example in Figure 3.1. It states that one of HR's responsibilities is to locate the talent the organization needs to fill critical human capital needs of the organization. The question posed by the evaporating cloud is: How do we achieve that goal? The cloud offers two different alternatives. One says the goal is fiscal responsibility, which requires the organization to stay within budgetary guidelines. The other option states that the goal is to recruit or promote employees to fill these critical openings.

The weakest link appears after this segment of the discussion because it directly compares the two approaches. On the fiscal side, the resulting action is to reduce the amount of relocation benefits provided to the human capital assets, while filling the positions is the paramount issue you need to increase the level of benefits. The conflict arises because you may not be able to reduce benefits and still get the level of talent that the organization is seeking.

The third component of the toolbox is the future reality tree (Figure 3.2). The design for growth methodology we discussed earlier is an example of this. We are asking ourselves what the future looks like.

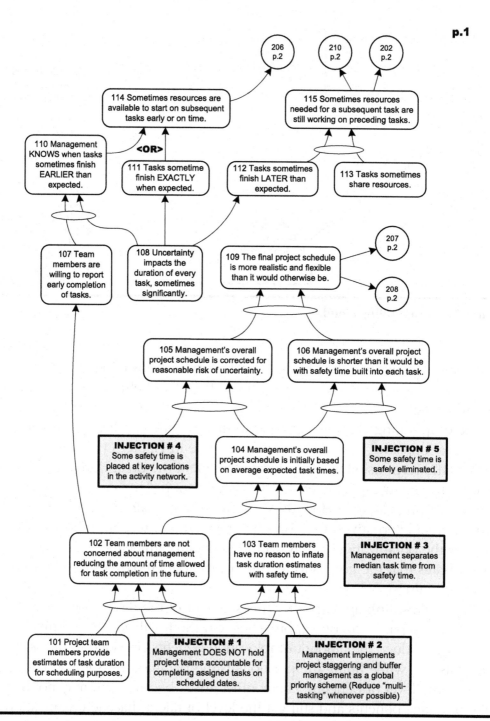

Figure 3.2 Future reality tree (Successful project management). (Continued)

Source: © H. William Dettmer 2010. Used with permission

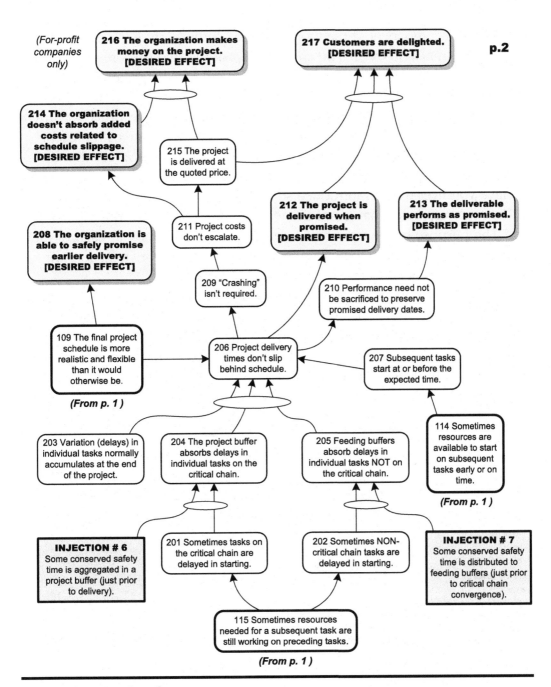

(From p. 1)

Figure 3.2 (Continued)

The fourth component of the toolbox is the combination of the prerequisite and the transition trees. The combination of the two trees responds to another one of Dr. Harry's KPIs. as discussed earlier. The prerequisite tree tells us what resources are going to be needed to resolve the system constraint. The tree is to some degree our initial roadmap of the process that we can use to create the various process maps. These resources represent manpower, materials, and financial resources. It is these resources that drive us forward.

Have you ever tried to introduce something new in your organization and got the response "that is not the way we do things here" or "it is not my job." The purpose of the transition tree (Figure 3.3) is to look at each of the prerequisites and seek to explore why some parts of the organization are not into why we need to take that route.

The final component of the TOC toolbox is the goal statement. Over time the goal tree (Figure 3.3) has been called many names. Whether you call it an IO map (intermediate objective map) or the goal tree, it serves the same primary focus. The purpose is to develop a mind map that displays the end goal along with the still smaller goals that must be obtained.

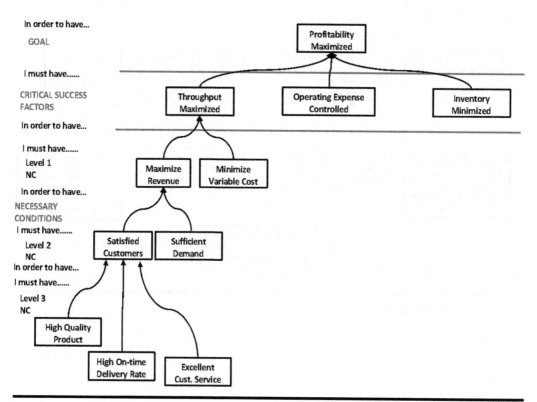

Figure 3.3 The goal tree.[5,6]

The goal tree begins with your goal. What is it you are trying to achieve? It then poses the question: What must be present to achieve the goal? The protocol for the goal Tree development is called the critical success factors. These factors must be created for you to achieve the goal. In the problems posed in this book, those critical success factors might be the removal of the barriers to process flow. It might be a better control system for the flow of parts to the factory floor.

With the critical success factors in place, the final step is to turn the critical success factors into goal statements and ask what is necessary for the organization to achieve the critical success. The goal tree and its uses and derivations will be discussed further in Part 3.

Principle #3: TOC's approach to root cause analysis, centered in the thinking process known as the current reality tree, starts with a range of diverse problems with which the system suffers and then builds rigorous cause-and-effect logic to identify one or very deep causes at the root of them all.

The root cause is a nonconforming factor in a process. It is the underlying factor in the existence of the system constraints. Karou Ishikawa, the creator of the Ishikawa fishbone diagram, tells us that in any process three types of causes exist. The first type is referred to as a common cause. It is called a common cause because it occurs in almost every process and is constantly active within the organization. One of our basic concerns that we will discuss more in detail later in this part of the book is the presence of variations. With the common causes, the variations are expected, and we can predict their impact on the processes. They are expected because they fall within our historical data on the performance of the organization.

Ishikawa's second type of process cause is that of special causes. Special causes appear in those conditions which occur in nonoperating environments. An example might be if there is a change in the work environment. The third type of cause is the root cause, and this is the type we are most concerned with. It is the root cause that is utilized by the first part of the toolbox, the current reality tree (Figure 3.4).

You can't even begin to analyze where the system problems are until you understand the current processes. The current reality tree logically looks at where you are now. It provides a view of the things that are disrupting the system and traces them back to where they intersect the system. It becomes the first indicator of what needs to be corrected.

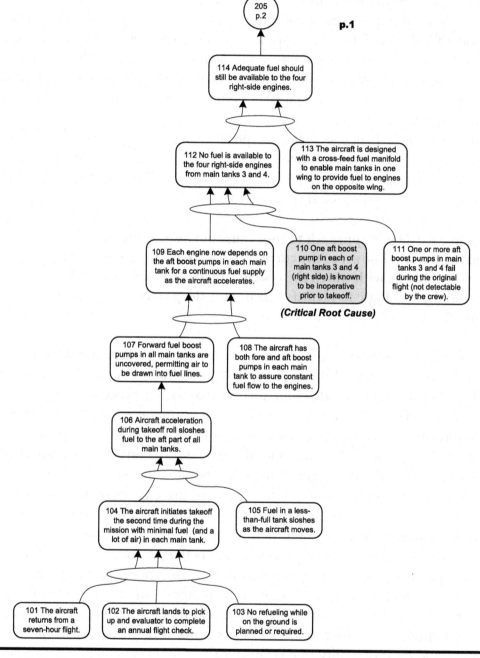

Figure 3.4   Current reality tree (Anatomy of a B-52 crash, part 1). (Continued)

Source: Dettmer, H.W. Breaking the Constraints to World-Class Performance (1998)
Used with permission

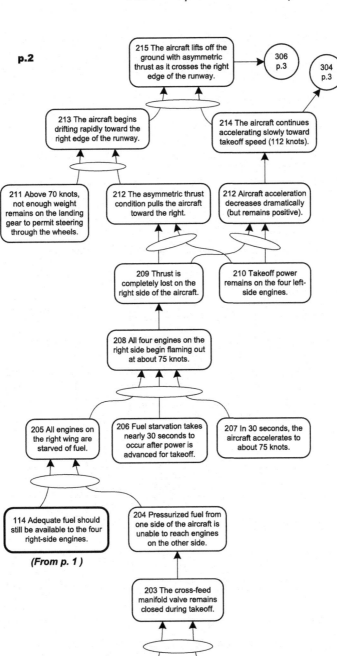

Figure 3.4   Current Reality Tree (Anatomy of a B-52 crash, part 2). (Continued)

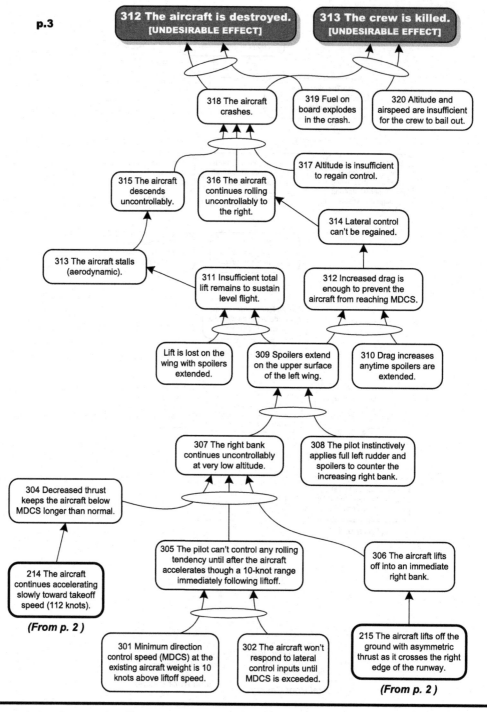

p.3

312 The aircraft is destroyed.
[UNDESIRABLE EFFECT]

313 The crew is killed.
[UNDESIRABLE EFFECT]

318 The aircraft crashes.

319 Fuel on board explodes in the crash.

320 Altitude and airspeed are insufficient for the crew to bail out.

317 Altitude is insufficient to regain control.

315 The aircraft descends uncontrollably.

316 The aircraft continues rolling uncontrollably to the right.

314 Lateral control can't be regained.

313 The aircraft stalls (aerodynamic).

311 Insufficient total lift remains to sustain level flight.

312 Increased drag is enough to prevent the aircraft from reaching MDCS.

Lift is lost on the wing with spoilers extended.

309 Spoilers extend on the upper surface of the left wing.

310 Drag increases anytime spoilers are extended.

307 The right bank continues uncontrollably at very low altitude.

308 The pilot instinctively applies full left rudder and spoilers to counter the increasing right bank.

304 Decreased thrust keeps the aircraft below MDCS longer than normal.

214 The aircraft continues accelerating slowly toward takeoff speed (112 knots).

(From p. 2)

305 The pilot can't control any rolling tendency until after the aircraft accelerates though a 10-knot range immediately following liftoff.

306 The aircraft lifts off into an immediate right bank.

301 Minimum direction control speed (MDCS) at the existing aircraft weight is 10 knots above liftoff speed.

302 The aircraft won't respond to lateral control inputs until MDCS is exceeded.

215 The aircraft lifts off the ground with asymmetric thrust as it crosses the right edge of the runway.

(From p. 2)

Figure 3.4   Current Reality Tree (Anatomy of a B-52 crash, part 3). (Continued)

Principle #4: TOC first strives to build "logistical" processes that are robust enough to deal with current variation, and through concepts like the five focusing steps and "buffer management," identify where attacks on variation will give us the biggest bang for the buck.

Goldratt tells us that once we have implemented the logical thinking tools, the next steps are to start to resolve the system constraint using the five focusing steps. The five steps allow us to plan out our effort to resolve the constraints. The first step is to identify the constraint. In most processes, there are typically four kinds of constraints that are identified. The first is that of internal physical processes. The constraints occur because the design of the physical facility does not have the capacity to perform at the required levels. The second is that of your internal policies and measures. If there is a system issue, nine times out of ten the reasoning behind them is the polices and how you measure the processes that are the root cause. We must reiterate at this juncture that the root cause is never the fault of your human capital assets.

The third type of constraint is the external market. The constraint may be caused by the supply and demand of the marketplace that governs your organization. The final type of constraints is those that are linked to the supply chain delivery of materials. You can't complete a process if you don't have the materials to do so.

You should have done that when you prepared your current reality tree. Once the constraint is identified, the next step is to decide how you can exploit the constraint. In Goldratt's Herbie example, he found that Herbie was the problem. The decision on how to exploit the constraint meant that Herbie was moved from the end of the line to the lead position.

The third focusing factor is the elevation of the constraint. Again, in the Herbie example, they timed the process based on the capabilities of Herbie, not the fastest person in line. This led to the fourth step, which is to elevate the constraint, making everything revolve on the operation of the constraint.

The fifth and final step is to review your process and start it all over again to resolve the next constraint that appears, and it will.

Principle #5: TOC extends its use of the constraints to define maximum value for a market segment or customer in terms of the constraint or core

problem of their system. Having identified that, positioning one's product and offering in terms of assisting with that critical issue is the main route to increased value.

By removing the obstacles in the chain, you remove those activities that are non-value-added in nature. It means the organization can concentrate more on the needs of the customer. It means that the process flow, even if it is temporary, is delivering products and services in a faster, cheaper, and defect-free manner. This change of focus brings about increased value to the organization.

Notes

1 Patrick, Frank. http://focusedperformance.com/srticles/tocsixsigma.html
2 Goldratt, Eliyahu. *The Goal.* 2nd Revised Edition. Croton-on-Hudson, NY: North River Press, 1992. Pages 94–119
3 Harry, Mikel. *Six Sigma: The Breakthrough Management Strategy Revolutionizing the World's Top Corporations.* New York, NY: Currency Random House, 2005. Page xii
4 The image of the evaporating cloud is taken from the Road to HR Excellence course offered by Daniel T. Bloom & Associates, Inc.
5 The image of the goal tree is from the Road to HR Excellence course offered by Daniel T. Bloom & Associates, Inc.
6 https://online.visual-paradigm.com/knowledge/problem-solving/what-is-current-reality-tree/

Chapter 4

The Principles of Lean Management

The second third of the pie is that of Lean management. Developed out of the foundations of the Toyota Production System, it is primarily based in the effort to remove non-value-added activities from the various processes found within our products and services. Non-value-added activities and associated waste are those actions that do not bring any value to the end user of our products and services. The concepts behind Lean management were first presented in detail by James Womack and Daniel Jones in *Lean Thinking*. We have taken the Womack-Jones principles and enhanced the list, once again turning to Dr. Lawrence Miller from his book *Lean Culture*.[1] We can take these concepts and create basic principles like we did in the previous chapter with the Theory of Constraints.

Principle #1: Lean establishes and communicates a sense of organizational purpose.

Remember that elevator speech you were supposed to learn for when you meet someone? Remember that last networking get-together when you were supposed to introduce yourself to strangers telling them what you did? Take a moment and answer these questions.

What business are you in?
What does your business do?
Why is your organization in business?

DOI: 10.4324/9780429029196-5

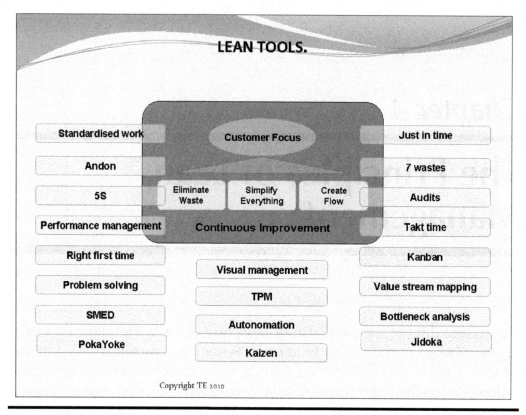

Figure 4.1   Lean toolbox.[2]

Questions with an easy answer, right? We can almost guarantee that your immediate answer would be centered around what your organization produces or delivers. You might have even responded in terms of what your job responsibilities are now. What is the real answer?

A basic tenet of the Theory of Constraints is that we are in business to make money. On the flip side, Dr. Tony Alessandra in his book *The Platinum Rule* suggests that we are in business to acquire and maintain customers. Both responses are semi-correct, but they do not fully answer the question. However, when we look at the question of establishing the purpose of your organization, we need to go further.

If we want to make more money or acquire and maintain more customers, we need to meet the needs of the customers by providing them what they want, where they want it, when they want it, and at the price they want it. To achieve that we need to listen to the voice of the customer. In order to enable your organization to do that we need to fully understand their needs and in turn establish our reasons for our organization to function in the marketplace.

To begin our discussion of the voice of the customer, we need to establish a theorem about why our organizations exist. A theorem is a general set of principles that we believe to be true. In the case of the voice of the customer, the theorem is that every organization exists to contribute something of value to the global marketplace. It is also critical that we recognize that your organization does not exist in a bubble. Your clients do not exist in a bubble. If we don't survive in a bubble, then what is it that we bring to the marketplace? That contribution usually is in the form of our products and services. Typically, thus, the first part of the voice of the customer paradigm are our core services.

Our core services are those products and services that we make available to the global marketplace. The voice of the customer paradigm tells us what products and services they need. It makes no difference whether these clients are internal to the organization or out in the marketplace. These customer requirements will not be the same with every customer, so as an organization we need to strive to have a wide variety of core services. It is also a necessity that you understand that these core services may be offered on an interim basis. As the client needs change, so must your core service package. That voice of the customer tells us what it is about those products or services that brought them to us rather than to one of our competitors. Our message tells the customers that we are able meet their basic demands. Failure to meet the voice of the customer means that we will not acquire and maintain customers. Failure to meet the vice of the customer means that we will not be able to make money. It means that the customer can look at the marketplace and see who else may also fit their needs. There is no such thing as customer loyalty in today's marketplace. The way we maintain them is to listen genuinely to the voice of the customer.

With the establishment of the organizational purpose, we need to tell the world what that purpose is. We need to communicate that message widely both internally and externally. To our organization and to the marketplace. The ultimate goal is for everyone to be on the same page on why we are serving the marketplace and our customers. The message must be totally aligned with the organizational processes.

Principle #2: Lean establishes the values of your organization.

As we institute our communication campaign regarding our organizational purpose, we must also pay attention to the undertone of those messages. Beneath our messages must be an alignment with mission, values, goals, and strategies. Consider each of these areas individually even though they are totally interdependent on each other.

Our mission tells both the organization and the customer why we exist. The mission statement tells all parties involved the answer to the question as to what our overall purpose is. Consider the website LinkedIn's mission statement: "To connect the world's professionals to make them more productive and successful."

With the mission statement in place, we then must turn to the value statement that explains what we stand for. What are our ethical beliefs regarding how the organization operates regarding the marketplace as a whole? Further, our values instill a sense of direction to our operations. With the purpose presented and the values declared, we have a sense in which direction the operations must flow.

The next step is to establish the organizational goals or performance targets. The goals provide an end spot for the mission statement. When we combine the purpose with the mission and values, we can develop our mission of the organization.

Charles Handy, in his classic work *The Age of Unreason*,[3] tells us that the purpose or vision needs to be different in nature. First, the vision must be different. We are talking here about the future state of the organization. As a result, the mission cannot be grounded in the present. Second, the vision must make sense to others. As a manager you may understand what you wrote, but does the human capital asset on the front line understand it? Third, the vision must be understandable. Is it free from a wide variety of jargon that only the management understands?

The prior criteria present themselves with two remaining criteria. First, management must walk the walk and talk the talk. The vision must become the corporate mantra. Second, as we will see later in this chapter, management must remember that it is the work of others. They must recognize the input of the cross-functional teams.

Finally with the other components in place, we can begin to develop the strategies that tell us how we will achieve the missions, values, and goals.

Principle #3: Lean identifies and eliminates those non-valued activities that are uncovered within the organization unless they are required to meet the need of the customer.

Shigeo Shingo told us that "the most dangerous kind of waste is the waste we do not recognize."

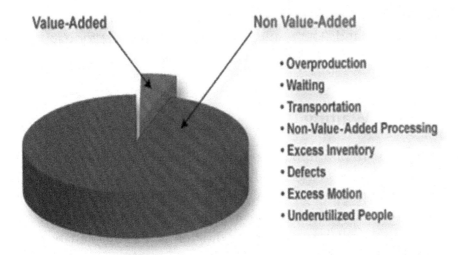

Figure 4.2   Types of organizational waste.[4]

Every process in the workplace is inclined to have hiccups. Those hiccups are typically due to waste or non-value-added activities of some kind. In many cases the reason why we don't recognize the wastes in our processes is because we don't look for them even though they are in plain sight.

It is also important that we recognize that some of the non-value-added activities are a necessary evil in resolving some change. With that said, we still need to identify their existence. There is some debate in the industry as to how many types of wastes there are. Depending on what source you reference there may be seven, eight, or nine individual types of waste in existence. Toyota's original list consisted of seven wastes. We like to view nine types of waste, and we will look at each of them later. The easiest rule of thumb is that the examples of waste we will see in this chapter are those activities that add nothing to the task of meeting the demands of the customer.

4.1 Waste from Overproduction

If you are on the manufacturing floor, many organizations operate in a push environment in which the materials needed on the floor are sent through the processes when they come into the building rather when they are needed. Part of the reason we do this is because as human beings we tend to believe that having more is better in the long run even if you have an oversupply on hand. The result is that we get a request for data, and we tend to produce way more than the customer asked for or needs.

4.2 Waste of Waiting

Put this book down for a minute and think about how you felt the last time you went to the doctor's office. Awhile back I was referred to a specialist for an 8:30 a.m. appointment, and when I got there, the nurse told me that based on his operating method, I would be lucky if I got into to see him before 3 p.m. in the afternoon. How would you feel in this situation?

The second of the nine waste types is that of waiting. Waiting is non-value-added because it is not requested by a customer. It plays no part in fulfilling their demands. We receive many reasons for the delay; however, anytime we delay the delivery of a product or service beyond when the customer requests it, it is waste.

4.3 Waste of Over-Transportation

Whether we are talking about the original works of Frederick Taylor and the Hawthorne Studies, every organization at one time or another has been concerned with the flow of materials and resources through the organization. I am sure you have all worked in an organization where it seemed that every time you turned around the organization had rearranged the office whenever the wind changed. Many times, there is a valid reason for the change. Other times, it is supposed to be to meet some reported need. The problem is that sometimes the movement creates more problems than believed because the total organization and the customer's voice were not reviewed. When this extra movement is present, it creates waste.

4.4 Waste of Overprocessing

A member of management attends a conference and hears of a new strategy and comes back to the office and implements it without seeing how it will fit into the total organization. Somewhere back in time a minor crisis occurred, and management decided to avoid it happening again so they will implement oversight controls. All of these could be great ideas, but if they are not taken in the context of your corporate culture, you are asking for added problems. These added steps were implemented to isolate the organization but not meet the needs of the customer. Failure to listen to the customer is waste.

4.5 Waste of Excess Inventory

Wikipedia defines excess inventory as a capital outlay in which there is no return from the customer. We usually consider this from the point of view of a physical item. However, you can also have excess inventory from a service perspective.

4.6 Waste of Excess Motion

In virtually every corporate facility in the world, if we utilize the spaghetti diagram tool or the stand in a circle tool created by Taiichi Ohno, we can see that we have designed the work floor not entirely in the most efficient way to move human capital within the system. The added steps required to complete the process based on the workflow create waste as we create less productivity.

4.7 Waste from Process Defects

By far this could be the largest segment of the waste types and includes many easily overlooked examples of non-value-added steps. Many of these defects may be simple slips as part of being human, but they do represent waste in the system. It refers to those opportunities where the wrong information is provided, and the result is a disruption to the customer. A disruption that requires that the process be reworked to correct the process so the customer requirements can be met.

4.8 Waste of Underutilized Human Capital Potential

Can any of you remember the United Negro College Fund's slogan that "a mind is a terrible thing to waste"? While this was referring to the opportunities for a young African American trying to get through higher education, the same question can be posed to the internal organization and how you treat your human capital. We can waste the contributions of our human capital assets when we place them in a less-than-optimal work environment, in work environments where there is no opportunity for them to build their skill portfolios.

4.9 Waste of Material Underutilization

The last of the nine types of wastes is that of material underutilization, and it refers to how we use materials within the organization. Every day we do things within the organizational structure that create waste in the processes and organization.

Principle #4: Lean requires a passion for constant improvement.

The top of the organizational wish list is that every one of our processes were perfect. That is an impractical expectation. Our organizations are confronted every day with the potential for process changes. Your front-line workers spot the imperfections. The critical outcome must be that you can't run away from the opportunity. Take Peter Pande at his word when he tells us there is always a better way. The goal of the organization must be that you come to work for the sole purpose of making your work environment better every single workday.

This belief that there is always a better way must become the corporate mantra. If you turn to your organization, is every person on board with your missions, goals, values, and strategies? Everyone understands what is in it for them and why the changes are required at this time and in this place.

Principle #5: Lean is based on the foundation that the organization will respect its human capital assets.

Our human capital assets are the crux of our organizations. There is no organization in the global marketplace that can survive without the presence of human capital assets. They are the ones who implement the organization's values. They are the ones who interact with the organizational customers. They are the ones who present the image of the organization in the marketplace. They are the ones who fulfill the customer orders. They are the ones who disseminate the expanse of the corporate knowledge database to the newly acquired talent. Take a moment and look at your organization, with an open mind, and respond to this question: How does your organization categorize your human capital assets? Do not jump to conclusions to a right answer because you more than likely are wrong. Your direct response to the question indicates whether you respect your human capital assets or not.

In 1969 on a global basis, this new tool came into existence called the Internet. The direct result of this new tool was a dramatic evolution of the workplace. The workplace shifted from the conditions of the industrial age to what now was referred to as the information age. This essential understanding is the crux of the creation of the empowered human capital asset.

Russ Moen, vice president of human resources at Express Services, Inc., explains the response to my question as how you categorize your human capital assets in a slide from one of his programs, as shown in Figure 4.3. As we moved from the farm to the factory floor, it became the norm for our human capital assets to be identified by a number. Look at your company identification badge; you are probably still provided a unique number

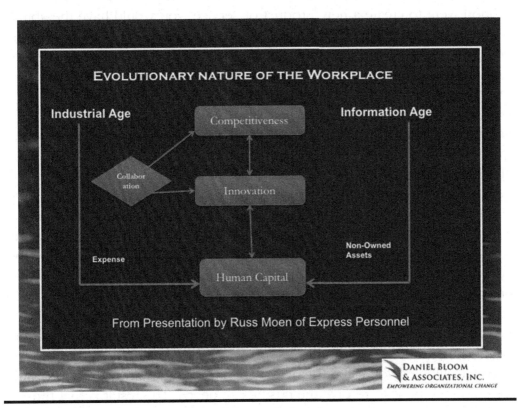

Figure 4.3   Russ Moen's Evolution of the workplace.[5]

to locate you in corporate records. This worked for a while. If our human capital assets were paid based on the hours worked and the number of pieces made, the number system worked fine. But times would change, and so would the nature of the role of the individual within your workplace, globally and internally. Russ Moen makes the argument that as an organization, we now compensate our human capital assets based not on what they make, but on what they dream. Charles Handy again defines this new picture of our human capital assets as the I^3, standing for intelligence, information, and ideas.[6] We do not employ the human capital assets to fill time and space. We hire them to derive new ideas, concepts, and processes designed to meet the needs of the customer. The knowledge of what the organization does now resides in their heads. As an example in point, not too long ago a company wanted to reduce its overhead, so it offered every employee with 20 or more years of service an early buyout. Every one of them took the offer. The company was out of business in six months mostly due to the loss of knowledge within the company. Russ goes on to suggest that in the knowledge age, today's human capital assets are non-owned, corporate-leased assets. Let's dwell on this idea for a moment. If your organization were to create a new product or service, you would have the ability to develop a brand, a trademark, or a patent because the organization owns the rights to that new product or service. With the advent of the knowledge age, you are not able to trademark what your human capital assets dream. The human capital assets' minds are not the property of the organization. There may be an agreement in place that provides your organization with the results of the idea, but you still do not own the mind itself. You still do not own the concepts, ideas, and potential solutions that the human capital assets develop. As an offshoot of the previous chapter, you do not own the results of the work of the empowered cross-functional team either.

The other aspect of Russ Moen's profile of the knowledge-age human capital asset is that they are corporate-leased assets. Leave the human capital assets in a classical workplace and they can take their knowledge, skills, and ideas elsewhere. They are leased assets because you only have them for as long as you meet their needs.

This new view of human capital assets has led to several major changes in organizations. First with the advent of new knowledge, it has enabled the organization to dominate the product niche you are basing your business on. It has allowed you to be the first to market with new concepts, innovations, and methods to resolve the customer's needs. The result is that the individual human capital assets are becoming empowered to deliver for the organization. Rather than being a number, the human capital assets are now valued and thus compensated based on their worth to the organization. This has come from a change in both the location and type of work being performed. It also means that there is no longer any type of censorship on what your human capital assets contribute. Consider, for example, what would have happened today if the 3M employee who suggested a new product we now know as Post-it Notes had his idea immediately censored because management did not like it.

Another change in the empowered organization is that management's view toward these new ideas plays out in the willingness to let human capital assets experiment with their ideas with the full understanding that if the experiment fails, that is okay. Management understands that failure is a natural part of experimentation.

We would argue that with the evolution of the human capital asset role, they are now the primary key in the model to empower your organization. They are the ones who better understand the nature of the organizational processes. Human capital resources are vital to the success of our businesses. You make the decision as to whether your organization maintains the status quo or heads in the direction of the new paradigm. This new paradigm calls for new strategies to maximize our human capital assets. This means we must gain a better understanding of the importance of their roles. In my mind, there are three key strategies that will carry us forward to the empowered organization. The three strategies consider engagement, ownership, and subject matter expertise.

Principle #6: Lean understands the limits of the organization's capabilities.

Your business development professionals go out into the marketplace seeking to acquire and maintain customers. We get it; that is their role. The key here is can the organization meet those promises? Do we have the skills and abilities to meet those promises?

The Lean part of the pie needs to be able to identify where the process breaks down and limits our ability to meet the customer's needs. It means that we need to fully understand what is in the orders coming in the door and the required resources to fulfill those orders. The ability to spot the system constraints is dependent on this knowledge.

Understand that there is no such thing as a perfect process. Every process, if measured over time, will contain variations in the deliverance. Part of understanding the capabilities of the process is to measure those variations and how they affect the process overall.

Principle #7: Lean is unequivocally customer-centric in nature.

Your organization is experiencing a problem with an order. Whose problem is it really? The problem resides with the customer. Your goal is to make the experience an infinitely great experience for the customer. You can only achieve that when we act on the principle of becoming customer-centric.

Your responsibility, as stated earlier in this chapter, is to acquire and maintain customers and therefore make money. We can only do that when we act and think like the customer does. We need to proactively recognize what they need and when they need it. We must recognize that the customer is the deciding factor as to whether we are meeting their needs.

Principle # 8: Lean recognizes the value of human capital assets owning the processes they are delivering.

If we see something wrong with a process, what is the path to correct it? Dictionary.com tells us that one of the definitions for ownership is legal right of possession.[7] In my view, this means we need to address who has control over the processes. On those occasions where a problem is uncovered, who has the responsibility for resolving the issue—only with the C-Suite, or does it permit the real SMEs in the company to make the correction?

Every time we encounter a change based on volatility of the workplace, we are forced to do things differently. Every time we encounter a change that is derived out of the uncertainty of the workplace, we need to prepare the organization for the next unexpected change. Charles Handy, once again in the *Age of Unreason*, refers to it as discontinuous change. The goal is to reach a point where the human capital assets take responsibility for both the successes and failures of the organizational processes. When things go bad, they take the responsibility to make things right. When things go right, they champion that success to the organization and to the world. They take ownership of the process to ensure that there are more successes than failures. They understand that under this ownership umbrella they have not only the ability but the right to stop the process to correct the problems. The Toyota Production System contains what is called the Anon System in which every associate has the right to pull the anon chord or push the anon button to stop the process in its tracks when a problem arises. They understand that in doing so, there is no retaliation for making the decision. Management understands the reasons why they did what they did. Their fellow human capital assets understand the reasons why they did what they did. The human capital assets are the crux to advancing innovation, process improvement, and change management. We asked earlier: How do you classify your human capital assets? The answer is simple: they are the organizational subject matter experts for several reasons.

First, the human capital assets are the ones who understand the processes. Management sitting in the corner office or the professionals at the lower management levels may think they know the processes, but your front-line human capital assets are the real processes experts. They are the ones who hear the voice of the customer in the form of the customer complaints. They are the ones who see when the production line is slowing down, so orders are late. They are the ones who see the end product and know if it is meeting the specifications of the product order.

For the human capital assets to become totally empowered, they must be provided the opportunity to go and see the various steps to deliver the end product and/or service to the customer. This means that they should be given the opportunity to see the stages of the supply chain that comes before your organization gets involved. The purpose of these aspects is that the human capital assets gain knowledge of the processes that they might not already possess. This allows them to have a clear concept of the process involved.

The final aspect of the empowered individual process ownership may very well be the most important. W. Edwards Deming said it best when he said in his 14 Points of Quality that we need to drive out fear. The initial facet of this is to empower the human capital assets to take the chance on a solution. They need to be able to take the first three steps of the design thinking methodology. They have asked: What is the current situation? They have asked: What if we did this? The final of the three steps is to conduct experimentation in some form to determine if the solutions or hypotheses will work. The other side of the coin is that an empowered management will not hold any failures against the human capital assets. Management understands that each failure is a sign of how close we are getting to the correct solution.

Principle #9: Lean is dependent on the organizational support of the systems.

In Lean the organizational structure is dependent on key elements of the organization. They do not survive as an island. Our project charter has a clearly defined area where the necessary resource required by the improvement effort is delineated.

As an organization, you need to determine if you are committed to the change effort. If you are, then you need to be sure that the required resources are available. This means the areas off the Ishikawa fishbone diagram: manpower, financial, equipment and management. It also means that each resource must understand what their role is in the process.

Principle #10: Lean must enable the flow through the system.

One of the goals of the TLS Continuum and the Lean segment is to remove the obstacles that inhibit the flow of products and services through the chain. We achieve this by seeking out the obstacles that the TOC logical tools uncover.

The created flow provides the organization and its stakeholders with a guide on how each operates within the business operation. Dr. Mikel Harry told us that we don't know what we don't know. The only way to really know and understand our processes is to prepare a process map that plots out the journey from your suppliers, to your organization, to your clients, and then to their end users.

The key at this point is to convert the system from a push environment to a pull one. In a push environment, we send materials that are needed to introduce a product or service upstream as soon as they arrive in our facilities. On the other hand, in a pull environment, we only send materials upstream at the exact time they are needed, not before.

Principle #11: Lean requires the organization to play the game.

The process of implementing the change process should be fun. But it is also serious. The success of these efforts is dependent on everyone playing their part. Every member of the associated cross-functional teams puts forth the maximum effort. No one should consider that the effort is someone else's job.

The proverbs tell us that if you don't have time to do it right, you must have time to do it over. That is what Lean management tell us. The goal is to ensure that everything that flows out of our organizations is as defect free as is humanly possible. Ford tells us that quality is job one. Toyota believes that is in their DNA to do it right the first time. This final principle suggests that it is your job as a human capital asset of the organization to do everything you can to ensure that the outgoing product or service meets the values established in the first principle for the client.

Notes

1 Miller, Lawrence. *Lean Culture: The Leader's Guide.* Annapolis, MD: LMM Publishing, 2011. Pages 11–18

2 Lean Toolbox. *Lean Manufacturing Tools Website.* https://leanmanufacturing-tools.org/

3 Handy, Charles. *The Age of Unreason.* Boston, MA: Harvard Business Press, 1990. Pages 134–135

4 Taken from the Six Sigma Black Belt Training Materials. St Petersburg College. Clearwater, FL. 2008–2009

5 Moen, Russ. *Love 'Em or Lose 'Em: Proven Strategies for Employee Retention.* Express Employment Professionals. January 21, 2009

6 Handy, Charles. *The Age of Unreason.* Boston, MA: Harvard Business Press, 1990. Page 141

7 Definition of Ownership. www.dictionary.com/browse/ownership

Chapter 5

The Principles of Six Sigma

While we have reviewed two parts of the pie, we still have the third and vital part of the TLS Continuum equation—that of the Six Sigma methodology. Like the previous two slices, it also has its unique toolbox as shown in Figure 5.1

During the golden age (1980–1990) of continuous process improvement, one company was seeking a more finite method of determining the prevalence of errors or defects in their processes. Under the experimentation of Bill Smith and his team, Motorola created and trademarked the term Six Sigma.

To understand the principles of the Six Sigma methodology, we need to have a basic understanding of two concepts. First, we need to understand what we mean by the term sigma and then what do we mean by the expanded Six Sigma? What is this term Six Sigma? What does sigma mean?

I have a little mental exercise for you before we continue. Think back to your high school or college days and remember that exam you swore you aced only to find the results for the total class were a disaster. What was your initial reaction? We would probably first think that there was something wrong with the grading, and then you or your class would go visit the instructor and plead that he change the scoring to reflect a curve. Remember your school days when we pushed instructors to grade on a curve? The intent was to identify where the average score landed and to grade the exceptions on a curve. When we grade on a curve, the premise is that we average the scores on a bell curve.

Covering the concept of nominal distribution of data, the bell curve identifies the "norm," or the height of the curve, as well as the outliers, which

DOI: 10.4324/9780429029196-6

DMAIC Step	SIX SIGMA Tools	LEAN Tools
DEFINE	**Voice of Customer** **Project Charter** **Project Critical to Quality Definition** **High Level Process Map**	Value Definition
MEASURE	Quality Function Deployment Measurement System Analysis	Value Stream Mapping
ANALYZE	Process Capability Analysis FMEA Benchmarking Hypothesis Testing Graphical Tools	Line Balance Takt Time Calculation
IMPROVE	Regression Analysis Design Of Experiments Risk Assessment	5 S Establish Flow / Pull System SCORE Events
CONTROL	Determine New Process Capability Statistical Process Control Control Plans	Poke Yoke Visual Management

Figure 5.1   Six Sigma toolbox.[1]

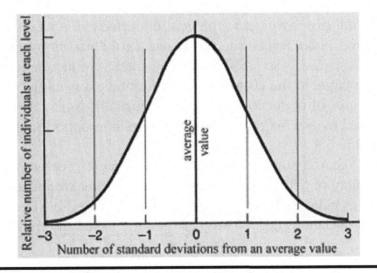

Figure 5.2   The bell curve.[2]

are shown as scores at the outer edges of the curve. With that consideration in place, our argument to the instructor is based on the scores that have been recorded and the scores that fell outside the expected grade ranges. If you are successful, grading on a curve will raise your score by a few points, which may get you to the score level that you were expecting. While we will never reach it, we are all seeking that sense of nirvana we call perfection.

Our goal both in life and within the workplace is to reach a point where our output is considered to be as free from defects or as close to perfection as possible. The bell curve provides us with the ability to view our data and determine how close we have come to reaching that goal. This all leads to applying sigma to our data.

Coming from the Greek, sigma refers to the summation of the numbers or quantities indicated.[3] In statistical terms, *sigma* allows us to measure the data in the bell curve and the rate of the variation within our processes. It represents the amount of variation that occurs relative to the specific customer's specifications. The bell curve tells us that in most cases, we allow for one standard deviation above or below the mean score. Each deviation from the mean is equivalent to 34% above and below the average point, or the point of error-free processes. The bell curve provides us with a clear perspective on how close we are to meeting the voice of the customer. We can take the bell curve and apply it to a DPMO chart.

If we review Figure 5.3, we find that as our defects per million opportunities decrease, the level of the yield, or those items that meet the required customer specifications, increases. The smaller the variation from the requirement, the closer we get to the goal of perfection. As a result, when we reach a level of Six Sigma, the defect rate, or the variation from the voice of the customer, is so small that the resulting product or service is 99.99966% on target to the customer's specifications. It is hard to get much closer to our goal of perfection than that. We usually display these results in what is referred to as a Six Sigma defects per million opportunities chart as shown in Figure 5.3.

The DPMO chart assumes a 1.5 sigma shift because processes tend to exhibit instability of that magnitude over time. In other words, although statistical tables indicate that 3.4 defects/million is achieved when 4.5 process standard deviations (sigma) are between the mean and the closest

Sigma Score	DPMO *	% Good
0	933,193	0.067
1	691,462	30.85
2	308,538	69.15
3	66,807	93.32
4	6,210	99.38
5	233	99.98
6	3.4	99.9997
* - Defects per million opportunities		

Figure 5.3 Defects per million opportunities (DPMO) chart.[4]

specification limit, the target is raised to 6.0 standard deviations to accommodate adverse process shifts over time and still produce only 3.4 defects per million opportunities.

Toyota, through their Toyota Production System, has shown that at its very essence, the Six Sigma methodology is a unique, structured system to resolve workplace-critical issues. Some organizations have tried to approach the process from the point of view of an established quality department. Six Sigma can't operate as a silo and expect to achieve the goals we anticipate from our continuous process improvement efforts. Its goal is to take the culture of process improvement and embed it in cross-functional personnel determining where the problems are and potential solutions to the issues that arise. These potential solutions are not a finance problem, nor an HR problem—they are an organizational problem. It is not necessarily squarely centered on the ultimate results, but rather on how we got there.

The process.st[5] website presents us with seven principles regarding the Six Sigma methodology: customer focus, workflow, process flow, waste removal, removing variation, organizational buy-in, and making efforts evidence-based. As we have done with the other segments previously, it is worth our time to review these individually.

Principle #1: Six Sigma utilizes tools to identify and reduce waste in enterprise processes.

As shown in Figure 5.1, the Six Sigma methodology has its own set of tools. They are not designed to look for the low-hanging fruit as we did in our view of Lean. The tools and their uses are laid out in a specific manner that is designed to get us from the identification of the problem to the problem resolution steps. Each step leads to the next based on the results of the previous one. We define the problem and then we must ascertain what the problem is doing. We do so via clearly defined metrics. With the metrics in place, we need to analyze the results compared to what the problem is telling us. The results in front of us we can derive the steps to resolve the problem in the form of action steps. Finally, we can institute a system to control the process going forward.

Principle #2: Six Sigma always focuses on the customer.

Jack Welch at a GE shareholders meeting told them that "the best six-sigma projects begin not inside the business but outside of it, focused on the question: how can we make the customer more competitive? What is critical to the customer's success? One thing we discovered with certainty is that anything we do that makes the customer more successful inevitably results in a financial return for us."

We need our customers to survive as an organization. That means that we need to listen to what they are telling us is the problem facing them and why it is happening in their minds. That said, every organization needs to make sure that they understand their customer. Who are they? What is their corporate culture? What are their values? What are their current needs? What are their future needs? Allow me to flip the coin for a moment. What is their lifetime value (total sales divided by years as a customer)? It is imperative that your human capital assets and your organization become one with the customer. You must learn to think like your customer. You must learn to act like your customer. There needs to be no daylight between each other.

Principle #3: Six Sigma understands how work really happens.

You know what your organization does, or we hope that you do. But do you know how your organization does what you do? As an organization, you and your human capital assets must obtain knowledge on how your processes operate in the workplace. Just because you think a process works in a particular fashion does not mean that is the way it operates. Dr. Mikel Harry has told us we don't know what we don't know. The goal is to know. You should be able to walk the entire process, of every process, within the building and externally to the building. At your suppliers. At your customers. You should almost be able to walk it blindfolded. This comes from constant interaction between all parties.

You must be cognizant of the impediments to the process. What is slowing it down? What is speeding it up? Taiichi Ohno made his managers stand in a circle and observe the process for errors. He would not accept the response that you could not find any.

Principle #4: Six Sigma makes the process flow smart.

Six Sigma is designed to identify and remove errors in the process of delivering your products or services. The reasoning behind this effort is to ensure that we are meeting the expectations of the customer base. When we remove these errors, the process tends to flow more freely.

So how do we know that the processes are flowing smartly? We gain that knowledge by utilizing mapping tools to create process maps and, by extension, value stream maps. A value stream map outlines our processes

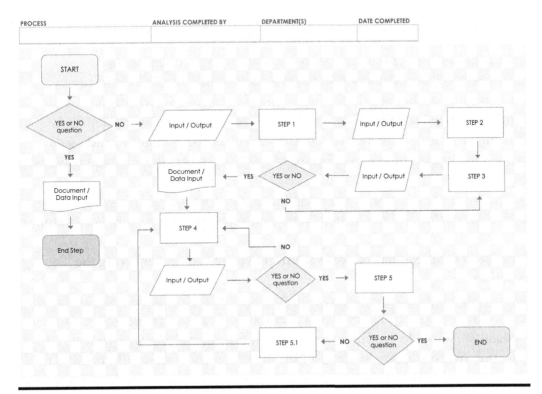

Figure 5.4 Process map.[6]

from the receiving deck to the shipping deck. Shown in the form of simple blocks, each block represents a step in the process. The tasks are connected by arrows to show the direction of the process flow.

We can supercharge the process map by converting it to a value stream map. The process map is converted by inserting the time intervals between the task blocks in the process map. In doing so, we now make it known in its current state exactly what the time interval is from the time the order is placed until we ship the order to the customer. This enables us to see visually where the process hang-ups might be occurring.

Six Sigma additionally places on us the obligation to review every day all our processes to understand how we can improve them.

Principle #5: Six Sigma focuses on value.

Our values include everything that in the long run affect the health and well-being of your organization and your customers. Michael George, in his book *Lean Six Sigma Pocket Toolbox*, tells us that there are three ways to classify our business values.

The first is value-added. These are the conditions that must be present to deliver the product or service to the customer. These are the value types that add to the service, enhance quality, or add an extra component.

The second are business non-value-added. While our goal is to remove the non-value-added activities, there can be occasions in which these non-value-added activities are necessary to meet the customer's demands. This might include activities required by regulations. It might include aids to the value-added activities. These examples are mandatory for the process to proceed.

The third are the non-value-added activities that we definitely want to remove from the process. It may very well represent the system constraint.

Principle # 6: Six Sigma reduces variation in processes by removing the variation.

One of the basics of the Six Sigma methodology is our processes must be repeatable. What do we mean by the term repeatable? Given a process, if the same process arises at some future date, the process should be able to be implemented using the same steps, the same instructions, the same players, and the same outcome.

Nature is funny and likes to play tricks on us. Even if we followed the exact same steps every time, there is no guarantee that the process will behave the same. As we stated earlier, every process is subject to some variation, usually about 1.5 Sigmas either above or below the mean. Thus, it becomes necessary to identify what type of variation we are dealing with. If you determine that it is a common cause or that it falls within the 1.5 sigma drift we discussed a minute ago, it is a common cause, and we can basically ignore it at this time. On the other hand, if the amount of the drift or variation exceeds that 1.5 sigma drift, then it is called a special cause, and the methodology tells us that our aim is to remove the variation.

By removing the special cause variation, we are enhancing the process at hand and therefore going forward the issue is moot, as the cause no longer exists.

Principle #7: Six Sigma understands that processes are an experiment and so approach change scientifically and according to the methodology.

It is important that we stress at this point that your role in the TLS Continuum is to perform as if you are a scientist. As such, when we enter

Scientific Method	DMAIC
Hypothesis	Define
Test Your Hypothesis	Measure
Analyze	Analyze
Draw a Conclusion	Improve
Communicate Your Results	Control

Figure 5.5   Scientific method steps vs. DMAIC process steps.

the process improvement effort, we take the same steps that you would undertake in a science experiment; we just use different terms.

The TLS Continuum is based on a concentrated process grounded in a path of discovery. Every one of you reading this book has been through a similar process. Take a minute and go back in time to your high school science classes. Each semester the science instructor began the first class with the same lesson for the day. Do you remember what it was? (I know what I am asking because I am a former science teacher, and I did it.) Typically the teacher began with a discussion of the steps of the scientific method.

The scientific method began with constructing a hypothesis, which represented your issue at hand. Once you identified that "what if" stage of the experimental process, you turned to testing whether your hypothesis was correct. You did that by taking measurements to prove or disprove your data, and from that you drew a conclusion as to whether your thinking was right or not. When you were done with the first stages, you then communicated your results to the indicated audience, whether that was your fellow students or the teacher. The scientific method is designed for the natural environment.

The Six Sigma methodology is no different. Both the scientific method and the Six Sigma methodology are designed to solve problems. The Six Sigma methodology is specifically designed for the business world.

Similar to the scientific method, the DMAIC method provides a roadmap for cross-functional teams to complete a process centered on improving the quality of your organizational transactional services or the products you produce.

As you can see in Figure 5.5, while the intent is the same, we just have changed the step nomenclature. You begin with defining the problem. What is the system telling you is the constraint that must be attended to? Once we have identified the constraint, we measure the effects of the constraint on the system to identify the impact of the problem on the organization. As with the scientific method, we take the measurements and analyze the data to find the cause of the problem. Then we use that analysis to improve the system and set up controls to ensure that the constraint does not return once we have removed it.

Principle #8: Six Sigma standardizes the various organizational processes.

The Six Sigma methodology has the expectation that all our organizational processes will be based on credible, verifiable, and repeatable data. From this data, the organization develops a set of instructions on how to implement the new processes.

Given these instructions, the organization develops a precise process for implementing the change process efforts each and every time the same type of process is called upon to resolve an issue. If you are producing a product or service, the delivery steps should be the same. The customer can expect that their order will be completed according to this process.

Notes

1 The Six Sigma toolbox is from the course materials in the Six Sigma Black Belt training at St. Petersburg College.
2 The bell curve is from the course materials in the Six Sigma Black Belt training at St. Petersburg College.
3 Dictionary.com. *Definition of Sigma.* http://dictionary.reference.com/browse/sigma?s=t. Based on Random House Dictionary, 2013
4 Process.st. *Principles of Six Sigma.* https://process.st/six-sigma-principles
5 The process map is from the course materials in the Six-Sigma Black Belt training class at St. Petersburg College.
6 The scientific method vs. DMAIC is taken from my book *Achieving HR Excellence Through Six Sigma.*

Chapter 6

The TLS Continuum Framework

Let's say we are having a holiday party. You have the table set. You have a voracious teenager who can't wait to get to the food. What do you expect his response would be if there was not enough dessert for everyone? That is or should be your reaction to the concepts presented in the previous three chapters.

Each of the methodologies (slices of the pie) are important in resolving the issues confronting your organization. In our presentation of the methodologies, we have tried to demonstrate the power of each of them: Theory of Constraints, Lean, and Six Sigma. Each on its own behalf brings to the table powerful tools and outcomes.

John Donne has told us that no man is an island. This is never more clearly presented than when you are looking at the world from only a third of the pie. If no single methodology can bring the improvements to your organization, what choice do we have?

Let us provide another perception of the issue at hand. Think back to the times when the family used to gather around the folding card table in the corner of the living room and worked to build that 1000-piece jigsaw puzzle. We can convert the jigsaw puzzle concept into Figure 6.1. The TLS Continuum framework is that jigsaw puzzle. If we do this, we come to realize that none of the methodologies can survive totally on their own. It is like putting the jigsaw puzzle together only to find you are missing the last piece to complete the picture.

DOI: 10.4324/9780429029196-7

Figure 6.1 TLS Continuum framework.[1]

As we stated, none of the pieces of the jigsaw can function totally on their own. Figure 6.1 allows us to see the interrelationships between the various pieces of the pie. Each of the slices of pie have their weaknesses. It is through the TLS Continuum that we can take the strengths of one methodology and apply them to the weaknesses of another. After some reflection, we need to change our focus from that of pieces of a pie to that of the pieces of the jigsaw puzzle. This realignment requires us to gain the knowledge and the understanding just how this relationship works in real time. The easiest way to do this is to look at the principles behind the TLS Continuum, as we did in the view of the individual methodologies.

Principle #1: The TLS Continuum views all processes (systems) as a chain.

We have several ways we can view how our organizations operate. The TLS Continuum requires us to view the organization from the socio-technical system (STS) view. STS requires us to view the world as a series of interdependent steps that are influenced by the work processes and the social skills of our human capital assets and our customers. These interdependent steps form a chain of events.

As we stated in Chapter 1, this chain needs to be viewed as a continuum rather than a cycle because our processes are the results of a series of chains. The chain represents the resources required and the interdependency of the various steps in the chain.

For the TLS Continuum to yield its maximum potential, we need to understand the chain and the steps of the chains not just for the immediate process but for all the processes within the organization. Sooner rather than later we will learn that all the processes are entangled within the chain. What finance does with their issues directly affects what HR does with their issues and so forth through the organization. The result is that the first principle of the TLS Continuum is to learn and understand the chains. Take the time to walk the Gemba walk and see the chains in action. Learn where the holdups are located.

It is also critical that you understand a primary point behind this view. If you have a problem in the chain, the problem is either caused by the process or by the policy attached. It is never the fault of the human capital assets or the customers.

Principle #2: The TLS Continuum understands that the expression of ideas is not a solution.

As an organization we tend to believe in the validity of groupthink. We believe that as Marshall Goldsmith said, "What got us here, won't get us there." We have a problem, so we rely on solutions from the past to resolve today's problems. Dr. Richard Feynman charges us to be careful not to believe things simply because we want them to be true.

Remember that all process improvement, as stated earlier, is an experiment. When we conduct an experiment, we arrive at thoughts about how to resolve the issue at hand. We do not arrive directly at solutions.

One of the keys to the TLS Continuum is the use of a revised toolbox of tools that we utilize to reach our goals. Part of that toolbox is the utilization of diversity in the methods we use to arrive at possible solutions in the form of ideas. We need to be open through collaboration to discover the initial thoughts on the causes of the problems. It is only through the remaining steps of the continuum that we propose the end solutions. However, before that we need to consider the second question of the Design4Gowth and ask ourselves what is possible out there to arrive at a solution. Understand that there is no such thing as a dumb idea as to the eventual resolution.

Principle #3: The TLS Continuum seeks out and identifies the system constraints.

Every day our organizations are confronted with a mire of issues. Each of these issues have some undesirable effect on the organization. But our focus is purely on the process and how it operates. We want to be able to walk through the process and identify where in that process we find some step, some policy, some part of the process that is telling the organization, "Sorry you don't get to proceed from here right now." We want to identify why those constraints appear, what caused them, and how to best remove them.

As we explained in Chapter 3, we need to begin with the premise that every process in existence has its hiccups. The problem is that we don't look for them. It is these hiccups that create the system constraints. Think about driving down a highway and suddenly there is a roadblock in your way. That roadblock says you are not going forward even if you want to. Your only recourse is to find a new way and take steps to remove the constraint. Welcome to the world of the TLS Continuum.

Principle #4: The TLS Continuum provides strategies to deal with excess system capabilities.

Utilizing the logical thinking tools, we answer the basic outcomes of the TLS Continuum. First, we identify what needs to change. This means we have identified the system constraint. Second, we determine how the process has to change and what the new normal looks like. Finally, we determine the strategies regarding how to make the change happen.

Once we identify the change goal, we take the steps to make it happen. What resources do we need both financially and manpower wise? Who do we need to buy into the new normal? How do we ensure that the stakeholders have bought into the process?

Principle #5: The TLS Continuum determines the most advantageous time to introduce the three pieces of the pie.

Bob Sproull, in his book *The Ultimate Improvement Cycle*, explains that as we proceed through the TLS Continuum there will be times when we realize that part of the improvement cycle is not fulfilled by the logical thinking tools alone.

For example, in the introduction of his book, Bob Sproull suggests that one of the weaknesses of the Theory of Constraints is that TOC does not directly address the need for cultural change, whereas Lean does. We can find numerous examples where the same circumstances will appear.

The TLS Continuum is by no means the magical answer to the problems confronting the organization. It is in the combination of the three methodologies that a vibrant model for process improvement is born.

Principles #6: The TLS Continuum methodology is a dynamic package of resources.

As we reach the conclusion of Part 1 of this book, it is the intent that the reader has begun to gain an understanding of the vitality of the model we

Focusing Step	TOC Tools	Six Sigma Tools	Lean Tools
Constraint Identification	Five Focusing Steps Current Reality Tree Evaporating Cloud	Voice of the Customer Project Charter Process Map	Value Definition Kaizen Events
Constraint Elevation	Pre-Requisite Tree	Benchmarking Measurement System Analysis	Value Stream Map Traffic Intensity SIPOC
Process Subordination	Drum-Buffer-Rope Goal Tree Transition Tree	Design of Experiments Risk Assessment Control Plans Determine New Capacity level	5S Pull Environment Visual Management Poke Yoke

Figure 6.2   TLS Continuum toolbox.

are proposing. It should be clear by now that we can't function with a third of a pie. It does not work in your holiday party, and it certainly does not work when management and your stakeholders expect—no correct that, demand— that you as a part of the critical chain will speak the language of business. That language of business is expressed in the principles of the TLS Continuum. Some of you are comfortable with speaking the language of business; still others are fighting tooth and nail to remain in the state of status quo. But this does not work in today's business world. You are faced with a wide assortment of paradoxes and dilemmas every day. Let us try and simplify it all for you.

Like Lean and Six Sigma before it, the TLS Continuum has its own toolbox. The toolbox is shown in Figure 6.2. It presents a graphic roadmap as to what tools we use when.

Note that unlike the Six Sigma toolbox, the TLS Continuum toolbox contains only three distinct steps. First we identify the constraint. Once have done that, we move to the task of making the constraint the primary task that the organization must work on. The final step is to make sure that the process progress is directly answerable to the constraint. If we are not resolving the constraint, then the process step can wait. The TLS Continuum focuses on continuously improving the *transactional process quality, getting the product or service to market faster,* and *reducing cost while improving the price to the customer.*

There is an axiom in the scientific community which states that the sum of the parts is greater than each contribution of the parts. Thus, when we make the observation that we only use TOC, or Lean, or Six Sigma at the expense of the rest of the pie, we are not delivering the ultimate capability of the process. We are approaching the continuous process improvement arena as if we are baking only a third of a pie. Stop and think for a moment and consider whether you are serving your customer by meeting his or her demands with only a third of the stable of tools. You owe it to your customers and to your organization to deliver the total package

As we have tried to present in Part 1, the TLS Continuum is as strong tool in the continuous process improvement effort with the agreement that its sister functions are critical to that resource. Let's try and visualize the process as we begin our journey through the process improvement path. Bobb Sproull, in his book *Epiphanized* (2nd ed.), presents the concept of a piping diagram. You can visually see the diagram in Figure 6.3.

Sit back for a moment and close your eyes. You are the head of public works for the city in which you live, and your phone is flooded with citizens calling to say that for some reason their water pressure has dropped significantly. Your job is to find and cure this problem. Your first task is to review the water system to see if you can discover the reason for the water pressure issue.

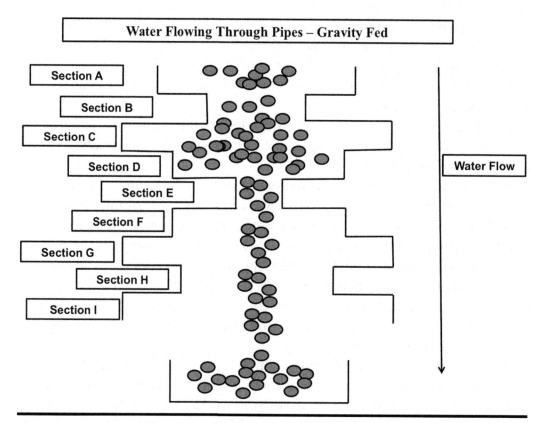

Figure 6.3 Bob Sproull's piping diagram.[2,3,4]

What you determine is the subject of Figure 6.3. Your water system is fueled by the force of nature called gravity. The gravitational force pulls the water down through the system until it ends in a receiving area at the end of the process. So where is the problem? What you know is that the water pressure has dropped. What you found, and almost anyone looking at the system will notice, is that the water flows through your system fine until it reaches point E. It is here that the water flow for some reason is constricted. Using the logical thinking tools, it is easy to determine that the solution is to clear the constraint at point E. Once we fix the flow at point E, it is likely that another flow obstacle will appear.

This an example of the TLS Continuum in practice. We used the logical thinking tools to establish the causes of the problem and then used the continuum toolbox to resolve the constraint. The remainder of this book will take us through that effort in specific terms and strategies, beginning with Part 2, where we discuss how to start the process off by identifying just what is wrong with it.

Notes

1 Taken from the book *How to Achieve HR Excellence through Six Sigma.*
2 Definition of a solution. *Merriam Webster Dictionary.* www.merriam-webster. com/dictionary/solution
3 Sproull, Bob. *The Ultimate Improvement Cycle.* New York, NY: CRC Press, 2009. Page xxxvii.
4 Sproull, Bob and Bruce Nelson. *Epiphanized.* 2nd Edition. New York, NY: CRC Press, 2015. Pages 13–15.

2

CONTINUOUS PROCESS IMPROVEMENT JOURNEY

The continuous process improvement is a unique journey. When you plan a trip (i.e., journey), you lay out a departure time and date, the route you are going to take, and the date of the expected arrival at your destination along with the length of the stay and the date you plan to return to your original location. The continuous process improvement journey is nothing like that. We can provide you with a departure date, but that is the extent of our knowledge in the beginning.

The continuous process improvement journey has no clearly defined destination, although we have some preliminary concept of that point using our goal statement or problem statement. It does not even have a clearly defined path or route you are going to take to get to your ultimate destination. The route is discovered by utilizing the business scientific method, as described in Figure 5.5. In Part 1 of this book, we laid the foundations of the TLS Continuum along with the role it plays in the resolution of problems within the critical chain. We still have not delineated just what the continuous process improvement entails. That is the purpose of Part 2.

Before we begin that exploration, we need to first deal with the "bull in the china cabinet" that we will find in many organizations today. This issue is the tendency for organizations to guard the status quo through the provision of reasoning as to why the continuous process improvement effort will not work. These reasons become the modus operandi behind every attempt to introduce change of any kind to the organization.

DOI: 10.4324/9780429029196-8

Reason #1: It is a manufacturing thing.

Your function is grounded in HR, finance, sales, etc. You have no direct involvement in the manufacturing floor. We recognize that the origins of the Lean and Six Sigma methodologies rest in the manufacturing floor. In the beginning of the total quality movement, the world was firmly entrenched within the industrial age following World War II. An organization's brand and reputation in the marketplace were based on the quality of the products it produced. Deming and those who followed him were reviewing problems that arose out of the resulting process. The constant goal was to produce end-user products that were readily available to the marketplace and that provided products that the end users would pay for. The end user is seeking product that is delivered and that fulfills the purpose for which it was intended. The end user is seeking products that are free from defects making them less valuable to their organization. Deming, Ishikawa, and Smith saw processes that were basically flawed from the very nature of their existence. These processes were not meeting the needs of their customers due to rework due to defects in the production process.

The organizational functions that are outside the manufacturing side of the business also have their widgets.

Like the production side of the coin, the transactional side also produces widgets. The difference is that our widgets are less tangible in nature. Our widgets, as Ken Miller argues in his book, *We Don't Make Widgets*,[1] are the process outputs that are generated by the transactional side of the business when it delivers its services in order to serve the stakeholders of the organization. Our widgets are items like applications for candidates, policy descriptions when we create handbooks and manuals, the end results of harassment investigations, and other final reports. However, these widgets are still a vital part of the organization. Because they are not tangible in nature, our widgets are not something that a staff person can necessarily turn to and say, "wait a minute something is wrong." While the widgets are not measurable like on the factory floor, the transactional functions are a factory of sorts. This means that the output is measurable just like if we were on that factory floor. Our transactional widgets are still able to produce credible, verifiable data measure points to solve the process defects.

Reason #2: That's not the way we do things here.

As humans, we tend to become ingrained with the status quo. When a new concept is presented to the organization, the tendency is for the organization to say, "wait a minute, this not how we do things here." The new solution is not part of the existing corporate culture, so it has to be wrong. This approach is limited in its focus on the world as it is. We view the world as if we were looking in a mirror. We express the view that we know what the organization is like and there is no need for a change.

Reason #3: We tried that, and it didn't work in our organization.

Business annals are filled with examples of management decisions to get the latest great tool. Business annals are filled with examples where management tried to take shortcuts to implement these tools only to be met with disaster. As human beings, we tend to want the newest and greatest tool that becomes available to make our lives "easier."

The implementation of TLS in an organization requires some fundamental changes to the organization. When we try and implement the latest tool without thinking it through, the premise going in is flawed. TLS Continuum–related improvement efforts fail because the organization has not made the required changes to the basis for making decisions. The perspective on the business marketplace needs to shift from the organization to focus on what the customer wants and needs. In many cases, as we will show later in this book, the first requirement is a culture change. Management touts the changes but wants to do it on the terms of the organization at that moment or in the past. It is these kinds of circumstances that bring about the response that the system does not work. These are the kinds of circumstances that bring out the response that it is not right for our organization. While management wants the successes that have been reported, they are not interested in making the changes we will discuss in future chapters. The TLS Continuum process is a structured response to a problem, but one of the critical factors here is that to fully realize the benefits to the organization and the customers, we need to create a new way of doing business. Failure to achieve this organizational change is what leads to the failure of TLS Continuum improvement efforts.

60 of TLS Continuum Field Guide

The failure comes from trying to take shortcuts to the end game. The failure comes from the organization fully accepting the new corporate normal and going back to the old way of doing things.

Reason #4: It is too highly complex to be used in most organizations.

Organizations tend to stereotype their human capital assets. We tend to believe that what we are asking of our human capital assets is beyond their capabilities. We believe that the changes of the journey being successful is very much in doubt.

The whole basis of the total quality movement was the work of Dr. Deming, who was by trade a statistician. His fellow champions of the total quality movement mostly were engineers. By their very nature, they are steeped in detailed analysis of data. We totally understand that high math is not everyone's cup of tea. Further, this strong demand for high-level math has lost followers on the way along our journey. Motorola today no longer offers the high-level training it used to due to the complexity of the data and the training requirements. With advances in technology today, you don't need to be a statistician. If you know how to use an Excel worksheet, you can obtain software in the form of Excel add-ins which will do all the data analysis for you.

Returning to our journey, Part 2 consists of three chapters that pertain to the beginning of the journey. In Chapter 7 we will discuss the nature of goals and where the concept came from. In Chapter 8 we will look at how to go about establishing the suggested destination. How do we determine what we need to improve? How do we utilize the TLS Continuum toolbox to establish the goal? In Chapter 9 we will look at how to present the goal statement. It is not a case of constructing a two-word answer. We need to make a clear statement as to the intent of this journey.

Before we begin, however, there is another factor that must be discussed. What makes a goal so powerful? In 1991, in her award-winning album, *Luck of the Draw* Bonnie Raitt presented her seminal single titled "Something to Talk About."[2] When we create that goal statement, we are left with two alternatives. First, we can determine the goal statement and keep it in our heads, maybe even write it down in some journal or database. This is all well and good, but the audience is limited as a result. The second alternative is to take Bonnie Raitt at her word and create something to talk about. Create that goal statement and circulate it inside the organization both to management and to your human capital assets. If they touch the problem, they need to be involved. Then share that goal statement with your external stakeholders. Every part of the TLS Continuum's critical chain must be knowledgeable as to what you are trying to achieve.

Reason #5: It's not my job.

In line with "that is not how we do things around here" is the excuse of a human capital asset based on the corporate culture stating that they can't do something because that is not in their job description.

Notes

1 Miller, Ken. *We Don't Make Widgets*. Washington, DC: Government Press, 2010.
2 Raitt, Bonnie. "Something to Talk About." Song #1 on the album *Luck of the Draw*. Capital Records, June 25, 1991.

Chapter 7

What Is a Goal?

Stop for a moment and think about what comes to mind when you are asked what a goal is. We suspect that you have different responses depending on your frame of mind. In my book, *Achieving HR Excellence Through Six Sigma* (2nd ed.), I faced the same dilemma when you were asked to define the term excellence. As we stated, the definition of excellence is in the eye of the beholder. We have the same scenario in determining the definition of a goal.

If you Google the question "what is a goal?" you get 8,650,000,000 results. If you Google "goal setting training," you get 489,000,000 hits. If we search Amazon for business titles pertaining to goal setting, we get 50,000 titles. If we change the search parameters to "what is a goal?" we narrow the search down to 672 titles. If we throw the issue of context into the equation, in the sports world, a goal is nothing more than the net at the end of the playing field.

The Oxford Dictionary of Languages defines a goal as "the object of a person's ambition or effort; an aim or desired result."

According to the blog Weekdone (https://blog.weekdone.com/what-are-goals-in-business-how-to-master-them-in-2020/), a goal is something you write down and discuss what a company or team would like to achieve before a set deadline. As we said in the introduction to Part 2, a goal provides us with something to talk about. The career website Indeed tells us that goals define what a business purpose is and the general direction that the organization will follow. In the TLS Continuum, it is common for us to replace the term goal with the term problem statement. Understand that going forward through the remaining pages of this book, we will see the

DOI: 10.4324/9780429029196-9

two terms interchangeably. It is the very first item in the project charter. One critical part of the problem statement is the description of what the problem is over time. Not an indefinite time, but a very precise time frame. Consider this problem statement from my earlier book, *The Field Guide to Achieving HR Excellence Through Six Sigma*.[1] An electronics firm in a Six Sigma–related project stated that they were seeking to reduce the average time to fill salaried positions from 111 days to 71 days. In addition, they sought to reduce their cost per hire from 13.5% to 9%. As we stated earlier, the goal statement is specific, explains a problem over time, and sets a metric to show successful completion.

The use of the word goal is not something new in our vocabulary. The website etymonline.com tells us that the first suggestion of a goal dates to the 14th century and originally referred to a goal, as the word gal. obstacle or barrier. In the 1530s unknown writings referred to a goal as the endpoint of a race. A decade later the term was referred to as the object of an effort.[2]

With the preliminary definition of a goal in mind, it is prudent for us to explore the conditions behind a goal's existence and chances for successful completion. Dr. Ayelet Fishbach, the Jeffrey Breakenridge Keller Professor of Behavioral Science and Marketing and IBM Corporation Faculty Scholar at the University of Chicago's Booth School of Business and one of the world's leading experts in goal research, defines in her phenomenal book *Get It Done: Surprising Lessons from the Science of Motivation* (I highly recommend that you obtain a copy and read it cover to cover)[3] the necessary conditions for us to create successful goals. These necessary conditions are discussed next.

7.1 A Goal (Problem Statement) Is Not a Proxy or a Means to Reach Another Goal

The Oxford Dictionary of Languages tells us that a mean is "a thing that is not valued or important in itself but is useful in achieving an aim." A goal or problem statement is not a thing that is not valued but is useful in achieving an aim. The goal or problem statement is the result of your organization identifying a system constraint. The goal or problem statement is your organization's belief on how to remove the system constraint so that your process system runs smoother. It is not to use the goal as a stepping-stone to another goal if you will. Many of you might be familiar with the term proxy in conjunction with your investments. It means that you are allowing some-one else to represent your interests. When we look at our goal, the process does not allow us to use the goal as a vehicle to someone else's goal. If you are a member of Generation X or Generation Y, you are constantly looking to add to your skill set by gaining those skills that will take you to the next level in your career. If you have ever been in a search for new employment, we guarantee that a friend or a recruiter has advised you to accept this posi-tion because it will advance your career. When I worked as an executive recruiter, I guarantee that on more than one occasion, I was guilty of advis-ing a candidate in this vein. In this scenario we are using the career decision in a proxy mode. We are using the career decision as a means to reach a future goal. While remotely the goal and a mean might be intertwined, they are not dependent on each other. Our goal is particular to this time and this place.

Within the TLS Continuum, the concept that one goal/problem statement can be a way to reach an entirely different goal is just not feasible. We can't use the current goal to resolve some nebulous goal at some point in the uncertain future. This is true for several reasons.

First, you can't predict the future. You are not able to predict if there will be another problem or system constraint even though the likelihood is strong that there will be one. Consider Professor Richard Feynman's state-ment: "I can't define a real problem; therefore, I suspect no real problem, but I am not sure there's no real problem." If Feynman is correct, you can't determine a future problem if you don't understand the current one. Don't misunderstand me by assuming that there will never be a future problem/goal because when we cure one system constraint, it is more than likely that another system constraint will raise its head almost immediately. This is because when you change a process flow, there are bound to be hiccups in the system.

Second, the goal (problem statement) contains a specific time frame. The expectation is that we are dealing with time as an essential element within our organizations. The time to resolve the system constraint is now, not at some undetermined time in the future. Using the goal/problem statement to reach another goal/problem statement additionally will lead to an extended process time and thus increased work in progress. A goal/problem statement is focused on a specific issue, at a specific time, and for a specific duration. When you are confronted with an organizational problem, it is not focused on some long-term condition, but rather it is based on real-time reality.

Your goals/problem statements are created based on your customers, internally or externally, telling your organization that there is a problem. That problem is facing their operations here and now. The purpose of the goal/problem statement is therefore to discover what the true nature of the problem is and why it is existing. The goal/problem statement is directed toward the plausible solutions to the problem.

7.2 A Goal (Problem Statement) Should Describe a Purpose Without Losing Sight of the Actions You Need to Reach Them

If you are representative of most organizations in the business world, you tend to look at your problems from a very narrow constrained view focused solely on the results. How you got there is not as important as obtaining the desired results. Did you resolve the problem so that the customer is satisfied?

The TLS Continuum looks at the goal/problem statement from a different view. The TLS Continuum views the goal/problem statement from the perspective of the critical chain. Our concern is what causes the process to slow down. So rather than concentrating on the results, we want to consider the various steps of the process. Where did we get the solutions from, and how relevant are they? Our center of attention is therefore not on the results, but on the various possible solutions to the problem. Since the continuous process improvement is in essence a science experiment, the tendency to want a quick result is a false pretense.

When we work to establish the goal/problem statement, we must be cognizant of the steps we need to take to reach the solution. As stated earlier, the steps are clearly delineated. We know what those steps are and how they are related to the goal/problem statement.

7.3 A Goal (Problem Statement) Should Be Attainable and Within Reach

Some of the writings around setting goals talk about the existence of SMART goals. The expectation is that the goals will be specific, as we already discussed earlier, but also measurable, relevant, and time bound. The best goals/problem statements are ones that cause the organization to stretch but that are still attainable. The selection of a goal should challenge all parties, but not at the risk of not reaching the goal. If we make the goals too far out in left field, we risk the possibility of reducing the motivation of the parties involved to try and reach the goals.

A key part of the continuous process improvement effort is to create so-called stretch goals. The website Wrike (www.wrike.com) tells us that stretch goals are a high-effort and high-risk effort. Stretch goals are intentionally set above normal standards to attract exponential rewards, opportunities, and experience. They are designed to challenge your organization to go beyond what you think possible. In our discussions of HR excellence, it is suggested that one of the aspects of defining HR excellence was that three areas came to present themselves.

First, the development of our goal/problem statements should be willing to risk more than others think safe to change the corporate culture. With the goal statement, we are changing the organizational norms. We are devising new processes. Second, the development of our goal/problem statements should expect more than others find possible from your human capital assets. Third, ensure that you remove any stereotypes as to what the organization can do. Be open-minded as to where the search for solutions can take you. The solution of the *Challenger* explosion came from a retired engineer fiddling around in his home workshop. Finally, be willing to be open to considering how much more your organization can achieve than others think practical.

7.4 A Goal (Problem Statement) Should Be Designed Around a Goal Even If It Has an Uncertain Chance of Success

I recently conducted a Six Sigma Yellow Belt training course in which one of the participants stated in his evaluation that the least useful part of the class was the final project since his management would never let him implement the project. He was missing the point.

As I stated in the introduction to Part 2, the TLS Continuum is a unique journey without a clearly defined destination. As a result, we don't know whether we will succeed in our efforts.

Even if we don't succeed in our journey, there are still benefits to the organization. Thomas Alva Edison told us that he never failed; he just found what didn't work. The important thing is that you tried to resolve the problem. Understand the initial problem statement is not written in stone. As we implement the TLS Continuum toolbox, we may very well find that the goal/ problem statement needs to be revised to meet the conditions uncovered in the process.

7.5 A Goal/Problem Statement Should Be Intrinsic In that Even If No One Else Cared, You Felt Good that You Tried to Reach the Top

Accept the fact that in every organization, there will be those who will tell you that you are wasting your time. There will be those who will tell you that what you are suggesting won't work. Understand in the long run that despite the naysayers' comments' they will all benefit from your goal/prob- lem statement. The cross-functional team should be embedded in the project solution despite what others in the organization or marketplace are telling us. The problem needs to be resolved despite what anyone thinks or says.

7.6 A Goal/Problem Statement Should Feel Exciting and Not Like a Chore

Think of your approach to the problem as if you were a scientist. If you do, you will find the excitement of the journey just as a scientist conduct- ing an experiment does. The excitement comes from not being sure what the experiment will find. The excitement comes from discovering new and powerful solutions to the problems facing your organization.

How do you feel about potentially changing your workplace? Are you gung-ho to get started, or are you harboring the attitude that you have more important things to do, so just get this assignment done so I can get back to what is piling up on my desk?

7.7 A Goal/Problem Statement Should Be Specific and Quantifiable

Think back to the goal/problem statement from the electronics company discussed earlier in this chapter. Their goal/problem statement met all the required conditions of any goal/problem statement. It was specific in nature in terms of what they wanted to achieve. It was quantifiable in that it set specific metrics to determine the performance levels. Finally, it was specific in nature of the time allotment to achieve the goal/performance statement. To be successful, the TLS Continuum must be credible, repeatable, and verifiable.

7.8 A Goal/Problem Statement Should Be Defined in Terms of Its Benefits Not Its Costs

The TLS Continuum challenges you to look at the organization through a different set of lenses. The age-old basis for problem-solving takes the problem and its associated solutions and looks at it from the point of reference as how much it will cost to implement the expected changes. This view is increasingly becoming obsolete in determining the outcome of potential project solutions. Today's view should be based on how the organization and its customers will benefit from the new corporate normal. In fact, the final section of the project charter provides you space to describe the project impact. The purpose of the project impact statement is to define what the stakeholders will achieve from the changes we have made to the corporate culture and the process at hand. The TLS Continuum achieves this change using throughput accounting which will be discussed in Chapter 25 of the book.

Notes

1 Bloom, Daniel. *Field Guide to Achieving HR Excellence through Six Sigma.* New York, NY: Productivity Press, 2016. Page 110.
2 Definition of a goal. www.etymonline.com/word/goal
3 Fishbach, Ayelet. *Get It Done: Surprising Lessons from the Science of Motivation.* New York, NY: Little, Brown Spark, 2022. Pages 2–3, 8, 10, 77.

Chapter 8

Goal Identification

Let's begin our journey. As in any journey, we have to begin by defining a starting point. In the case of the TLS Continuum, that starting point is the identification of the goal of the continuous process. If we take the old adage from the field of journalism, we need to begin with the who, what, where, and when of the journey. The goal/problem statement represents the who and the what of the journey. The goal tells who has the problem and what that problem is.

The first step is to identify the what of the equation. What exactly are we facing? In my book, *Achieving HR Excellence Through Six Sigma* (2nd ed.), I introduced the ten commandments of project selection. It is these ten steps that define how we identify the goal.

8.1 Thou Shalt Become One with the Customer/ Client Internally or Externally

To properly identify our goal, we must understand our customers. Both the ones inside and outside our organizations. The initial understanding you need to ascertain is that if there is an actual problem, the customer is going to be the first one to see it. Do not make the mistake of thinking that just because a customer tells you that they have a problem, they are just trying to game the system. Their problems are real.

Dr. Tony Alessandra, in his book *The Platinum Rule*, tells us that the reason organizations exist is to acquire and maintain customers. Joseph Juran tells us that quality planning consists of developing the products and

 DOI: 10.4324/9780429029196-10

processes required to meet customers' needs. Jack Welch, in a presentation to GE stockholders said,

> The best Six Sigma projects begin not inside the business but outside it, focused on answering the question—how can we make the customer more competitive? What is critical to the customer's success? One thing we have discovered with certainty is that anything we do that makes the customer more successful inevitably results in financial return to us.

Kathy Schissler, of Destination Breakthrough LLC, tells us that to play in the game, we need to choose to play, stop and think, seek to appreciate your customers, and learn to execute by hearing the voices of the customer. As we will see in Chapter 10, a critical part of understanding our customers is to recognize the difference between a shareholder and a stakeholder. We do not care whether the customer has any equity in your organization. Our concern and interest are in what they need from us in the way of products and services, which in turn advances their operations.

8.2 Thou Shalt Remember That the Customer Is the One That Pays the Bills

In line with the previous step, we need to return to Dr. Tony Alessandra's charge that our goal is to acquire and maintain our customers. We need to look at Eliyahu Goldratt's view that our organizations exist to make money. Where does that come from? The monies to operate our organizations come from the purchases of our products and services by our customers.

Principle #3: Thou shalt become engaged in constant communications to all stakeholders.

Remember in the introduction to Part 2 we suggested that you listen to "Something to Talk About" off Bonnie Raitt's *Luck of the Draw* album. The key to identifying the goal/problem statement and to resolving the issues at hand is to communicate, communicate, and communicate. We want to communicate our failures as well as our successes. The communication flow should not be an off thing you do. Every one of our stakeholders deserves to be fully informed about the progress of the efforts to resolve their problems. They should share the same access as your managers and your cross-functional teams have.

8.3 Thou Shalt Never Stop Questioning Everything

Part of the goal identification process is that you need to change your mindset. You are now a business scientist and as such you need to question everything. Our processes are not set in stone. They are subject to change as circumstances change. We can only begin to establish the changes if we question what it is we are doing, why we are doing it, and what the obstacles are to change—both real and imagined.

8.4 Thou Shalt Never End the Improvement Process Because You Think that You Solved the Problem Early

Once again, we can refer back to Prof. Richard Feynman who told us that we must be careful not to believe things simply because we want them to be true. There is a constant attempt to try and speed up the solutions to the process problems. It is incumbent on us to avoid the temptation. We are not done with the improvement process until the process tells us based on credible, verifiable, and repeatable results that we have truly resolved the issue. If you have resolved the issue early, go back and recheck your data, your conclusions, and your new normal characteristics to ensure that you met all the milestones of your project. Don't try to rush an improvement because you are trying to save time.

8.5 Thou Shalt Always Be Available to Stakeholders, Responding Promptly to Inquiries

We talked earlier about the need for constant communication. This also applies to when the stakeholder calls with a question regarding the status of the improvement effort. The TLS Continuum recognizes that we are all partners in the improvement effort and must be equal partners. Stakeholders deserve your attention if they have a question. They deserve that response sooner rather than when you think you can get around to it.

8.6 Thou Shalt Strive to Meet the Customer Demands Faster, Better, and Cheaper

Our customers have needs and deadlines which are established by their customers. As a result, our ultimate goal should be to deliver our products and services before they need them, which enables them to deliver to their customer sooner. It also means that in doing so, we must work to deliver the product or services with as little presence of defects as possible.

8.7 Thou Shalt Recognize the Importance of the Entire Human Assets to the Process

As we will see in Part 3, our efforts to make improvements and thus to identify our goal/problem statement do not happen in a vacuum. The human capital assets that are involved in the entire process—both ours and our customers—are critical to our success.

Therefore, it is mandatory that no one at any level try and stereotype our subject matter experts. They must be recognized for the contribution they make to identifying the goal/problem statement and then the implementation of the selected solutions.

8.8 Thou Shalt Ensure that Improvement Efforts Are Aligned with Corporate Missions and Strategy

The final step is that whatever solutions we define must be in total alignment with our organization's missions, values, goals, and strategies. Goals are more than the goal/problem statement we are discussing here. In this instance, we are referring to what your organization stands for and how you plan on delivering on that message.

With those steps having been completed, we can turn our direction to how we identify the goal/problem statement that provides the basis for the improvement effort. The state of Michigan tells us that our goals should begin by establishing an idea or objective as to why we are choosing this particular goal. Michigan says that objectives are developed to help achieve goals by dividing them into manageable components. Successful completion of multiple objectives is needed for each individual goal. Some objectives may themselves have components that can be expressed as "action steps," but it is vital to eventually identify in the goal identification all the details that will guide and encourage concrete actions to be taken.[1]

As we begin the process of identifying the goal/problem statement, we need to remain cognizant of the factors that ensure our success in doing this. First, we must lay out a logical path to reaching the established goal, including the various steps we will utilize to reach the goal. Each of these steps needs to be looked at as if you are a journalist. You need to define the who, what, where, and when of each of the solutions suggested.

Once you have determined the goal/problem statement, you must be fully committed to its conclusion. Further, the goal needs to be specific, with a time limit and a plan for rewarding your successes. Once we have determined the goal/problem statement, it is critical that we make that goal/problem statement public, so all stakeholders understand what it is we are seeking to achieve.

To gain a better understanding of the identification of the goal/problem statement, the most efficient way to do this is to undertake a business tool called role playing. The purpose of role playing is to put you in someone else's shoes who may be facing a similar dilemma to the one you are facing.

The scenario: *A member of management receives a telephone call in which your largest customer informs you that there is a major problem with your product or service delivery.*

If you are like a vast majority of members of management, your first reaction would be "that can't be right." No one in the organization has provided even a hint of anything wrong. This typically leads to further questions such as: What else is wrong?

With the realization that the organization has problem, the organization or management would want to review the process involved. The quickest way to do this is to map out the process using a process map like the one shown in Figure 8.1.

The creation of the process map begins to show you where the problem might be residing within your organization. Carefully review the completed map to see if there are any obvious steps that could be causing the problem. Follow this action by asking the five whys. This concept was created by Sakichi Toyoda, who firmly believed that by asking the question why surrounding a problem, both the problem and the indicated solutions become clearer.

With the responses to the five whys collected, we then can begin to determine the causes of the problem at hand. For everyone involved to

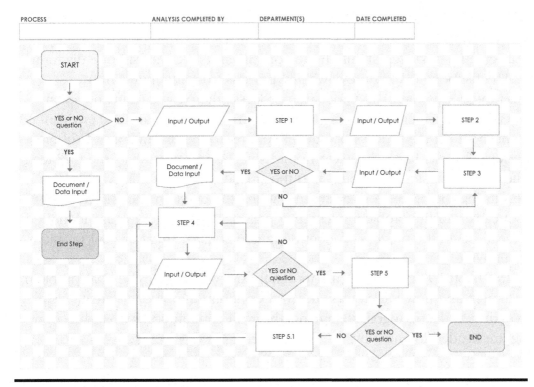

Figure 8.1   Process map.

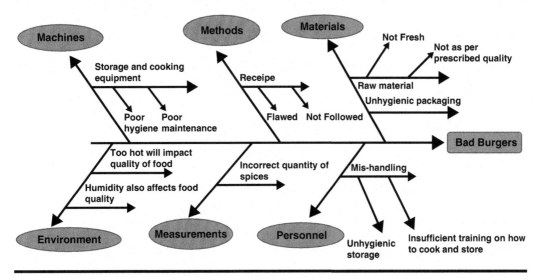

Figure 8.2   Fishbone diagram.

better understand the causes and effects, it is necessary that we meet the various ways individuals intake information. To meet the needs of visual learners, the next step should be to compile an Ishikawa fishbone diagram.

The fishbone diagram reviews any process from the inputs from machines (equipment), methods (the process), the people (human capital assets), management (your managers), materials, metrics, and the environment in which the process operates. We refer to the diagram as a fishbone because it looks like the skeleton of a fish. The rear represents the problem. The arms represent the inputs, and the smaller bones look at what might be causing the problem in each area. When the diagram is completed, the root causes of the problem become apparent. With the root cause identified, we can begin the process of identifying and constructing our goal/problem statements.

In Chapter 9, we will discuss in detail how we develop the goal/problem statement and how we can use the TLS Continuum toolbox to create clear, dynamic, and strong goal statements that will communicate what direction we are headed in and why.

Note

1 www.michigan.gov/documents/8-pub207_60743_7.pdf

Chapter 9

Creating the Goal Statement

We have utilized the various tools from the TLS Continuum toolbox to identify our goal/problem statement, and we have determined what we believe is the right path to resolve the issue that the client or stakeholder has brought to our attention. The next task is communicate that path to the entire breadth of the stakeholders. How do we present that goal/problem statement so it is clearly understood by everyone?

Remember Clint Eastwood's movie *The Good, the Bad and the Ugly?* When we look at the goal/problem statements, we can find the same scenario. The ugly is simple—it is not worth the paper it is printed on. We have all seen them. They might very well read similar to this: "we will fix the recruiting process." The statement does not tell us much. There is no time frame for reference. There is no performance metric discussed. There is no specific reference to what you are fixing. The response might appease management, but it does not resolve the issue at hand.

The bad is equally worthless. The problem might be slightly better presented and a time reference might be provided, but the specificity of the problem is still lacking. The discussion of the problem may be broader than the ugly version, but it is still lacking the complete picture. Joseph Juran tells us that "Goal setting has traditionally been based on past performance. This practice has tended to perpetuate the sins of the past." The bad goal/problem statement adheres itself to what we have done in the past. There is no indication that we are conducting experimentation to see what the true causes are.

What, then, are the characteristics of the good goal/problem statement? The University of Sheffield in the United Kingdom tells their students that

DOI: 10.4324/9780429029196-11

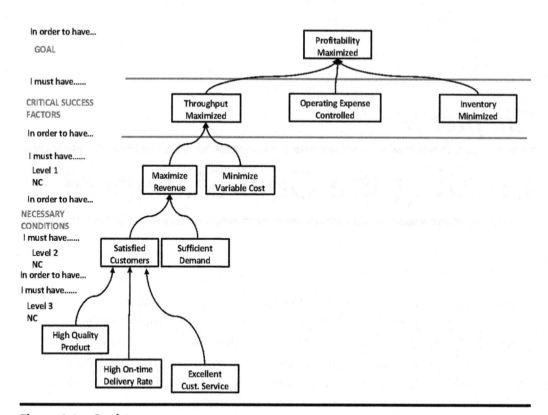

Figure 9.1   Goal tree.

In 1995 at a Goldratt Institute event, Oded Cohen of TOC Strategic Solutions Ltd. described the concept of the intermediate objectives map or IO map. The idea behind the IO map was to keep the organization focused on what made the system work successfully. We have stressed throughout this book so far the need for a standard of work. The IO map provides a vehicle for measuring a standard of system performance. It provides a way for your organization to determine how far from that standard of performance you are operating at. It thus provides a graphic presentation of the goal/problem statement and the intermediate steps necessary to reach the goal/problem statement. Additionally, the IO map helps set the boundaries of the process improvement effort. It identifies what efforts of change are located within the system and which are extraneous to the process improvement effort. In the article "Intermediate Objectives Map" by H. William Dettmer, he tells us that the IO map is explaining that knowing what we know now about our system and its environment, if you want to achieve this goal, these are the things—the building blocks—that must be successfully accomplished.[1]

a problem statement is **usually one or two sentences to explain the problem your process improvement project will address**. In general, a problem statement will outline the negative points of the current situation and explain why these matter. Let's break this down to its essence. First, it is not one or two words; it is a complete sentence or sentences and presents a detailed explanation of the problem at hand. It points out the negative issues and why the problem resolution is important. It is important to understand that we are not at this point suggesting solutions, as we have not completed the steps to identify them. It is also critical that we understand at this juncture that we are not talking about the final project impact, so the problem statement is not written in stone and can be changed as we proceed with the process of removing the system constraints. Going back to our previous discussions of the journalist creed, the statement should answer five very specific questions (who, what, why, when, and where).

This chapter will look at two different versions of a goal/problem statement. One looks forward in the form of the goal tree, and the other looks backward at the problem resolution tree.

9.1 Goal Tree

In 2002 H. William Dettmer reconsidered the concept when he changed the name from an IO map to that of a goal tree. The goal statement combines the five different logical thinking tools to make it easier to understand where we are headed in the improvement efforts.

Dettmer found that the industry was struggling with the development and presentation of the current reality tree, as we will see in Chapter 14. Part of the difficulty was that the current reality tree and the related tool, the evaporating cloud, lacked a focus on the problem at hand.

The goal tree begins with clearly defining the boundaries of your system. Let's be perfectly clear right from the start. Your organization is a system. Your processes have one responsibility and only one responsibility. Your organization must deliver something of value to your customer. The website https://searchwindowsservertechtarget.com/defiition/system tells us that a system is a collection of elements or components that are organized for a common purpose (i.e., your processes).

With the boundaries in place, the next step is to determine the end outcome of your system improvement. This more than likely is going to be what your customer is demanding. What is it you are trying to achieve? The response becomes your goal/problem statement.

With the goal/problem statement established, we need to move to the next level in the goal tree. You have established the goal/problem statement, so now look at it again and determine the key performance indicators that will tell your organization that you have achieved your goal. These are the critical success factors or CSFs. The CSFs are the must-haves.

The North Carolina State University IES program contends that there are five main CSFs for project managers that should be considered. First, agree on the project goals. Second, have clearly developed plans with assigned responsibilities. Third, manage the project scope effectively. Fourth, cultivate constant communication, and finally, gain management support.

CSFs represent high-level performance metrics, and there should never be more than three to five such factors for each process within your organization. These CSFs are placed in your goal tree immediately below the block representing the goal/problem statement and connected with arrows running upward showing the relationship between the CSFs and the goal/problem statement.

Stop for a moment and consider this scenario. You have decided to take a trip and drive Orlando. Your goal/problem statement is the trip to Orlando. Your CSFs are you need a car and then you need to determine the next step.

That next step is referred to in the goal tree as necessary conditions. These represent what must happen for you to achieve your CSFs. In our Orlando trip, that necessary condition may very well be that you have gas to fuel the car. There are no limits to the number of necessary conditions that you can have. If you look at Figure 9.1, you can see that the example shows seven necessary conditions. While you are not limited in the number of necessary conditions, you do want to ensure that the ones you do identify are within the boundaries of the system that you have recognized.

As we did in the case of the CSFs, we draw arrows up from the necessary conditions to the CSFs to manifest the relationship between them.

The completed goal tree is read as follows: with the necessary conditions in place, we can achieve the critical success factors that are vital to us obtaining our goal/problem statement successfully.

In my book *Achieving HR Excellence Through Six Sigma*, I decided to turn Dettmer and Cohen on its head if you will. During our discussion earlier we talked about the progression through the various steps of creating the goal tree. In considering the intentions behind the goal tree, which is designed to be proactive in nature, why couldn't we also be reactive at the

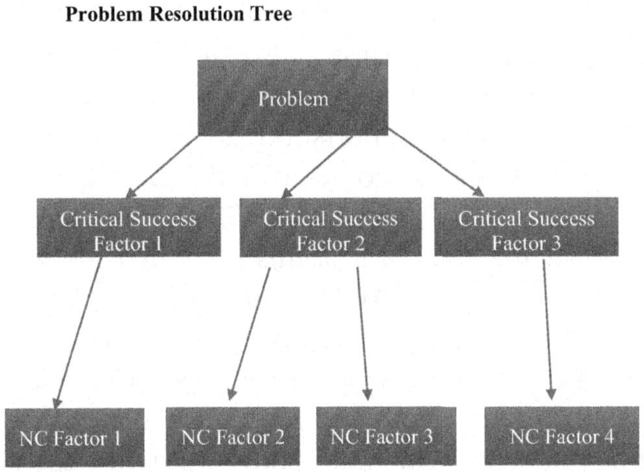

Problem Resolution Tree

Figure 9.2 Work problem resolution guide.[2,3]

same time? To test that theory, I created the TLS Continuum problem resolution tree (PRT).

The PRT begins with the problem brought to our attention by the customer. Remember when the customer does so, our immediate reaction was why had we not heard about this sooner? As shown in Figure 9.2, the tree begins with the problem. As with the goal tree, we change the initial question from what are the CSFs to what are the reasons why the problem exists? We are not concerned with key performance indicators. We are instead interested in why the problem exists. Once we have identified those conditions, we draw the same arrows as we did in the goal tree, except we reverse the direction. The direction now flows from the top down rather than the bottom up.

Once we have completed those steps, the following task replaces the necessary conditions with the answer to the question. If we have the problem and we understand what is causing the problem to occur, then we need to know what conditions in our processes are leading to the problem. Take our earlier example of the road trip to Orlando. We are driving down the road and the engine quits. We have a problem—the car won't move. The problem seems to be that the automobile is missing a critical element to allow it to move. On further examination, we find that we are out of gas. Let's break this down even further. We begin by asking a question: Why did the car stop moving? The answer to the question is that the engine shut off due to the car running out of gas.

The combination of the goal/problem statement with the PRT provides us the opportunity to envision what the next step in the journey is. With the information obtained from the two tools, the cross-functional team can now take the problem resolution efforts to management for review of the direction the organization should go in to identify and remove the system constraints. This includes your proposed solution and recommendations for changes within the organization. It is at this point that the naysayers may begin to express their disapproval of the route you are planning on taking. They are the ones who will try to convince the organization and management that the path forward won't work. Based on your evidence-based metrics, you need to stick to your path and proceed to the next step.

In Part 3 of this book, we will look at how we define the inside boundaries of the improvement process, including the roles of each of the participants.

Notes

1 Goal tree image used with permission of Bob Sproull.
2 Dettmer, H. William. *The Intermediate Objectives Map.* https://goalsys.com/books/documents/IOMapPaper.pd
3 Bloom, Daniel. *Achieving HR Excellence through Six Sigma.* New York, NY: Productivity Press, 2021. Page 118.

3

DEFINING THE BOUNDARIES

The TLS Continuum and the continuous process improvement efforts are not the Wild Wild West, nor are they a free-for-all. For over 20 years we dealt with the Wild Wild West as an environmental condition. We recruited and trained new real estate agents. Part of the training program was how to go about attracting clients. As long as their client prospecting was within the boundaries of that state and it was legally and morally alright, they were free to go for it. In real estate that might be good, but in the TLS Continuum world that does not work. In the continuous improvement world that is not sufficient. In the continuous process improvement journey that does not get us to the end game—locating the solutions to resolve our problems.

To begin our journey through the TLS Continuum, it is necessary that we establish the boundaries of our projects. What is a boundary? The website Etmyonline defines a boundary as "that which indicates the limits of anything," The concept of boundaries dates back to the 13th century when reference was made to a "boundary marker," from Anglo-Latin *bunda*, from Old French *bonde* "limit, boundary, boundary stone" (12c., Modern French *borne*), variant of *bodne*, from Medieval Latin *bodina*, which is perhaps from Gaulish.[1]

If we can't utilize the Wild Wild West or the free-for-all, what can we use to determine our ultimate goals? We need to determine those boundaries by considering which criteria are closely aligned with the nature of the problem. They are instrumental in determining the nature of the project scope, the performance metrics, and what needs to be eliminated from the process environment due to being unrelated to our goal/problem statement. The boundaries delineate not only the scope of the project but also identify

DOI: 10.4324/9780429029196-12

the project milestones that represent the project deliverables. They represent what the project is and why the project is important.

The Association for Project Management[2] based in the United Kingdom has suggested that there are seven distinct boundaries to the project management field.

Boundary #1 — Upwards to Direction

By necessity, the direction of all continuous process improvement, and thus the TLS Continuum, must always be in the direction of the flow through the critical chain. The flow is toward the end of the chain and the needs of the customer and their voice. The flow must be centered around this voice and what the voice is telling us is required to resolve those needs. The TLS Continuum therefore flows towards the problem the customer is having and what seems to be throwing up roadblocks in the form of system constraints to achieving the improvement of the system flow.

There are many responses that your organization can deliver when confronted with a problem. The quality of the response comes from how we apply the TLS Continuum.

If we treat the problem as a nonissue. then the upward boundary is ignored. If the system constraint is determined to be a nonissue, then the system constraint can be relegated to some future date. If it is a nonissue, it is not having any meaningful impact on the chain flow. We typically refer to these nonissues as representing common causes.

If we treat the problem as a vital issue, then we need to take concrete steps to resolve it. This means that we can move forward in meeting the customer demands. If we treat the problem as a vital issue, we need to drive the organization forward in the direction of the customer.

Boundary #2 — Downwards to Administration

Management has a vital role to play in most organizations. They are responsible for the establishment of the corporate mission, values, and strategies. But that role is not one of master of the universe. The TLS Continuum does not recognize the command-and-control environment that many organizations operate under. We do not take the solutions that we discover and fit them to the wants and needs of the management of the organization.

Management edicts do not resolve the system constraints. Management edicts do not resolve the reasons why we do something a certain way other than believing in an outdated corporate culture. We do not implement the TLS Continuum to satisfy an individual's fascination with the current fad.

Boundary #3 — Outwards to External Skills

Part of the project charter is the identification of the required resources to complete the project. This means that we need to be aware of all the available skills in the global workplace. The expectation from the TLS Continuum is that your organization will take advantage of all the appropriate skills that exist outside of the organization boundaries but available in the global marketplace. Consider the explosion of the *Challenger.* The solution came from a retired engineer's garage workshop.

What is required is the completion of a skill inventory to establish the skills that will be needed and when they will be utilized.

Boundary #4 – Inwards to Internal Skills

The same strategies apply internally as well as externally. We must recognize that we also have a source of skills inside the organization. They are found within your centers of excellence. They are found within the potential of your human capital assets. We need to be careful not to stereotype those available skills. Believing that just because someone presents a certain profile that they are not able to contribute to the successes of the organization is looking for trouble.

One solution is to take a page from John Ricketts which he explained in his book *Reaching the Goal.* John suggests that we develop a skill bench that represents all the available skills, and when projects arise, we take the required human capital assets off the bench that represents the required skills. When the project is finished, they are returned to the skill bench until the next time they are needed.

Boundary #5 – External Focus on Socioeconomic Factors

One of the central tenets of the TLS Continuum and the continuous process improvement efforts is that you should expect a return on your investment. You should expect that the removal of the system constraints should increase your bottom line. The real question is how do we go about doing that?

If you are like most organizations in the marketplace, you operate under the assumption that if you reduce costs, you will improve that bottom line. You operate under the view that trimming costs is the answer to your problems. We get it. Your organization is embedded in the theory of cost accounting, which legally imposes requirements on the organization. The governing body of this legal requirement is referred to as GAAP, or general accepted accounting principles. GAAP considers five major rules: accrual accounting methods, depreciation and capital expenditures, how we report historical costs, and reporting of bad debts. In some ways the methodology behind GAA mirrors the TLS Continuum.

1) The principles are applied as standard practice (process standardization).
2) The same standards are applied through each step (repeatable process).
3) Objective and accurate information is used (need for credible data).
4) Consistency is used in processes (verifiable data).
5) There is no compensation for achieving certain results.
6) Data is based on documented facts (the use of experimentation to determine results).
7) The data collection should not interrupt normal business operations (the TLS Continuum expects that as we identify the system constraints, the organization will continue to serve the voice of the customer).
8) Data should be reported according to schedule (the TLS Continuum follows the process flow).
9) GAAP requires the use of material facts (once again credible, verifiable data).
10) Data should be honest ad complete (metrics must be valid).

It is apparent that there is an interrelationship between the legally required GAAP requirements and the outcomes sought by the TLS Continuum. The Association of Project Management underplays the complete influence here. APM presents the argument that while the process improvement effort is governed by legal boundaries, it is also governed by technical boundaries. The TLS Continuum further introduces social factors on top of the rest of the boundaries. This can be shown more completely by introducing the socio-technical system of organizational structure to the picture.

First proposed by Eric Trist and Fred Emery in 1960 and then enhanced by the work of Lou Davis at UCLA, it proposes that organizations are composed of two interdependent systems. The first is that of the technical aspects, which are various processes and the social aspects that represent the methods we use for decision-making, the skill levels of those involved in the process, and their motivation for the change.

The APM underplays the complete influence here. While the TLS Continuum boundaries are influenced by both the social and economic factors in which the system constraints operate, they are also influenced by the technical aspects of the boundaries. These are discussed in the seven boundaries we are discussing here. It would help for our later discussions to look at the STS concept more in depth.

The University of Leeds[4] in the United Kingdom suggests that the STS can be viewed as a hexagonal model consisting of six components: the people, the infrastructure, the technology, the culture, the processes, and the goals/ metrics. The model is shown in Figure Part 3.1.

Boundary #6 – Internal Focus on Project Tasks

The TLS Continuum and the project charter along with the gap analysis results, which we will discuss in Chapter 13, tell your organization what must be done in order to reach your goals. The organization must be totally focused on those tasks. The organization must not put off for another day what needs to be done today. Further, the organization must understand that each task is dependent on the prior task being completed before you begin a new task.

The tasks do not operate in a vacuum, and they are all part of the process of system improvement.

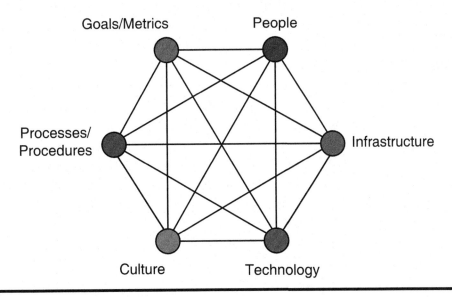

Figure Part 3.1 STS model.[3]

Boundary #7 — Irrational Complexity and Quantum Management

The final boundary is that of understanding that we are operating in a new business environment. Our working parameters are different. Our working influences are different. This change requires a new way of making decisions. We now need to focus on irrational complexity and quantum management.

Irrational complexity comes from our existing in a VUCA world, one characterized by volatility, uncertainty, chaos, and ambiguity. It makes our decisions contingent on new ways of thoughts. In their 2018 operational blog, McKinsey and Company[4] states that the phenomenon of human irrationality illuminates why leading people is a challenge for even the smartest, hardest-working, and well-intentioned leaders and why so many "textbook" recommendations miss the mark. Messages are sent but not heard, actions are misunderstood, and incentives create unintended consequences. These are all factors of the VUCA world that are brought about by rapid change.

The other factor in this last boundary is a change in management focus. For decades the focus of management has been based on the work of Frederick Taylor and his principles of scientific management. Quantum management changes that focus. It redefines the essential principles of management that are present in the 21st century. It picks up on the last factor in the VUCA world and embraces the use of flexible organizations and agile management concepts.

The website Think 50[5] looks at this view more deeply in a blog entry. Think 50 states that quantum management comes from a different field within the physics realm. The new view comes from quantum physics and the nature of complexity science.

According to Think 50, quantum management has its origins, and draws its management principles from, the nature and behavior of Computer Assisted Designs (CADs), and describes companies as complex, adaptive, living quantum systems. Quantum management draws its authority from an *actual* description of companies and suggests an *actual*, scientific way of managing them. It further suggests that this in turn means that our organizations will function at their peak performance levels when they function as human systems.

In the first two parts of this book, we looked at the fundamentals of the TLS Continuum and its applications. In Part 3, we begin the process of laying out the TLS Continuum roadmap by investigating the parties that are involved. In Chapter 10, we will look at how to identify the stakeholders who have an investment in the outcome of improving the system. In Chapter 11, we will consider the role of cross-functional teams in the process, and finally in Chapter 12 we will dive deep into the various roles and responsibilities of the various team members.

Before we engage in that conversation, we have one other issue that needs to be explored. As stated earlier, this is not the real estate market. The identification and the construction of our improvement efforts are confined by the environment in which the problem exists. Initially, then, we must establish the boundaries of our efforts. What needs to be part of the process and what does not? This does not mean that if something is deleted as a boundary component in this instance, it is not of any use as a boundary component in another issue later.

Notes

1 Definition of the term boundary. www.etymonline.com/word/boundary
2 www.apm.org.uk/news/the-7-boundaries-of-project-management/
3 https://business.leeds.ac.uk/research-stc/doc/socio-technical-systems-theory
4 www.mckinsey.com/business-functions/people-and-orga-nizational-performance/our-insights/the-organization-blog/be-rational-about-irrationality
5 https://thinkers50.com/blog/the-quantum-management-revolution/

Chapter 10

Identification of the Supply Chain Partners

As we discussed earlier, as an organization, it is our responsibility to make more money and to acquire and maintain customers. The subsequent question that arises is how do we achieve that ultimate goal? Two alternative responses have plagued our organizations for decades.

The first response is based on the work of the economist Milton Friedman, who believed that your organization has no responsibility to the public as a whole since its only concern is to increase the corporate bottom line through increasing the corporate income. The needs of the public would be met by the shareholders' actions. The basis of this belief is that the shareholders own equity in the organization. The Pearse Trust tells us that shareholders are the owners of the company and provide financial backing in return for potential dividends over the lifetime of the company. In other words, a shareholder is a person, company, or institution that owns at least one share of a company's stock, which is known as equity. Because shareholders are essentially owners in a company, they reap the benefits of a business's success. They also suffer the losses when the business does not perform as well. The problem with Friedman's view is that it does not take into account the contribution of the various components of the critical chain except in vague terms. It does not take into account that under the shareholder theory, management is an agent of those who own the organization.

The second view is that expressed by R. Edward Freeman who put forth the concept of the stakeholder theory. Stakeholder theory[1] is a view of capitalism that stresses the interconnected relationships between a business and

DOI: 10.4324/9780429029196-13

its customers, suppliers, employees, investors, communities, and others who have a stake in the organization. The theory argues that a firm should create value for all stakeholders, not just shareholders.

We believe that to fully implement the TLS Continuum we must operate from the latter perspective and focus on the stakeholders. The University of Virginia Darden School of Business, which implemented this alternative view, tells us in their principles and purpose statement that five distinct types of shareholders exist.[2]

The first type are our customers. As we will see later in this chapter, the customer dictates the direction in which the TLS Continuum directs its actions, tasks, and efforts. It is the customer who tells the organization what is wrong with the processes. The second type are the human capital assets, who are our subject matter experts who know and understand where the system constraints are found. This is because they see the process in its functional state. The third type are the suppliers. The suppliers govern the supply chain and thus the supply and demand of materials needed to ensure that the processes run smoothly. The fourth type are the communities in which we operate, whether we are talking about the local community or the global workplace. The fifth type are the shareholders. By accepting the stakeholder theory, we are not negating Milton Friedman's view of organizational structure; however, we are saying they are not the primary focus. The shareholders' contribution to the organization is in the form of the basic funds to operate.

The first step in the TLS Continuum journey thus becomes identifying who the appropriate stakeholders are in the process at hand. The TLS Continuum toolbox provides us with a tool called the SIPOC form in order to facilitate this task.

To better understand who the stakeholders are, it is imperative that we understand the roles each of the stakeholders play in the process improvement efforts. The easiest way to achieve this is through the usage of a tool called the SIPOC diagram. Remember in Chapter 2, we said the TLS Continuum is just that. It is a chain of a series of actions resulting in process improvement. In order to begin implementation of process improvement within your organization, you need to gain an eagle's-eye view of the processes and the performance gaps from the customer's point of view. The SIPOC can fill that need.

The first step in the journey is to look at the organization from above and identify the players in the mix. Using the form seen in Figure 10.1, the

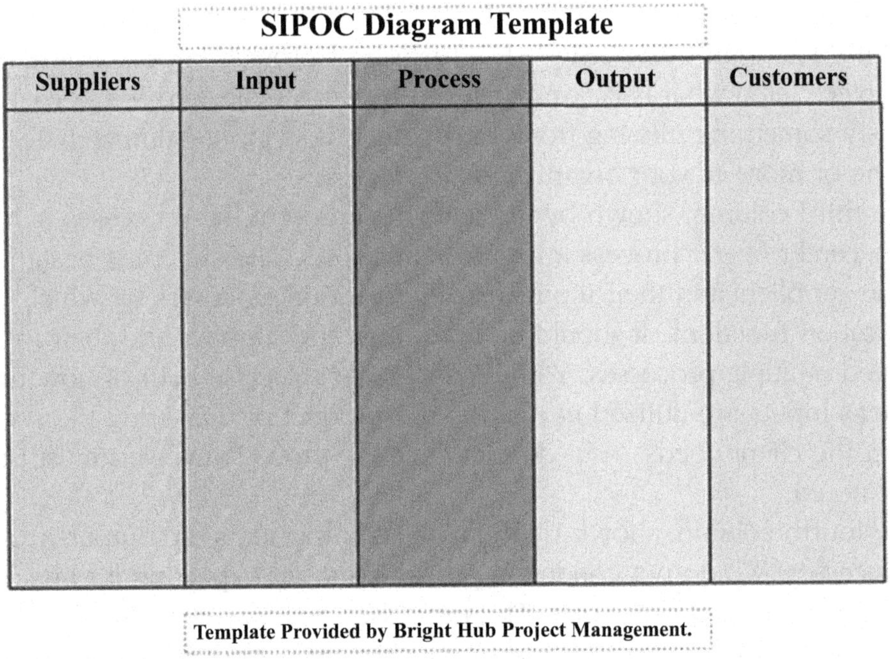

SIPOC Diagram Template

Suppliers	Input	Process	Output	Customers

Template Provided by Bright Hub Project Management.

Figure 10.1 SIPOC diagram.[3]

process begins with the construction of a SIPOC analysis of your operation. The SIPOC is divided into five segments or columns which lay out the steps in the process chain. While we eventually will be concerned with the critical few, at this macro viewpoint we want to include all that are applicable to the process in each column.

The first column in the SIPOC tool (represented by the S in the form) represents the suppliers to the system. These are the entities that contribute the materials that are used to produce our products and services. Initially, you want to look at the potential suppliers from a macro view. If a potential supplier may contribute to the process, they should be included. When we are ready to begin the problem-solving stage, we can narrow down the suppliers to those with the most to contribute. It is the goal of the suppliers to deliver something of value to the various processes that they are involved in. These things of value are represented in the second column shown by the letter I.

These materials are delivered to the organization in the form of an input of some kind. As an organization, you seek out suppliers to provide you with something. Whether it is materials or software, you still seek out their inputs. These process inputs come both from within and outside our organizations. The inputs are designed to furnish or provide (a person, establishment, place, etc.) what is lacking or requisite or to make up, compensate for, or satisfy something missing from a process. These inputs ultimately feed into one or more of your organizational processes.

The third column, shown by the letter P, represent the processes, which are the center of our process improvement efforts. The system is designed so that the suppliers and their inputs feed the various processes by which your organization functions. It should be noted that the supplier and their inputs may feed multiple processes. You need to have a precise path of how the supplier's inputs are utilized in making the product or delivering the service to meet the client needs. Your definition of the process involved must be clearly noted.

The fourth column, shown by the letter O, represents the outputs from the processes. We do not conduct a process without expecting it to result in some sort of product or service. The processes deliver something of value to the end user in the form of outputs. Our processes need to produce something tangible. When we complete a process, the process creates the end product or service, which we deliver to the customer.

The fifth and final column, shown by the letter C, represents the end user or customer, who delivers the product or service to their customer, thus completing their own SIPOC. This is a clear manifestation of the continuum since the critical chain flows both forward and backward, and thus you could develop SIPOC forms for both ends of the processes.

10.1 Stakeholder Analysis

With the SIPOC completed, the organization is now in a position to establish where the stakeholders are in working toward the completion of the process improvement effort. The TLS Continuum does this through implementing a stakeholder analysis. A stakeholder analysis groups the stakeholders according to their levels of involvement. Typically, the analysis considers the involvement from the aspects of participation, interest, and influence. Once this step is done, the organization then determines how to best involve and communicate to each level throughout the process. As can be seen in Figure 10.1, the form demonstrates each stakeholder and where they fall in the spectrum. It is critical that we identify those stakeholders that are critical for success and what their current level of involvement in the process is.

Stakeholder Analysis Matrix

Stakeholder Name	Contact Person *Phone, Email, Website, Address*	Impact *How much does the project impact them? (Low, Medium, High)*	Influence *How much influence do they have over the project? (Low, Medium, High)*	What is important to the stakeholder?	How could the stakeholder contribute to the project?	How could the stakeholder block the project?	Strategy for engaging the stakeholder
EXAMPLE **Nurses & Midwives Union**	*Carlos Davida cdavida@ nu.org 0998 765 287*	High	High	*Maintaining working conditions for nurses*	*Agree for union members to implement the new reforms*	*Going on strike*	*Monthly round-table discussions*
Patient Advocacy Group	*Viki Chan vchan@ pag.org 888 587 101*	High	Medium	*Maximising quality of care for patients*	*Communicate with other stakeholders to express their support for reforms*	*Making complaints about quality of service after the reports*	*Information and feedback meetings every 6 months*
Sunday Times Newspaper	*Jane Smith jsmith@stn. com 888 587 101*	Low	High	*Getting a good story*	*Print stories that support the new reforms*	*Printing stories that oppose the new reforms*	*Quarterly press meetings*

Figure 10.2   Stakeholder analysis form.[4]

The reasoning behind the stakeholder analysis can be delineated for several areas. First, the stakeholder analysis helps management to enlist the assistance of key organizational players. The project charter asks us to identify several levels of parties. We have the executive sponsor, who is the key management individual who is pushing the project. We have the project sponsor, who is charged with being the gatekeeper for the project through the various levels within the organization.

In the end, the project outcomes must be aligned with the organizational goals, values, and strategies. It is easier to obtain this alignment if the organization starts early to begin the process of getting everyone on the same page as we make the journey through the continuum.

We are all human, and as a result we may not see eye to eye all the time. One of the outcomes of the stakeholder analysis is the potential to uncover areas of conflict where certain individuals are not totally onboard with the improvement efforts. It is these individuals who can add a constraint to the improvement effort.

10.2 Voice of the Customer

With the stakeholder analysis completed, it becomes necessary that we turn to the most critical stakeholder in the form of the end user or customer. Remember that we can't take the TLS Continuum improvement journey without some credible data. So where do we get these data points? The easiest way is to ask the customer what is on their mind. The difficulty here is that their immediate answers may not be the full story.

Our goal is two-fold. First, we want to understand what they think the problem is that is confronting them. They see the world as they see it. The supposed deficit in your product or service delivery is what they see as an assumption of what is wrong with the process. This assumption is the starting point in our experiment to determine the system constraint. Second, the results of utilizing the TLS Continuum will show the real determination as to the cause of the system constraint.

To assist us in making this determination, the TLS Continuum toolbox contains a specific tool that is essential in arriving at that answer. The TLS Continuum toolbox contains a tool called the quality function deployment (QFD) tool as shown in Figure 10.3. The QFD is a process within a bigger process and is designed to more effectively define that all-important voice of the customer. The end goal is that with the customer telling us what is critical to them, your organization is better able to establish those products and services that meet those voices. It is the completion of the voice of the customer matrix that completes that goal.

To get a better understanding of how the matrix works, turn back to Figure 10.3, and I will take you through the various components of the matrix and their interactions with the rest of the form.

Running horizontally across the top of the matrix is the delineation of the phases of the process in question. In this case the phases are laid out as plan, develop, market, deliver, and support. Under each of these are three options that might be undertaken for each phase. For instance, in the planning stage the options shown are internal consultant, customer surveys, and the cross-functional team.

On the far left is a vertical column denoted by the three goals of the TLS Continuum. We want to strive to get your product or service to the end user better (fewer defects), faster, and cheaper (not in total cost but in the outlay of funds to produce the product or service).

By entering this data into an Excel-type spreadsheet you construct a grid between the components. The next step is to ask the customer what would characterize a "perfect product for them." Your final task is to then identify

		Voice of the Customer													
		Plan		Develop				Market			Deliver			Support		
Customer Requirements ● 4 Strong ○ 2 Medium △ 1 Weak	Importance (1-5)	Internal Consultant	Customer Surveys	X functional Team	Internal controls	Talent Screening	Dept partnerships	Policies	Procedures	Process	Sourcing vehicles	Talent search	Employmnt offers	Pre-Interview steps	Pre-hire steps	Onboarding
Better Treat me like you want my business	5	1	2	2	4	2	4	4	2	2	2	2	2	1	1	2
Deliver services that meet my needs	5	2	2	2	2	2	2	2	2	2	2	2	2	2	2	2
services that work right	3	2	2	2	1	2	2	2	2	2	2	2	2	2	2	2
Be accurate, right the first time	4	2	2	2	1	2	2	2	2	2	2	2	2	2	2	2
Source us the right candidate	5	2	2	2	1	2	2	2	2	2	2	2	2	2	2	2
Faster I want it when I want it	3	2	2	2	1	2	2	2	2	2	1	2	2	4	2	2
Make commitments that meet my needs	4	2	2	2	1	2	2	2	2	2	2	2	2	4	2	2
Meet your commitments	4	2	2	2	1	2	2	2	2	2	2	2	2	4	2	2
I want fast, easy access to help	4	2	2	2	1	2	2	2	2	2	2	2	2	2	2	2
Don't waste my time	5	2	2	2	1	2	2	2	2	2	2	2	2	2	2	2
if it breaks, fix it fast	4	2	2	2	1	2	2	2	2	2	2	2	2	2	2	2
Cheaper Deliver irresistable value	4	2	2	2	1	4	2	2	2	2	2	2	1	2	2	2
Help me save money	5	4	2	2	1	4	2	2	2	2	2	2	1	2	2	2
Help me save time	5	4	2	2	1	4	2	2	2	2	2	2	1	2	2	1
Total Weight		135	120	120	80	148	130	130	120	120	117	120	106	137	115	115

Figure 10.3 Voice of the customer matrix.[5]

the customer priorities in their response on a scale of 1–5, with 5 being the strongest want. When you enter the priority ranking into the column, the matrix is preloaded with weighting formulas for each square. The last horizontal row is the calculation of the totals of each column, giving you the ability to identify those customer needs that are critical to the improvement effort. It is these critical few items that must be worked on immediately.

Notes

1 Freeman, R. Edward. *Stakeholder Theory.* www.stakeholder.org
2 University of Virginia, Darden School of Business. *Stakeholder Principles.* https://ideas.darden.virginia.edu/principles-and-purpose-a-statement-on-stakeholders
3 SIPOC diagram. https://drive.google.com/file/d/17gj65PNuqIuZ5EeWVn3EAwR NSV5Ao8Xr/view
4 The stakeholder analysis matrix template by tools4dev is licensed under a Creative Commons Attribution-ShareAlike 3.0 Unported License.
5 Voice of the customer matrix. Taken from the Black Belt Training Program at St. Petersburg, College.

Chapter 11

The Role of Cross-Functional Teams

In the previous chapter we discussed how to identify our organizational stakeholders. Having completed that task, the question becomes: What do we do with the stakeholders we identified?

If we look at the business world, the subject of teams is a major area of concern. Are the teams operating in person? Are the teams operating remotely via vehicles such as Microsoft Teams or Zoom? What do we do with the output from the team's efforts? Obviously, the concept of workplace teams is a point of critical discussion. The real question is: How do the teams operate within our workplaces? To answer these questions, it is important that we look at the creation of the teams, both historically and the currently empowered teams.

The concept of cross-functional teams has existed since the 1700s. The first teams most likely existed on our family farms, where each member of the family was assigned a certain task that needed to be completed to harvest the fruits of their labors.

In 1909, with the publication of his *Principles of Scientific Management,* Frederick Winslow Taylor first introduced the idea that workers and managers needed to cooperate with each other. From this idea Taylor began a series of time and motion studies to discover how to run the workplace more effectively.

These studies resulted in Taylor's four principles of scientific management.[1] In his first principle Taylor advocated that organizations should replace working by "rule of thumb" and instead use the scientific method

DOI: 10.4324/9780429029196-14

to study work and determine how most efficiently to perform specific tasks. In other words, Taylor suggested that we have a process to complete a task. The second principle suggested a different way of assigning tasks. Rather than simply assigning workers to any job, we should assign workers based on capability and motivation. One of the tenets of my *The Road to HR Excellence Through Six Sigma* course is that team members should be selected based on their skills and attitudes. From this point Taylor, in his third principle, suggested that worker performance be monitored and workers provided with instructions and supervision to ensure that they are using the most efficient ways of working. This principle reinforces the Toyota premise of the manager as a coach. The final principle advocated that the work between managers and workers be allocated so that the workers were allowed to perform their tasks efficiently. The drawback to these principles is that they are based on the idea that there is only one way to do something and that it does not allow for innovation or expanded views of the problem.

11.1 Hawthorne Studies

Sixty-one years later, with the *Principles of Scientific Management* embedded into the global business workplace, a team of Harvard business professors (Elton May, F.J. Roethlisberger, and William J. Dickinson) were contracted by Western Electric to conduct a series of studies at their Hawthorne plant in Cicero, Illinois. The initial scope of the studies was concentrated on the physical and environmental issues surrounding the plant and its effect on the human capital assets.

Shortly after beginning the Hawthorne studies, the Harvard anthropologists discovered that in addition to the physical and environmental issues, there was a social issue to the workings of the Cicero plant.

May et al. looked at the social dynamics of the groups within the plant. Like Frederick Taylor, they discovered that the relationships between supervisors and workers govern the success of the team. They further expressed the view that the workplace is a social system made up of many parts. These social dynamics have a direct correlation to the total productivity of the organization.

However, I had heard this concept before from Abraham Maslow, who in his hierarchy of needs suggested that the third level of the pyramid was the need for belongingness and love. To carry this forward, it is that need for belongingness that empowers organizational teams.

Our organizations are confronted with a choice. They can continue in their time-tested mode or create a new paradigm for team construction. The rest of this chapter will show the difference between the two types of teams. It is worth mentioning at this juncture that Robert Mathis in his seminal work *Human Resource Management* suggests that in every organization there exists three types of teams: special-purpose teams, self-directed teams, and virtual teams.[2] My concentration in this book is primarily centered around the self-directed teams, although the same principles can be applied to all of them.

11.2 Classical Workplace Teams

We would expect that everyone reading this book has at one time or another served on a team within their workplace. We would also expect that many of these teams fit the model of the classical team.

The classical workplace team, no matter the type they are,[3] are constructed identically. Management asks certain members of the organization to be part of a team designed to solve a particular problem that confronts the organization. The typical team is composed of a member of management and possibly five to eight individuals from the rest of the organization. They come together periodically to discuss the nature of the problem and possible solutions.

The problem comes when we gather around a table and the management representative asks for our suggestions and then management decides the solution. Or after the end of the discussions, the team decides to experience "groupthink," and everyone coalesces around a single solution, whether it is the best solution or not, usually suggested by the member of management.

Groupthink presents the classical team and your organization with a double-edged sword. From one side, groupthink provides a relatively swift way to resolve process problems. The team tends to use lateral thinking to look at the problem in the light of previous problems and try and apply the same logic as the previous problem to the new situation. It is valid to point out that there is a form of synergy among team members involved, and that sense of synergy comes from the preliminary sharing of information among team members. The presence of groupthink can also contribute to the presence of management control of the process. As we will show later, overmanaging a team is not the way you empower cross-functional teams. Safi Bahcall, in his book *Loonshots*, describes these actions as falling into two traps:[4] the Moses trap in which the manager listens to the possible solutions and decides which solution will be implemented and the PARC trap in which the solutions are totally disregarded.

The first organization to utilize cross-functional teams in the form of quality circles was Nippon Wireless and Telegraph, starting about a decade after the introduction of Deming's work in Japan. Quality circles functioned essentially the same regardless of the organizational structure.

The concept behind the operation of quality circles was that it was composed of small groups of managers and employees who voluntarily got together to solve intercompany problems. The members were trained in the tenets of statistical process control, giving them the basis for identifying and analyzing processes within the organization. The meetings were held around the normal work schedule, occurring either during lunch breaks or before or after work. It should be noted that the solutions were designed to handle

HUMAN RESOURCE EXCELLENCE 101: QUALITY CIRCLES

Mary Johnson has been a member of the human resource function at Excellence Manufacturing for nearly 15 years. One day she is reviewing an e-mail from a department manager in which they are lamenting the length of time it takes to obtain approval for a new hire to take place. Mary talks with both the manager and some of her fellow department members to determine where the process is breaking down.

Based on the conversations, the people directly involved decide they will try and improve the process. The team consists of Mary, two of her fellow HR team members, and the department manager. They begin to meet once a week after hours looking at the current process. From their review, they identify what the problems are, select the final issue that needs to be resolved, and analyze the impact of the problem on overall operations.

Following the completion of their studies, they compile a report on the problem that was identified and the recommended solution and present their report to the organizational management team. Management, after review of the completed project, gives the team the go-ahead to implement the solution.

Their solution decreased the new hire process, saving the organization approximately $100,000 in cost reductions. In turn, the quality circle members received a 2% bonus in their pay due to their efforts.

issues ranging from safety and health to product design and manufacturing process improvements, so we are not talking about large-scale problems. Further, despite the principles set forth by Deming, the circles were more than likely within the same department or silo. Once a solution is developed, it is presented to management for permission to implement the steps to change the process. After gaining management approval, the solution is implemented. In some cases, the members of the quality circle are awarded bonuses based on the amount of savings generated by their solutions. The following box provides you with a simple overview of their operations.

As can be seen from the description, the quality circles were the perfect example of the classical team format. While the other members of the team arrived at solutions, it was left up to management to decide whether the solutions were implemented or discarded. General Electric under Jack Welch saw the folly in this method, and they implemented the GE Workout and the change acceleration process (CAP) to counter the classical team outcomes.

Do not construe from the discussion that we are totally alienated against classical teams. They have their place and purpose. If you are trying to decide whether to purchase a supply of copy paper or whether to purchase an office service, the need might not be there for the scope of problem solutions we are discussing in the empowered team section later. And that is fine.

The other side of the double-edged sword includes the negatives of the classical cross-functional team. The classical cross-functional team is characterized by a command-and-control process. The outcomes of the team result in management stating "thanks for your efforts but we will do it this way." The downside is further represented by several outcomes. First, when we sideline team members' views, it can ruin relationships that have been developed within your organization. In her writings, Adrienne Rich said,

> When those who have the power to name, and to socially construct reality choose not to see you or hear you, . . . when someone with the authority of a teacher say, describes the world and you are not in it, there is a moment of psychic disequilibrium, as if you looked into a mirror and saw nothing.[5]

The classical team runs the risk of having team members who feel like the person in Adrienne Rich's poem. The argument is that your views are not valid because the management-controlled view is considered the majority opinion of the group.

The second downside is that because ideas are discarded, the ability to potentially find a breakthrough solution is sometimes overlooked. The tendency is to operate on the premise that if the problem resembles a previous problem, why not use that solution in the current situation? The result is that not all the available solutions are considered.

The third downside is that false decisions tend to lower the quality of the process and the organization. The classical cross-functional teams tend to try and assume what the voice of the customer is saying even if the true nature of the problem is misunderstood by the team. Remember that in the Six Sigma end of the spectrum, we don't know what we don't know. The result is that the team takes on a false sense of security by believing that the right choice has been made, when in fact we have left out some part of the equation in arriving at the conclusion.

One of biggest downsides not only with classical cross-functional teams but further with the HR function is that many of today's professionals either were never taught or have forgotten what it means to critically think through the daily challenges. If they were never taught this, it is the fault of the educational system; if they forgot how to use those skills, it is because they have never been asked to do so in their organization. As we will see later, the empowered cross-functional team demands that we critically think through the problems that confront us.

Another downside is that due to the way classical cross-functional teams operate, there is an inherent lack of engagement. The teams believe that they are invulnerable and can do no wrong. They are the masters of knowledge of the organizational processes. This leads, as I suggested

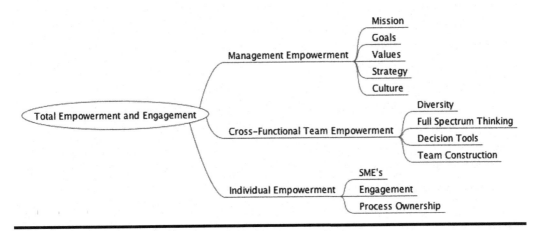

Figure 11.1   Empowered team mind map.

earlier, to the belief that they are always right. That their beliefs should not be questioned. The beliefs are required to be inside a set of mind guards designed to ensure that the corporate culture is not challenged even if that means that you are making decision that may harm the organization or the client.

11.3 Empowered Workplace Teams

Unlike the classical team, the empowered team is a whole new look for the organization. It takes advantage of the best resources to resolve organizational issues based on the voice of the customer. It expands the focus of the organization into new areas. It adds new resources that are often overlooked by the classical teams. The true cross-functional team is introduced to a set of new tools that will enhance the team's problem resolution options.

Tool #1: Diversity of Ideas

Is your organization one of those involved in a diversity campaign? Does your management team include a chief diversity and inclusion officer? If so, you are among the numerous organizations that have picked up on this trend. The goal behind these efforts is to move toward the inclusion of multiple backgrounds within the organization both educationally and ethnically. I agree with the assessment that it is a critical issue, but we are looking at a different type of diversity. I am looking at the idea of diversity in a different light.

Diversity in the empowered team arena looks at who is included in the deliberations. There exists in any organization a spectrum of thought if you will. To completely resolve the issues confronting the organization, it is necessary that you include everyone who touches the problem in any way or manner. So, who are we talking about? Consider as you construct your teams the entire supply chain from start to finish. Your major customer says that the product or service you are delivering to them fails to meet their needs and they are threatening to take their business elsewhere. The question is: Who do you call first? You want to reach out to everyone involved in the production of that product or service at both ends of the spectrum.

Take, for example, the car you drive. Who touches that automobile even remotely in getting the car to you? You have all the parts in the car, each made by a separate supplier. You have all the suppliers that service the part supplier, and you have all their suppliers. Once the car is assembled at the plant, you then have the supplier who delivers the car to your dealership. After delivery, you have whoever services the vehicle when it needs maintenance. This is the concept behind the consideration of stakeholders versus shareholders.

The stakeholder theory talks about the community. We would suggest that community should also include the openness to outside solutions, as we discuss in the next section. In their book *New Power* by Jeremy Hines and Henry Timms, they suggest one characteristic of the new business world is the need for collaboration. The Millennials have no hesitation to resolve a problem by jumping on their computer and asking for assistance from whoever in resolving the issue. NASA, using the power of a site called InnoCentive,[6] resolved problems that the in-house experts could not.

The empowered team will ensure that the solution that is arrived at includes the widest spectrum of thought regarding the issue at hand. It needs to identify and include the openness to diverse thoughts on the solution. Not the confined view of most organizations.

Tool #3 Full-Spectrum Thinking

In part, this VUCA age is based on what Michael Hayden in his book *The Assault on Intelligence* refers to as an era of post-truth.[7] It is an era where we base our decisions on personal beliefs and appeals to emotions. In my nearly 50 years in the business world, I have seen this play out on numerous occasions. When something goes wrong in the office, it is always their fault. A customer complains something is wrong with an order and it is the employee's fault, so you fire them. It is an age where we make decisions at the expense of facts and data. There is a solution to this dilemma, and it is called full-spectrum thinking.

What is full-spectrum thinking, you may ask? Throughout my writings I have talked about seeing a problem, feeling a problem, and changing the corporate culture. One aspect of that concept is that we have to exercise our power of judgement in order to think. Daniel Kahneman, a professor of psychology and public affairs emeritus at the Woodrow Wilson School, the Eugene Higgins Professor of Psychology Emeritus at Princeton University, and a fellow of the Center for Rationality at the Hebrew University in Jerusalem, in 2011 presented his views on business decision-making in his book *Thinking, Fast and Slow*[8] in which he suggested that we need to make our decisions based on two levels.

Kahneman refers to the first level as system 1 thinking. We use this form of thinking everyday both personally and professionally. It inspires quick decisions.

The base of the system is emotional. When was the last time you got near a hot stove and jerked your hand back? When was the last time that you needed to order a resupply of say copy paper and you just went online and ordered it? These are examples of system 1 thinking. I find system 1 very prevalent in the groupthink workplaces, where the power of the organization rests in the hands of management. The decisions are made based on past experiences and memoires. As stated earlier, when you have a process problem, you determine the solution based on similar events from the past. You almost automatically determine that because something worked in a similar situation in the past, the same solution should work in this situation. It seemingly works because it takes no effort to make the decision.

System 2 thinking is slower, more methodical in nature. System 2 thinking requires us to critically think about a solution. It asks us to take into consideration that just because the solution in front of us sounds right, it may not be the best solution to fit the problem. Think about the last time you had a problem to resolve. Was it easy to resolve the issue? My guess is probably not.

The further we get away from picking up the telephone or hitting a key on the keyboard, the more the solution requires multiple aspects to resolve. The more complex the solution, the more the demand for further investigation. Astrid Groenewegen and Tom De Bruyne, founders of SUE Behavioural Design, created a quick study guide to the differences between System 1 and System 2 thinking.[9] While my intent is not to redo their quick study guide, I do want to provide some added emphasis to several aspects of system 2 thinking as it applies to the question of empowered teams.

One of the basic principles of the TLS Continuum is that our solutions are based on credible and verifiable data. The System 2 side of the spectrum is based on evidence, not on thoughts. Consider this scenario. On one hand you determine a solution to a problem by saying "well, when we have had similar issues in the past, this is the way we resolved them," or "we have a problem; how can we determine what the causes are?" The latter scenario used to resolve the issue influenced by facts, logic, and evidence. It is ingrained in intentional thinking rather than intuition. The empowered team performs its "experiments" to arrive at the correct solutions. The reasons behind the selection of a particular solution are based on the conscious reasoning abilities of the team. System 2 thinking comes into play whenever you do not have the conditions present to make a quick decision. I would suggest that other than ordering new supplies or some minor issue with a product or service, the TLS Continuum empowerment model would expect that System 2 thinking would be the standard problem-solving method. Full-spectrum thinking requires the empowered cross-functional team to weigh all the available options. The empowered team understands that to find the right solution, there must be a change in the way we approach organizational problems. Part of that is the introduction of new decision tools.

Tool #4 New Decision Tools

The Theory of Constraints, Lean, and Six Sigma each offer your organization a set of tools. This Six Sigma toolbox is shown in Figure 11.2. Note that the toolbox covers both the Lean tools and the Six Sigma tools. The Lean toolbox should be your first call in solving the problem. They are usually the low-hanging fruit solutions.

In the book *Achieving HR Excellence Through Six Sigma*, I discussed many of these tools in more detail. However, the Theory of Constraints brings its own critical thinking tools to the table. An in-depth discussion of these tools can be found in H. William Dettmer's *The Logical Thinking Process*. While there are a number of tools in the TOC critical thinking

DMAIC Step	SIX SIGMA Tools	LEAN Tools
DEFINE	Voice of Customer Project Charter Project Critical to Quality Definition High Level Process Map	Value Definition
MEASURE	Quality Function Deployment Measurement System Analysis	Value Stream Mapping
ANALYZE	Process Capability Analysis FMEA Benchmarking Hypothesis Testing Graphical Tools	Line Balance Takt Time Calculation
IMPROVE	Regression Analysis Design Of Experiments Risk Assessment	5 S Establish Flow / Pull System SCORE Events
CONTROL	Determine New Process Capability Statistical Process Control Control Plans	Poke Yoke Visual Management

Figure 11.2 Lean Six Sigma toolbox.

process, as Dettmer describes, for our purposes, we want to concentrate on two of the tools at this juncture. The goal tree and the conflict resolution tree.

11.4 The Goal Tree

The goal tree is a clear method to demonstrate the empowerment of the team. The team is constructed, and then they begin to deliberate the questions that we get from the design thinking field. The beginning is asking the question "what is?" which represents the problem or goal, as can be seen in Figure 11.3. Once the goal or problem is in place, the next question: What are the critical facts that must be in place to reach that goal? With the critical success factors in place, your next task is to determine what necessary conditions must be in place for the critical factors to be created. You would do this for each of the critical factors in your journey to the goal.

The purpose of this book is not to discuss the tool in detail, as Dettmer's *The Logical Thinking Process* has full chapters just on this tool. In addition, we would refer you to Bob Sproull's *The Focus and Leverage Improvement Book*. On pages 68–90, Bob lays out a simulation of a team creating the goal tree.

Another powerful aspect of the goal tree is the ability to go back to your completed goal tree and develop the performance metrics for the process by asking yourself: What does the successful achievement of each level mean to the organization? The procedure is you reverse the arrows on the diagram to run from bottom up to the goal. At each level ask yourself what would

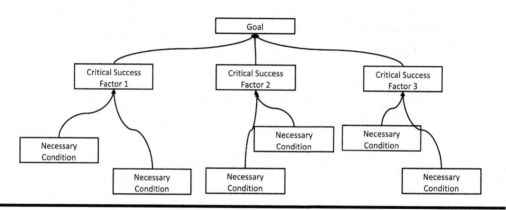

Figure 11.3   The goal tree.

tell you that you have the right condition in place. For example, you need to fill your hiring needs, and one of the necessary conditions is that you have qualified individuals in the pipeline. What would tell you that they are qualified individuals. What would they look like?

11.4.1 The Evaporating Cloud or Conflict Resolution

The second tool from the Theory of Constraints toolbox of interest here is the evaporating cloud or the conflict resolution tree. The evaporating cloud is designed to uncover the conflict within your processes. Consider for a moment the example in Figure 11.4. It states that one of HR's responsibilities is to locate the talent the organization needs to fill critical human capital needs of the organization. The question posed by the evaporating cloud is: How do we achieve that goal? The cloud offers two different alternatives. One says the goal is fiscal responsibility, which requires the organization to stay within budgetary guidelines. The other option states that the goal is to recruit or promote employees to fill these critical openings.

The weakest link appears after this segment of the discussion because it directly compares the two approaches. On the fiscal side, the resulting action is to reduce the amount of relocation benefits provided to the human capital assets, while filling the positions is the paramount issue you need to increase the level of benefits. The conflict arises because you may not be able to reduce

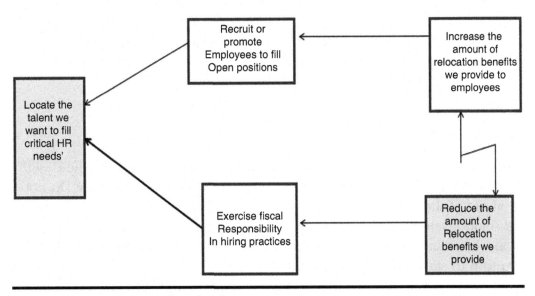

Figure 11.4   The evaporating cloud.

benefits and still get the level of talent that the organization is seeking. The evaporating cloud contains three parts. The first is the objective or the problem/goal. This is supported by both a requirement (critical success factor) and a prerequisite (necessary condition). Much like the goal tree, the CRT is read for each branch that in order to have your goal, you must have requirement 1 in place. In order to have requirement 1 in place, we must have prerequisite 1 in place. The conflict is created when prerequisites 1 and 2 are in conflict.

Steven Johnson, in his book *Far-Sighted*, suggests some additional tools that the empowered team can utilize to enhance your organization.

11.4.2 Mapping

I am sure that most of you have had experience with process maps or value stream maps, but this tool goes beyond those mapping exercises. Here I am referring to the use of mind mapping efforts. My two favorites are free mind and draw, IO. You will see examples of mind maps in Figure 14.3.

The process is that the team begins with a parent node, which represents your problem. From the parent node you brainstorm the potential solutions to the problem. Each what-if solution is represented by a sibling node. You can continue to add to the chart as you come up with additional factors that contribute to the issue resolution. The benefit of the mind map is that it allows for the introduction of alternative solutions that otherwise might have been overlooked. There is no such thing as a dumb solution suggestion here; your goal is arriving at the broadest array of possible solutions that may or may not have a bearing on the problem. You want to make sure that the mind maps are shared with all the stakeholders. This sharing effort must allow for the stakeholders' input as to problems with the proposed solutions and any additional solutions they see that you forgot.

11.4.3 Premortem

The second tool is the use of a premortem. The third question of the design thinking methodology is the answer to the question of what works? Do not be afraid of the risk of failure; you will. The idea is to take the more promising solutions and try them out with a narrow set of stakeholders to see if the proposed solutions accurately work in real time. This does not mean that you turn to stakeholders and ask them if they think the solution will work; you actually set up a demo model of your solution and let them take it for a test run. Let them help you find the flaws in the solution. Let them provide you with a good and bad analysis of the solution.

11.4.4 Solutions

The final tool is the determination of the solution menu to resolve the issue at hand. All too often we rush to judgement as to a solution. It comes from the use of the first idea that comes to mind. It comes from a view that this is what we should do. Francesca Gino, in her article for the *Harvard Business Review*, suggests that the right question to ask is not what we should do, but rather what we could do.[10] Changing the focus from should do to could do opens the discussion to more creative suggestions for applicable solutions. In particular, as we discussed earlier, part of the success of the empowered team is collaboration. So, if you go out to the wide range of ideas, they could do mode should be more inclusion of the diversity of ideas on the market.

11.4.5 Team Construction

The last subject that we need to discuss in summarizing the empowered team level of the TLS Continuum empowerment model is to discuss the construction of the teams themselves. As referred to earlier, Safi Bahcall in his book *Loonshots* suggested that the magic number for a team is 150 members. Before you start shouting that is absurd, I agree with you, but there is a better method that can be implemented here.

The team should start out with a core constituency. This is not necessarily exact persons, but rather the functions they play. I would suggest that every team should contain representatives from management, HR, finance, sales, customer service, logistics, and the floor manager. It is important to stress here that no member of this core is empowered to revert to a command-and-control environment. The chosen solutions are the compilation of the ideas of the whole team, not a team of one. Notice I am referring to a team of seven in the core. So where are the other 143 members?

John Ricketts, in his book *Reaching the Goal*,[11] suggests the creation of a talent bench. The rest of the 143 team members are rotated in and out of the team as their particular skills are needed. Once they have made their contribution, they are rotated back to their normal duties. The process enhances the outcomes by utilizing the strongest human assets in the development of the solutions.

To summarize where we are at this point before moving on to what I believe is the most important part of the TLS Continuum empowerment model, we have looked at the role of both management and the cross-functional teams in the model.

There is one other aspect of a successful cross-functional team that I would be remiss if dismissing. The members of the team as individuals must be empowered through ownership of the process. The organizational management must be open to allow the team, through their ownership of the process, to initiate changes to the process if it enhances the problem resolution. Take Toyota, for example, which allows its employees to activate the anon if they notice something wrong in the process. By activating the anon, the process is stopped in its tracks until the problem is resolved.

Notes

1 Mindtools. *Frederick Taylor and Scientific Management.* https://mindtool.com/pages/article/new/TMM_Taylor.htm
2 Mathis, Robert et al. *Human Resource Management.* 12th Edition. Mason, OH: Thomson South-West, 2008. Pages 168–169.
3 There typically are four types of teams: project teams, self-managed teams, virtual teams, and operational teams. https://study.com
4 Bahcall, Safi. *Loonshots.* New York, NY: St Martin's Press, 2019. Page 148.
5 Rich, Adrienne. *Blood, Bread, and Poetry: Selected Prose, 1979–1985.* New York, NY: Norton, 1986.
6 Epstein, David. *Range: Why Generalists Triumph in a Specialized World.* New York, NY: Riverhead Books, 2019. Pages 177–178.
7 Hayden, Michael. *The Assault on Intelligence.* New York, NY: Penguin Press, 2018. Page 3.
8 Kahneman, Daniel. *Thinking, Fast and Slow.* New York, NY: Farrar, Straus, and Giroux, 2011.
9 Groenewegen, Astrid and Tom De Bruyne. *System Thinking Quick Study Guide.* https://SUEbehaviouraldesign.com/sytem-1-2-quickguide/
10 Gino, Francesca. When Solving Problems, Think About What You Could Do, Not What You Should Do. *Harvard Business Review.* https://hbr.org/2018/04/when-solving-problems-think-about-what-you-could-do-not-what-you-should-do
11 Ricketts, John. *Reaching the Goal: How Managers Improve a Service Business Using Goldratt's Theory of Constraints.* New York, NY: IBM Press, 2008.

Chapter 12

Team Roles and Responsibilities

In the previous chapter, we talked about the existence of cross-functional teams and their responsibilities within the TLS Continuum. But the teams do not operate in a "spaghetti against the wall" method. Rather, each member of the team has a distinct role to play. With the suggestion that an ideal team size is around 150, we are not suggesting that the team operations are nothing but a free-for-all. Every team has a hierarchy of roles and responsibilities, which the team utilizes in its search for the right solution. Notice we did not say result, but rather solution. We will repeat over the following chapters that the real key to success is how you resolve the problem, not how you solved the problem.

We can get a better handle on these roles if we look at them in depth. These roles are not to say that we are talking about command-and-control here, but rather who has the responsibilities to guide the ship and make sure that the team is staying on task. This section will look at each of the roles, the training required, and what their contribution is to the finished product.

12.1 Senior Executive

The first role is that of the senior executive, whose role in the process is to gain management buy-in to the change process. The senior executive is the gatekeeper between the team and upper management. They are the ones who make the pitch to the senior management on what the problem is, why we need to solve the problem, and why the proposed project is the correct route to take. They are also responsible for conducting reviews of project progress and reporting the results of the review to the cross-functional teams, the rank-and-file human capital assets, and the senior management of the organization.

12.2 Executive Committee

Composed of the members of senior management, the executive committee pushes the methodology out into the organization. While there is some degree of discussion about the role of senior management in the process, if the executive committee and thus the senior management do not buy in to the process, it will not result in successful conclusions. They also have the responsibilities to ensure that the required resources needed by the project team are made available.

While it would be helpful, there is no published requirement that either the senior executive or the members of the executive team have any training in depth into the methodology and how it works.

12.3 Champion (Project)

The role of the champion is to be the rudder of the project. They are the ones who make sure the teams stay on target and are working to delivering the milestones when they say they will be delivered. They are responsible for reviewing the project's long-term impact on the organization. If the team runs into an obstacle, it is the champion who helps them get around a solution. The champion also holds the purse strings for the project, authorizing the release of funds for various aspects. Because of the nature of the duties of the project champion, the person in this role should have earned at least a Yellow Belt in Six Sigma so they have some understanding of the process the team is working through.

It is also critical that the champion ensure that the actions of the team are in alignment with the organizational goals, vision, mission, and strategies.

Level	Years of Experience	Training Requirements	Responsibilities	Reporting Path
Champion	None	Should ideally have Six Sigma yellow belt	Translates company vision to develop plan	

12.4 Process Owner

Since the first word in this book, I have mentioned the critical factor in the success of the TLS Continuum methodology is the voice of the customer. The project owner is that voice. They are the ones who have a direct impact on the project. In today's business climate, many managers and employees ask the question: What is in it for me? The process owner is no different. They know they have a problem and have asked the cross-functional team to assist in determining a solution. The expectation is that the process owner is going to be able to find the positive solution to the problem because of the process we have undertaken, and thus we will have met the voice of the customer. It is also important that you understand that the process owner may be inside your organization but just as likely may be external to the organization.

From this point on, the roles begin to require more in-depth training in how the process works. There are many sources out there to obtain the training, both live and online, and I will not suggest which is the best direction in which to obtain the training. I did, however, need a standard source to describe the basic training requirements going forward, so I turned to the certification section of the American Society for Quality as a basis for the resources in this area.

Level	Years of Experience	Training Requirements	Responsibilities	Reporting Path
Process owner	None	None	Stakeholder with the eventual benefit from the project	

I need to divert our attention for a moment to an issue within the quality industry at the present time. There is much discussion underway about whether we have since its inception at Motorola trained too many "belts" within our organizations. If you poll professionals within the quality field, you will receive a mix of responses. Motorola had the formula that you needed one Master Black Belt for each ten Black Belts and one Black Belt for each ten Green Belts. GE went so far as to require anyone seeking leadership positions within the organization to have at least their Green Belt. The real question, then, is have we concentrated too much on the certification process and not enough on the system for resolving the organizational problems?

12.5 Master Black Belt

A Master Black Belt is expected to have a minimum of five years of experience or successfully completed ten Six Sigma Black Belt projects showing expertise in three areas: teaching, coaching, and mentoring; occupational experience and responsibility; and technical knowledge and innovation of the field. It is inherent that a Master Black Belt have clear knowledge of strategic plan development and deployment, cross-functional competencies, and mentoring responsibilities.

The Master Black Belt is the leader of the Six Sigma improvement process and in some cases also will take on the responsibilities of the project champion in smaller organizations. They are also responsible for the implementation of programs that will aid the continuous improvement effort along with training the Black Belts and Green Belts in the Six Sigma methodology. In the cases where you have constructed the HR center of excellence, the Master Belt can be the lead of that center of excellence.

The role of the Master Black Belt is considered a full-time position within the organizational infrastructure.

Level	Years of Experience	Training Requirements	Responsibilities	Reporting Path
Master Black Belt	Five or more years in the role of Black Belt or Master Black Belt	Completion of ten projects	Trains and coaches Black Belts and Green Belts; internal Six Sigma consultant	Reports to champion or sponsor

12.6 Black Belt

The next level down in the pyramid is that of the Black Belt. Black Belts are expected to have completed two projects with a signed affidavit on each plus three years of work experience. In order to be successful, they must be able to explain the philosophy and principles to others within the organization. It is also preferred that they have at least a four-year college degree. They become the first-line supervisor of the process. The immediate supervisor is the Master Black Belt. It is the expectation of the organization that a Black Belt will complete projects that will lead to $250,000 to $500,000 in savings to their organization per year spread over between four and six projects per year. Like the Master Black Belt, the Black Belts are full-time in their responsibilities, so their primary vision is on how to improve the organization from the perspective of removing waste and variation from the processes.

Level	Years of Experience	Training Requirements	Responsibilities	Reporting Path
Black Belt	Three or more years of experience	BA degree and two completed projects with signed affidavits	Leads problem-solving projects; trains and coaches project teams	Master Black Belt

12.7 Green Belt

The Green Belt, like the Black Belt, should have at least three years of experience in quality efforts so that they are familiar with the tools. Under guidelines from ASQ, the candidate for a Green Belt will have completed 64 hours of instruction in a classroom situation learning the methodology.

In the course of their duties, they will analyze and solve elementary quality problems. They may also lead smaller teams. In most organizations the role of a Green Belt is a part-time one in nature. The projects they work on are in the range of $25,000 and $50,000 in potential savings for the organization. Their improvement efforts pay for the program training.

Level	Years of Experience	Training Requirements	Responsibilities	Reporting Path
Green Belt	Three or more years of experience	64 hours of training	Assists with data collection and analysis; leads smaller projects	Black Belt

12.8 Yellow Belt

The Yellow Belt certification is reserved for those individuals who will be assigned as team members on the improvement efforts. It typically requires between 16 and 20 hours of training into the tools of the Six Sigma methodology. While they will not be leading specific projects, it is necessary that they understand when and how they should use the individual tools at each stage of the process. They also learn how to relate these concepts to the overall business strategy. Remember that the ultimate results of the project process are the creation of credible, verifiable data, so they need to understand how to read the data points so they can be interpreted correctly.

Level	Years of Experience	Training Requirements	Responsibilities	Reporting Path
Yellow Belt	None	16–20 hours	Participates as team member	Black Belt

12.9 White Belt

The bottom layer of the roles within our cross-functional teams is the White Belts. This could be open to anyone within the organization who wants a general knowledge of the process. Typically, a White Belt candidate undergoes only about eight hours of training, which are centered on an overview of the process and the tools.

Level	Years of Experience	Training Requirements	Responsibilities	Reporting Path
White Belt	None	Eight hours	Works on local problem-solving teams	Black Belt

The culmination of the work of the teams is to create the environment in which the centers of excellence successfully function and flourish. These centers of excellence require the coordinated efforts of the results of the cross-functional teams in alignment with the organization and the new normal culture.

4

IDENTIFICATION OF THE SYSTEM CONSTRAINTS

How do you define success? First of all, I totally get the immediate response that the question appears to be off base with the topic of this book, but bear with me for a moment. Your response to that question very well might be dependent on your family environment. We grow up with the idea put into our thought stream that in order to be successful, we need to find the perfect spouse, find the perfect organization to work for. That perfect organization will provide us with the perfect job. We will find the perfect house and drive the perfect car. I was in the doctor's office this morning, and the nurse's assistant informed me that she was perfect. We all have that wish. Brian Swinder and his colleagues at the University of Florida wrote in the *Journal of Applied Psychology* that there is no evidence that perfectionists perform any better than the rest of us.[1] This striving for perfection is not only found in life but in business as well. Michael Brainard, writing for *Forbes Magazine*, tells us that "we have developed an unrealistic, mythical expectation that things in business are to be perfect." Even when we say that "we don't expect perfection," we really do. I think many leaders have an unconscious bias that they are perfect and that others ought to be perfect as well. And they apply this same standard to the product launch, the budget performance, the return-on-investment capital (ROIC) of new initiatives, and their newest hire. They must all be perfect.[2]

Consider these evidence-based findings regarding perfectionism from Momentum leaders. In a study they found that:[3]

DOI: 10.4324/9780429029196-16

- **86%** believed perfectionist expectations impact their work.
- **72%** believe perfectionism is harmful to relationship-building.
- **68%** believe perfectionism leads to burnout.
- **66%** believe perfectionism leads to fear of failure and conflict avoidance.
- **66%** of workplaces struggle with perfectionism.
- **One-third** of employees are considering leaving their workplace because of perfectionist expectations.

Perfection might sound good; however, there are drawbacks. If everything was perfect, life would be boring. If everything was perfect, you would not need any employees because they would have nothing to do. Your employees would become less engaged with the organization. Here is the problem: we can't reach perfection in our processes. It just won't happen. In reality, it does not happen in the natural world. Bill Smith at Motorola narrowed down his presence of defect to defects per million opportunities as seen in Figure Part 4.1.

Note that even at 6.0 sigma, we don't get to perfection. We almost get there, with our processes being 99.9967% error free. There is also another factor that kicks its head up. How many of you have ever heard about Murphy's Law? Created by Captain Edward Murphy in 1949, Murphy's Law states that **if something can go wrong, something will go wrong, and at the worst possible time**! (I attended a conference recently where the presenter asked the audience how many people had heard of Schultz's Law, which simply states that Murphy was too damn optimistic.)

In reality we can't reach a state of perfection, which your organizations disguise under the pretext of getting it right the first time. This then means we have to find a way to deal with the errors in our lives. Every process in

Sigma Score	DPMO *	% Good
0	933,193	0.067
1	691,462	30.85
2	308,538	69.15
3	66,807	93.32
4	6,210	99.38
5	233	99.98
6	3.4	99.9997

* - Defects per million opportunities

Figure Part 4.1   Defects per million opportunities (DPMO) chart.

our organizations has hiccups. The problem is that we have not looked for them.

In Part 4 we are intent on identifying the system constraints. We are intent on finding the hiccups within our processes. Over the next three chapters we will consider how to find those hiccups. In Chapter 13 we learn how to observe the current state of the process. We will do so using three tools from the TLS Continuum toolbox: the current reality tree, the process map, and the Gemba walk. This will also utilize the first stage of the Design4Growth as we consider the answer to question what is? In Chapter 14, we will look at the next step, which is to determine what the future process will look like. These questions answer the second stage of the Design4Growth process by asking the question: What if?

The final chapter takes a look at what this presents to us. We have a clear picture of what the process looks like currently. We have a potential picture of what the process will look like, assuming that Murphy's Law does not rear its head. What are the differences between the two? In Chapter 15 we will delve into a discussion of gap analysis—how do we determine the gap between the two pictures and what do we do with the gap results.

Notes

1 Harari, D., B. W. Swider, L. B. Steed, and A. P. Breidenthal. Is Perfect Good? A Meta-Analysis of Perfectionism in the Workplace. *Journal of Applied Psychology*, 103(10), 1121–1144, 2018. https://doi.org/10.1037/apl0000324
2 www.forbes.com/sites/forbescoachescouncil/2020/12/16/busting-the-myth-of-perfection-in-business/?sh=3e00892435b4
3 https://momentumleaders.org/2022/04/14/perfectionism-in-the-workplace/

Chapter 13

Establishing the Current Process State

As we mentioned on page 30, Dr. Mikel Harry, in his seminal work, *Six Sigma: The Breakthrough Management Strategy Revolutionizing the World's Top Corporations*,[1] laid out for us some key performance indicators that dictate how we begin the process of implementing the TLS Continuum. Dr. Harry tells us that:

- We don't know what we don't know.
- We can't do what we don't know.
- We won't know until we measure.
- We don't measure what we don't value.
- We don't value what we don't measure.

Making the assumption that Dr. Harry is correct in his assumptions, then in order to identify the system constraints, it is critical that we understand the nature of the system at hand in its current state. The TLS Continuum provides us with several tools to achieve this goal. In order to utilize these tools, we must base our efforts around walking the walk, talking the talk, and taking the Gemba walk. To start with let's break down the first two parts of the process.

DOI: 10.4324/9780429029196-17

13.1 Walk the Walk

Walk the walk is a critical part of the TLS Continuum and its successful implementation. While eventually as you will see later in this chapter, a physical walk will come into the picture, in and of itself walk the walk does not necessarily mean a physical walk. We are referring to the fact that beneath everything we promise in the talk, the talk is a process. This does not mean we are solely concerned with a silo in the form of a function. We are concerned with the organization as a whole.

If you are going to purchase new materials or equipment, there is a process. If you are actively involved in talent acquisition, there is a process. If you are producing a product or service, there is a process. If you are turning on your computer in the morning or shutting it down at night, there is a process.

What it all comes down to is that the processes do what we say they do. Are the processes designed in such a way so we can deliver on those promises without the requirement of rework? This means that there is a logical sequence to the steps in that process that makes sense to the marketplace.

Walking the walk is only one part of the message that your organization delivers every time we interact with a customer. Walk the walk consists of the expectations that the customer gains from our communication efforts as an organization.

13.2 Talk the Talk

The other half of the equation is the talk the talk. When we talk the talk, we are telling the customer base that we are good at what we do and will deliver what we say we will. It is the basis of our message to the marketplace. But what happens if the two messages don't match up? Dr. James Holt, professor emeritus at the University of Washington at Vancouver, gave us some insight into that with the creation of the Keeping the Promises calculator[2] (https://docs.google.com/spreadsheets/d/1RybrAxysJFRxiG4Tz8BkRpgBnF--aiTW/edit?usp=sharing&ouid=10719538 5541289798559&rtpof=true&sd=true). The Keeping the Promises calculator consists of seven columns:

◼ The first column is labeled Item, which refers to a particular job or a particular human capital asset.

- The second column is labeled Type, which refers to the task at hand.
- The third column is the value of the task on a scale of 1–10, with 10 being the most important.
- The fourth column is labeled Due, which is when the customer submitted the order.
- The fifth column is labeled with the date the task was due.
- The sixth column is labeled with the date the task was completed.
- The seventh column is the number of days the task was late.

All your responses are then graphed according to Value = Late-days; Value = Inventory-days, and Value per Day. What the control charts show us is what happens to the organization when we don't meet our milestone delivery times. Some reword the phrase to indicate that when we are all done, the messages we deliver is that what we tell the customer are what we deliver.

There are two pieces left in our discussion. The first is how do we prove that the two sides of the equation match? The second is what tools do we have to demonstrate evidence-based data that we are doing so?

13.3 Take the Gemba Walk

The way we prove that the two sides of the equation match is through conducting the Gemba walk. W. Edwards Deming told us that "if you can't describe what you are doing as a process, you don't know what you are doing." The Gemba walk delivers that requirement. The Gemba walk delivers the evidence-based tools through which we can describe the process.

The blog Gemba Solutions tells us that Gemba in its literal translation from the Japanese is a real place, and in business it refers to the real place where value is created, which is typically the bottom line. In our discussion of the TLS Continuum, that bottom line is the individual processes that you are considering.[3]

Taken from the book *Gemba Kaizen* by Masaaki Imai, the Gemba walk is based on five primary principles. First, when a problem arises we must go the Gemba first. We need to start at the process. Second, check for the relevant objects to find the possible root causes. Determine the special causes, the root causes, and the common causes. Third, we should take temporary countermeasures to lessen the impact of the problem. Fourth, we need to identify the root causes using the five whys and Pareto analysis. Finally, we need to standardize the corrections so that the problem does not return.[4]

The Gemba walk process visits the front line to glean firsthand knowledge of the process. We are especially concerned with how the services are provided to the customer and what challenges your organization is currently facing in achieving that delivery promise. Finally, it is looking for ways to improve the processes along the way. We can further delineate the purpose of the Gemba walk by looking at the key performance indicators that arise out of it.

13.4 Gemba Walk Key Performance Indicators

When we look at the Gemba walk KPIs, we discover there are eight primary KPIs that directly impact the walk process.

First, as I have already stated, is to gain firsthand knowledge regarding how the process is performing. Are there obvious process system constraints that are holding up the process? Every process contains milestones with a definitive delivery date. Are we reaching them and on time?

Gemba Tool – *Taiichi Ohno introduced the stand in the circle exercise. The stand in the circle exercise required managers to stand on the factory floor in a circle and observe the process. At the end of 25 minutes the managers reconvened with Ohno, and he asked what they observed. If they could not definitively explain what they saw was wrong in a process, he sent them back to the floor to look again.*

Second is the ability to observe where the gaps are between the promises and actual performance. Later in this part, we will look at the use of gap analysis in more detail. At this point consider our discussion of process hiccups. Consider when the customer tells us that they want this product or service at this price and delivered on this date and we don't meet those requirements.

Third is having a coordinated effort in reviewing the process in question. You have the front-line worker who sees the process every day, day in and day out. When you become too comfortable in the way things flow, it is easy to overlook certain details. With the introduction of management's eyes on the process, this allows us to look at the process with a fresh set of eyes.

Fourth, in conducting the Gemba walk management gets to stress to the organization the need to actively consider both quality and safety. We don't reduce quality to deliver sooner if it hinders the safety of the process and our human capital assets.

Fifth is the critical part of the Gemba walk. It gets everyone out of the corner office and allows for the interaction between all parts of the organization, which is the basis of the cross-functional teams. It emphasizes that management may not have all the answers and allows for the introduction of the diversity of ideas we discussed on page 100.

Sixth, as I stated in the golden rules of Gemba and in my discussion of the principles of Six Sigma, is to develop the standard of work so all facets of the organization are provided with a roadmap to success. Successful continuous process improvement works best when our processes are, among other attributes, repeatable. This means that if we conduct a process on Monday and then again on Tuesday, the same steps and outcomes are achieved.

Seventh is that the Gemba walk leads us to better alignment of the organization, which is absolutely necessary in order for the TLS Continuum to deliver on its potential. Everything we do must be aligned with the corporate values, mission statement, goals, and ultimate strategies for implementation.

The eighth and final KPI is that the basis of all communication becomes the explanation of both the value of the work being performed and the importance of that work to the overall organization. The communication vehicle must paint a clear picture for all the stakeholders as to where the processes are going and what needs to be improved.

The Gemba walk process is not a haphazard one. KaiNexus, in their blog, suggests that there are seven steps to a successful walk:[5]

Step 1: You need to prepare your team.

The team needs to understand what a Gemba walk is and what its purposes are. They further need to understand how the Gemba walk is conducted and the expectations for each step of the process. This includes what the team responsibilities are as a whole and on the part of the individual team members.

Step 2: You need to plan the walk.

We already mentioned earlier that the Gemba walk is not some haphazard effort. It needs to be planned out down to the details. The plan should include what questions are going to be asked along the way. The plan should also detail how the Gemba walk will be conducted. Where is the starting point and where does it end? The tacit understanding ought to be that you start at the "receiving dock" and end at the "shipping dock." How much time is allotted for this to take place?

Step 3: Follow the value stream.

Using the same analogy earlier, we begin at the beginning of the process and end at its conclusion. You want to follow every step in order and be observant of the areas where non-value-added activities are showing up and take note of the effect of those activities on process performance.

Gemba Walk Tool – *Make sure you take with you a clipboard and record every step in a process map. You should also bring along a stopwatch to record process times. Don't rely on your wristwatch. If you have a smart phone, go to the Utilities folder and locate the app for the clock; you will find a stopwatch embedded into the phone. Further with your iPad or tablet, locate and download Metrologic's Process Writer, which allows you to create the process map.*

Gemba Tool – *Create a process map on steroids. Between each step of the process, insert the duration time of each task. This will become useful later in your TLS Continuum journey as you plan the drum-buffer-rope tool.*

Fourth, understand that the problem is arising due to the process, not the role of the human capital assets. Therefore the goal of the Gemba walk is to concentrate on the specific process. If you have a process problem, it is never with an individual; it is always the process.

Fifth, one of the requirements of the Gemba walk is that you document everything. We will explore that later in this chapter.

Sixth, during the Gemba walk you must ask questions in order to understand fully the process sequence. Who, why, what, when, and why are important questions to be asked at each step. Seventh, the Gemba walk is not the place to offer suggestions. The purpose of the Gemba walk is to observe only

Eight, remember that the Gemba walk team involves all interested stakeholders. They must be involved at a level that allows them to understand why the organization is doing something. Ninth, the Gemba walk should be staggered and never at the exact time or place. This is in order to get a clear picture of the process from all aspects. If your organization works on shifts, the problem may not be taking place on the first shift, but rather on one of the other shifts.

The tenth rule is the sharing of your findings with the total organization. It is the critical communication piece I discussed earlier. We want to communicate both successes and failures.

The final and eleventh step is that the Gemba walk is not a one-off thing. They should be periodically scheduled throughout the year. They should be conducted without much prior notice so that if there are problems, they are not artificially covered up.

There is one other important factor here. In an ideal world, we should not be conducting one Gemba walk. You should be conducting three of them. Your client informs you that you have a problem. Where is it arising from? Why is it arising? When is it arising? The answers can be found by conducting first a Gemba walk of your organization. Then follow it up with Gemba walks through your suppliers and your customers. This allows you to identify if the problem is arising outside of your organization.

Remember earlier I said that every process has its hiccups. The Gemba walk is no different. The hiccups in this case stem from your attitudes going into the walk.

Hiccup #1: Preoccupied mindset

I totally get it. We all have busy schedules in today's VUCA world. We have numerous deadlines on the horizon. But in order to conduct an effective Gemba walk, we need to leave all that behind us. Your mind must be confined to the results of the walk, not the other things before you. A clouded mind will not provide the vehicle for you to see the whole picture.

Hiccup #2: Predetermined outcomes

Unfortunately, management tends to have a superiority mindset. Many believe they already know and understand the answers to the problems facing the organization. Forget about them. You need to enter the Gemba walk with an open view of the process without determining the solutions before you have all the facts.

Hiccup #3: You are there to learn, not to tell

Your goal for the Gemba walk is to observe, not to tell. As I stated earlier, Taiichi Ohno asked his managers to conduct a stand in the circle exercise. He asked them to stand in a circle on the factory floor for 25 minutes and observe the processes. At the conclusion of the time limit, he would ask them what they observed and what was wrong. If they said they did not find anything, he would send them back to the factory floor and conduct the exercise all over again.

Hiccup #4: Relying on a checklist

Along with the predetermined outcome is the tendency to enter into the Gemba walk with a checklist of what you think the problems are and the questions to ask. Don't do it.

Here is the problem. What happens if something arises and it is not on your checklist or a question arises and it is not one of your checklist questions? diminishes the walk.

Hiccup # 5 Chore mindset

Gemba walks can be fun. It gives you the opportunity to interact outside of your silo. The result is that if you enter into the Gemba walk with the attitude that you have to do this whether you want to or not, you will diminish the effectiveness of the walk.

Hiccup # 6: Conqueror mindset

Finally, don't go into the Gemba walk with the idea that you and only you know what the solution is. Don't enter the Gemba walk with the attitude that only you can resolve the problem.

13.5 The Next Step Upon Completion of the Gemba Walk

We mentioned earlier in this chapter the need to document everything. One of the reasons to do so is to describe in detail the conditions of your current process. One of the tools available to do this is through the use of William Dettmer's Logical Thinking Process and the current realty tree.[6] In the course of ten steps you can gain a clear picture of the current state of your processes from your notes. It would be worthwhile to investigate these ten steps.

It should be noted at this point that I am not attempting a full discussion of the various tools here, but to provide an overview of them. For those who

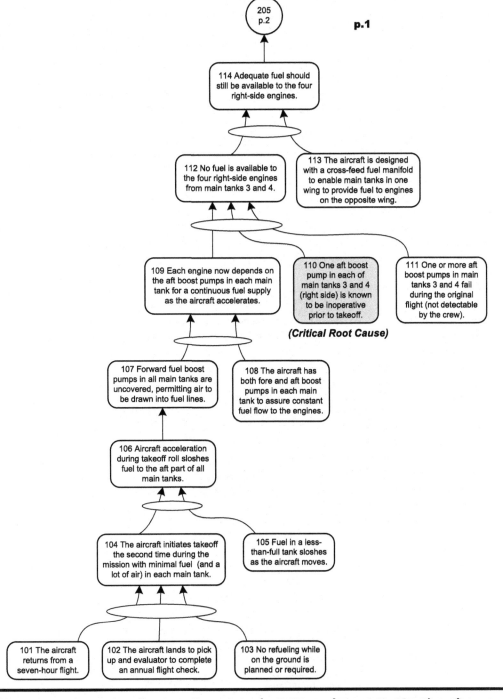

Figure 13.1 **Current reality tree (Anatomy of a B-52 crash, part 1). (Continued)**

*Source: Dettmer, H.W. Breaking the Constraints to World-Class Performance (1998)
Used with permission*

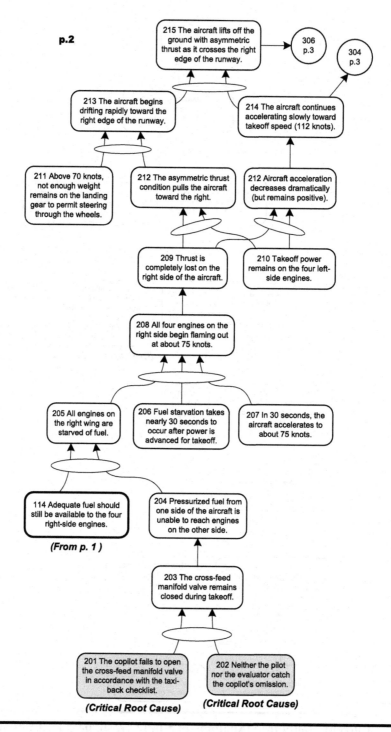

p.2

215 The aircraft lifts off the ground with asymmetric thrust as it crosses the right edge of the runway.

306 p.3

304 p.3

213 The aircraft begins drifting rapidly toward the right edge of the runway.

214 The aircraft continues accelerating slowly toward takeoff speed (112 knots).

211 Above 70 knots, not enough weight remains on the landing gear to permit steering through the wheels.

212 The asymmetric thrust condition pulls the aircraft toward the right.

212 Aircraft acceleration decreases dramatically (but remains positive).

209 Thrust is completely lost on the right side of the aircraft.

210 Takeoff power remains on the four left-side engines.

208 All four engines on the right side begin flaming out at about 75 knots.

205 All engines on the right wing are starved of fuel.

206 Fuel starvation takes nearly 30 seconds to occur after power is advanced for takeoff.

207 In 30 seconds, the aircraft accelerates to about 75 knots.

114 Adequate fuel should still be available to the four right-side engines.

(From p. 1)

204 Pressurized fuel from one side of the aircraft is unable to reach engines on the other side.

203 The cross-feed manifold valve remains closed during takeoff.

201 The copilot fails to open the cross-feed manifold valve in accordance with the taxi-back checklist.

(Critical Root Cause)

202 Neither the pilot nor the evaluator catch the copilot's omission.

(Critical Root Cause)

Figure 13.1   Current reality tree (Anatomy of a B-52 crash, part 2). (Continued)

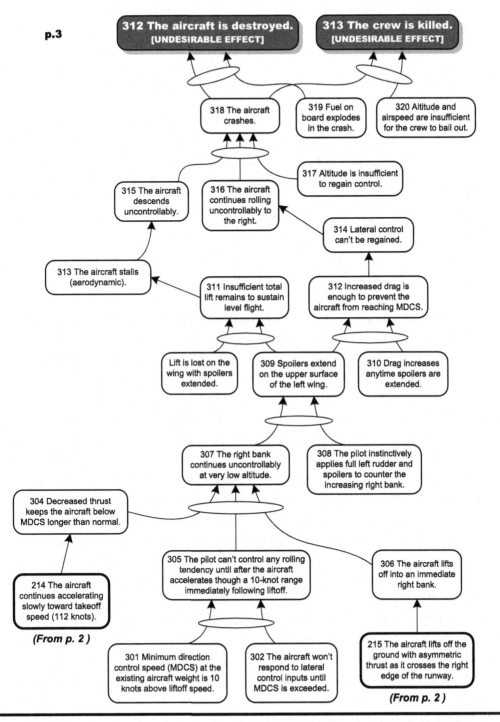

Figure 13.1   Current reality tree (Anatomy of a B-52 crash, part 3). (Continued)

want a more in-depth discussion of the tools, pick up a copy of H. William Dettmer's *The Logical Thinking Process*.

Step #1: Identify your span of control and the sphere of influence

Answer a simple question: Is your customer complaint based in the emergency evacuation plan or the HVAC plan? The chances that you will be dealing with a universal problem facing the entire organization are small. As a result, we need to concentrate on a limited-scope problem that may affect a segment of the organization.

Once we recognize that the customer's problem is a confined one, we need to take steps to understand both how it is manifested and how the problem affects our organization. We begin the process by seeking answers to two questions. The first is: What is the span of the problem?

The Human Capital Hub tells us that this span comes in two formats: a wide span and a narrow one.[7] In a wide-span situation, management oversees a wide breath of functions that influence the process. This is true when the impact of the problem is spread across multiple areas of the organization. In the long run the wide span is of more benefit to the organization because it allows for your subject matter experts to take on added responsibilities and higher degrees of engagement and empowerment. This can be a good thing.

The second question regarding the sphere of influence of the team is the case of the other option, that of a narrow span of control; it simply means that the number of functions involved in resolving the problem is lower. The type of problem will dictate whether you want to have a wide span of control or a narrow one. It also means that the level of the span of control will determine how you go about compiling suggestions for the removal of the system constraints. It will also determine the scope of the problem.

Another way to look at the span of control issue is to consider who is resolving the problem. If you have a wide span of control, the tendency is to use a fully implemented cross-functional team. On the other hand, if you are resolving the problem through the use of limited resources such as a quality circle, you are utilizing a narrow span of control.

The second issue in the problem-solving effort is the question of the sphere of influence of the cross-functional team. The website Rethority tells us that the sphere of influence is the collection of people who know you or know of you.[8] Why is the cross-functional team in place? Is it to appease the customer? Is it to make it appear like you are trying to resolve the problem? Or is it that the team has a legitimate purpose and goal for resolving the problem? In the latter case, the organizational parts know the team is working on resolving the issue and have trust in their ability to do this. The goal then must be for the team to gain the trust of the remainder of the organization.

The website The Muse tells that sphere of influence is determined in four distinct ways. Each of the ways increases the level of trust and impact of the team.[9] The first is exemplified by the vast majority of management. You have a problem, and management tells you this is how you are going to resolve it. They survive in a command-and-control environment. They tell the human capital assets and the stakeholders, here is the problem and this is the way we are going to resolve it. This brings to mind the title of a recent book by Carol Leonnig and her colleagues, *I Alone Can Fix It*. In today's VUCA world, this is the least acceptable method for exercising your sphere of influence.

In the second type of influence management is tasked with selling the organization on the benefits of the suggested resolution. This is still a limited involvement. It is like when you went and purchased your new car and the salesman at the dealership was preaching the virtues of the new vehicle. You may not think the solution is the one for you, but management is still pushing the option to get you to accept the new vehicle.

In the third type of influence, management utilizes Dr. Tony Alessandra's Platinum Rule and gains buy-in on the problem resolution through the use of nonmanipulative selling. The concept may rattle some within your organization because that is not the typical way of selling an idea. The goal is to demonstrate for the customer how the solution will resolve their problem.[10] You are the organization consultant, not the organizational prophet. You are there to offer advice to the organization, not once again tell the stakeholders that this is the way it will be.

The fourth type of influence is paramount of the influence types. It asks you to discover the solutions through collaboration. The cross-functional team in conjunction with the stakeholders work to discover the solution together with the input of everyone who touches the process that is presenting the problem in any way. If you have even minimal involvement in the process, you should be involved in the solution to the problem.

We can't expect to meet the needs of the customer to resolve the problem without influencing others. We need them to understand what is in it for them and to act accordingly. The dynamic combination of span of control with the level of influence the cross-functional team exerts on the organization is the key to continuous process improvement success.

Step #2: Create your list of undesirable effects

I discussed earlier the natural reaction when a customer calls for the first time to alert you to a problem. The organizational defense mechanisms go up, and you begin to list all the reasons why the problem can't exist. Here is reality. There will be problems. It is your charge to find a resolution to the problems. The initial task is to identify how the problem is manifesting itself.

Once again, during our discussion of the project maps, we talked about the use of a tool referred to as a goal tree. As we discussed, the goal tree begins with your goal and then establishes the critical factors that must be present to reach the goal. It then sets out the necessary factors that you need to obtain the critical success factors.

I want to turn the Dettmer's goal tree on its head, if you will. My suggestion is that we change the name of the goal tree to the TLS Continuum problem resolution guide, as shown in Figure 13.2.

Using the same nomenclature as shown in the example earlier, we redefine the components. In place of the term goal, place the problem statement. This problem statement should be in the form of a full statement. For example: The XYZ product is not performing according to specifications, or the applicant tracking system is referring us candidates who do not have the requisite skills according to the job requisition. Granted, the job requirements may have been off to begin with, but the problem can still exist.

Having determined the nature of the problem being presented, the next level down in the problem resolution guide is to ask: What is the reason for the problem to be appearing? How is the problem manifesting itself? What the customer is telling you is that the presence of the problem means

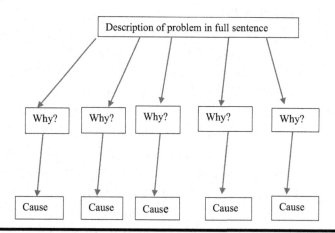

Figure 13.2 TLS Continuum problem resolution guide.

that their needs are not being met. Be specific. You want to know precisely why the problem exists. The next level down is not the critical success factors, but rather answering the question of how the product is not meeting their demands. You want to try and present at a minimum five reasons why the problem is presenting itself.

The final stage of the problem resolution guide may be the most difficult to complete. You need to take each of the five areas being presented and define why they are happening. Define the cause and effects of each condition to gain knowledge of why they are happening.

Gemba Tool – *The TLS Continuum takes from the Lean side of the equation and implements the five whys. Using a cascading series of five questions, you can reach a conclusion of what the root cause of the problem is.*

Consider this example:

> The problem: John printed too many e-mails in violation of corporate policy.
> Why: John did not know about the policy regarding printing e-mails
> Why: Management had not told John about the policy.
> Why: The policy was not part of the onboarding process.
> Why: The policy was not in the employee handbook.
> Why: The policy was not written down anywhere.
> Root Cause: The policy was not in written form.

Gemba Tool – *The continuum also offers up a tool called the Ishikawa fishbone diagram, which graphically presents the determination of the cause-and-effect relationships using the skeleton of a fish. The diagram looks at the contribution of man (people), machine (equipment), materials, management, and the environment. It is a graphic way to show the five whys. It is a useful tool when the team is in a rut in determining the root causes of the problem.*

Step #3: Begin the current reality tree

Select the worse reasons why the problem exists, and create the relationships between the problem and the results of the problem. You clearly want to establish a definitive relationship between your undesirable effects and the problem. If we review the undesirable effects carefully enough, we will find that more often than not, two of them will relate closely to each other. These should be the start of your current reality tree. By doing so can you identify any missing steps in the process? If so, add those steps to the process.

Step #4: Connect the first two undesirable effects

Take those two interrelated undesirable effects and draw the connection between them to your problem. These become the first parts of your current reality tree. It begins to show the interrelationships between the problem and what damage it may be causing to the organization and its stakeholders.

Step #5: Connect the other undesirable effects

Having established the relationship between the first two undesirable effects, go back and connect the remaining undesirable effects to the tree.

Step #6: Build the cause-and-effect chain downward

Remember in our discussion of the goal tree, the arrows of relationship ran from the bottom to the top or the goal statement. In the problem resolution guide, we do just the opposite. The arrows of relationship run from the top *down* to the bottom of the guide. This demonstrates that the flow of the relationship runs from the problem statement to the effects of the problem to the root causes of the problem.

Step #7: Redesignate the undesirable effects

What happens if in the course of getting to this step, you find additional undesirable effects? It is at this point that you can add them to your tree. Once you have them all connected, go back and look at your tree. As you progressed through the construction of the tree, are all the undesirable effects still undesirable? If not, remove them from the tree. Remove any potential causes if they are no longer of value to the issue at hand.

Step#8: Identify the root cause of the problem

Go back to the Gemba walk, the five whys, and the Ishikawa fishbone diagram and single out the root cause of the problem. With the root cause identified, the cross-functional team can begin the discussion regarding how to remove the root cause from the equation.

Step #9: Look for missing connections

With the root cause in place and the solutions discussed, go back and look at your tree and seek out any apparent missed connections. At this point you need to make sure that the new connections are connected to the remainder of the tree.

Step #10: Decide which are the priority root causes to be resolved

The final step in your construction of the current reality tree is to review all the potential root causes that have been identified and determine which are the most important. It is the root cause(s) that need to be removed that should take priority. It is these priority root causes which should have the greatest impact on why the problem exists, and with the consult of the stakeholders, they should be addressed to resolve the problem.

Notes

1 Harry, Mikel. *Six Sigma: The Breakthrough Management Strategy Revolutionizing the World's Top Corporations.* New York, NY: Currency Random House, 2005. Page xii.
2 Holt, James. *The Keeping the Promises Spreadsheet* was introduced in Dr. Holt's Class EM530 Applications in Constraint Management. https://netorg5223078-my.sharepoint.com/:x:/g/personal/dan_dbaiconsulting_com/EZs_qm-zLstHlEvpXxbOuLYB0g24jApK4zx3VeecrbOveQ?e=ELCtRE
3 Gemba Solutions. *What Does the Word Gemba Actually Mean?* https://gembasolutions.com/what-does-gemba-actually-mean/
4 Hash Management Services LLP. *Five Golden Rules of Gemba.* https://www.hashllp.com/golden-rules-of-gemba/
5 KaiNexus. *11 Steps to an Effective Gemba Walk.* https://blog.kainexus.com/improvement-disciplines/gemba-walks/11-steps-to-an-effective-gemba-walk
6 Dettmer, H. William. *Goldratt's Theory of Constraints: A Systems Approach to Continuous Improvement.* Milwaukee, WI: ASQ Quality Press, 1997. Pages 89–99.
7 www.thehumancapitalhub.com/articles/types-of-span-of-control
8 https://rethority.com/sphere-of-influence/
9 www.themuse.com/advice/types-of-influence
10 Alessandra, Tony. *Non-Manipulative Selling.* New York, NY: Prentice Hall, 1987. Pages viii, 4.

Chapter 14

Determining the Future Process State

In Chapter 13, we looked at the methods behind understanding how our processes operated in real time. By this time, you should have a basic idea of what the problem is and what effects the problem is having on your stakeholders.

Continuous process improvement and the TLS Continuum are a serious matter that have profound effects on your organization, but that does not mean you can't have fun at the same time. Stop for a moment and let your mind run wild.

Chapter 14 takes us on the next step in our journey. Ask yourself what would the perfect process look like? The Design4Growth methodology suggests that it is the response to looking at your process and discovering "what if." If you had a magic wand and you could wave it in the air, what would your process look like in the future? Eliyahu Goldratt provided us with a logical thinking process tool called the future reality tree to help us find the answer to the future. Further, we can combine the various facets of Design4Growth[1] with those of Dettmer's Logical Thinking Process[2] to define how we construct our vision of the future.

Step 1: Gather the information and materials

Presented in Chapter 13, the cross-functional team has taken the first critical step in identifying what the current process is telling us. You have identified where the system constraint resides in the process. In accomplishing that, you

DOI: 10.4324/9780429029196-18

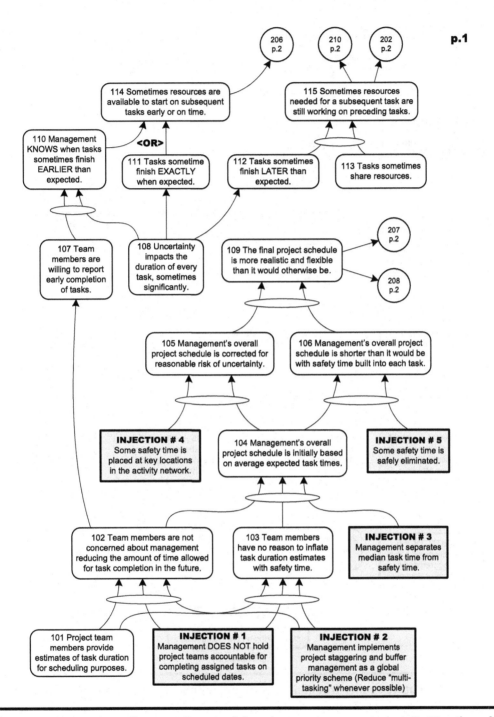

Figure 14.1 Future reality tree (Successful project management, part 1). (Continued)

Source: © H. William Dettmer 2010. Used with permission

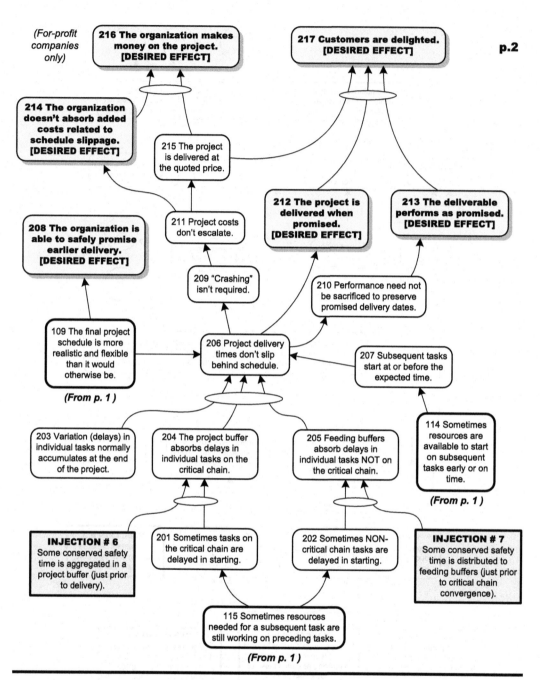

Figure 14.1 Future reality tree (Successful project management, part 2). (Continued)

have also been able to determine what the effect of the system constraint is having on the process at hand. At this juncture you need to move to the next step, which is to identify potential solutions. Now you are charged with discovering the best solutions to resolve the problem. The intent of the solution discovery is to resolve the voice of the customer issues to their satisfaction.

The project sponsor now is charged with assembling what is needed to complete this next step. The first ask is to return to the project charter, and specifically to the section where we identified the required project resources. Before we can begin to look at potential solutions, we need to confirm that those resources are in place. In order to take the next step, we need to be sure that we suddenly are not discovering resources we forgot about in the current phase. Each of these resources must be readily in place as you begin to evaluate potential solutions.

The project sponsor should begin by compiling all the documentation from the current stage effort and ensure that you have sufficient copies of all the materials for each member of the team participating in this next phase. This means that each member of the cross-functional team should receive a packet that contains copies of the notes from the Gemba walks, the process maps, the value stream maps, the project charter, the Ishikawa fishbone diagram (if applicable), the current reality tree, the goal statements, and any other corresponding documentation. They will be necessary as a reference point as we plan a future process. Your documentation should reflect a clear understanding of the current state of the process. It is critical that each member of the cross-functional team have the same understanding.

Prior to continuing in this phase of the process, the project sponsor needs to be sure that everyone is on the same page at this juncture. Every participant needs to see the current process and feel the effects of that process on the total organization. Ensure that they are entering the potential solution phase free from any biases as to what the solution may look like. A vital part of this is to ensure that we are meeting each team member in a way that fits their learning style. Some of us learn by touching. Some of us learn by hearing the material, and some of us learn by seeing what is in front of us. As you proceed, make sure you are taking these learning styles into consideration.

Gemba Tool – *In the recently released book Goldratt's Rules of Flow, the author Efrat Goldratt-Ashlag (Eliyahu Goldratt's daughter) suggests using a tool called the full-kit.[3] Be honest: How good is your memory?*

The full-kit provides in written form each resource that is required to complete the task at hand. You should not continue until you are totally sure that you have listed every required resource. This should include any ancillary resources you might need. For example, if you are going to paint a room, you will also need drop cloths, brushes, etc.

Step 2: Re-examine the project scope

Marshall Goldsmith tells us that what got us here won't get us there. In continuous process improvement, the same concept applies. If we don't know what got us here, we have no way to resolve the issues that we face. Deming told us that "if you can't describe what you are doing as a process, you don't know what you are doing."[4]

How do we define the process? We return to the initial phase of the project charter to the section devoted to the problem scope and impact. At that time, we detailed the various aspects of the intended project. We outlined what the ultimate goal of the project will be. We laid out the milestones or deliverables, the various tasks, and the anticipated costs.

Now, as we are projecting what our future system is going to look like, we need to complete that initial task all over again. Remember I stated that the project charter in its entirety is a living document and that it changes over time. This means that as we move from the current state to the future state, the scope most likely will change.

The process champion thus begins this step by ensuring that each member of the cross-functional team has been given a copy of the original project charter with a concentrated look at the project scope section of the charter. This will allow the team and management to refine and collaborate on what the future of the process look like. It also demonstrates whether we are on track going forward.

Re-examining the scope takes into consideration several key components of the examination process. First, we need to remind ourselves that we are not talking about a universal issue. Our scope is refined to a particular set of system constraints that pertain to a set series of events which are causing the problem at hand. Further, the scope applies to a specific issue, at a specific time, and in a specific place. Second, the cross-functional team needs to review the project requirements when we set out on this journey. With that in mind, we need to review those requirements in line with our current reality model and determine from our initial establishment of requirements, if the requirements list has changed as we begin to assess the future reality of our process.

Third, the team must establish whether because of the system constraints discovered in our first pass of the process if the needs of the business have changed. Is the issue behind the problem still appropriate, or did the Gemba walk discover a whole new set of needs that must be attended to? The list of business needs are reflected in the daily activities we undertake to respond to the voice of the customer and to bring a return on the investment of those activities to both the organization and the customer. The Alberta Motor Association[5] suggests that these basic needs are represented by beginning with an idea or a dream as to what the future looks like. Thus, the reasoning behind the future reality tree. Not generalities but specifics.

No idea or suggested solution is viable unless there is total buy-in from the organization. When we began this effort to improve the system flow, it was necessary to obtain approval from the management of the organization to try to improve the process. But as with most things, as time goes by, views change. So, as we begin the process of constructing what the future may look like, we need to go back and ensure that the same level of buy-in is present. This buy-in needs to determine that the same passion for the change process is still at a high level. If it is not, the champion must take steps to get everyone back on board. Being on board means that everyone involved has an equal or near-equal belief in the tenacity of the effort, the same level of knowledge about the issue, and the training to complete the effort.

Before we continue, we need to go back in time a bit. Your organization took the time and the effort to develop a new product or service. Your phenomenal sales team took the product or service to the marketplace and achieved orders for this product or service. The customer came away with a view in their mind as to what this new addition was going to do for their organization in the form of expectations. Jump forward in time to that communication where the problem arose. The customer's expectations changed to represent how they expect your organization to correct the problem. These expectations may or may not be the same as when they purchased the product or service. Jump further to the present. We are now involved in the process of identifying what the solution may look like. It is highly probable that the customer's expectations have changed again as the result of their involvement in the cross-functional team.

From here, the champion has one final task. They must develop a road-map or plan as to how we are going to construct the future view of the system constraint. This should reflect the likelihood that the plan may change again before we are all finished. If it does, how do we incorporate the changes as we proceed? These should all be included in a detailed scope statement.

The new plan should also identify the work breakdown structure or process tasks along with how we will monitor the process track as we continue.

Gemba Tool – *One tool to use to help with the new scope statement is to use the standard work combination worksheet, first introduced by Toyota. As shown in Figure 14.2, it combines the fill sheet with some other factors to provide you a clear view of the scope.*

The worksheet consists of several parts. The first column represents the various tasks involved in the process, which can be taken from the fill sheet. The following three columns ask you to define the task as a value-added task, a non-value-added-task, or a motion task, meaning that you are walking between process steps. In each column you should identify the duration of each task.

The fourth column totals the run times. The fifth column provides a running total of the run times that have been established. The columns to the right graphically plot out the standard work process.

Step 3: Plan and schedule a team meeting

The third responsibility of the project champion in the future reality process is to plan and schedule the cross-functional team in order to work through the potential solution selection. It is necessary for the champion to not assume what the best format for these meetings are. We all learn differently. Circumstances, especially in this post-COVID era, dictate different work arrangements.

If your organization has adapted the Results Oriented Work Environment (ROWE) method, the key is the deadline for solution, not how, when, and where you do it. In the case where the team is meeting remotely, plan on utilizing a remote meeting platform such as Zoom, Go-to-Meeting, or Microsoft Teams. Be sure that everyone has access to adequate Internet bandwidth so everyone can participate equally. Set aside a time and location for the meeting that accommodate everyone's needs.

Standard Work Combination Sheet

Process:

Item #	Description	Manual Task Time: value-add	Manual Task Time: non-value-add	Manual Task Time: walk-time	Manual Sub Total	Auto RUN (MACHINE CYCLE TIME)	TOTAL CYCLE TIME	COMBINATION TIME
1					0		0	
2					0		0	
3					0		0	
4					0		0	
5					0		0	
6					0		0	
7					0		0	
8					0		0	
9					0		0	
10					0		0	
11					0		0	
12					0		0	
13					0		0	
14					0		0	
15					0		0	
16					0		0	
17					0		0	
18					0		0	
19					0		0	
20					0		0	
	TOTALS:	0	0	0	0	0	0	manual, auto-run, walk, wait

Figure 14.2 Standard work combination worksheet from AllAboutLean.[6]

Step 4: Brainstorm potential solutions

There is no such thing as a stupid answer. One of the highlights of the cross-functional teams is the availability of a wide diversity of ideas. The best tool we have at our disposal is the act of brainstorming and benchmarking.

Remember in the establishment of a view of the future process we are letting our minds run wild. Just like the people at MIT Labs and their Design4Growth process, we are asking the question: What if? Brainstorming is the way we achieve that goal. By looking at all the evidence gained during the current process state, the cross-functional team throws out on the table ideas as how to resolve the issue. Once the list of ideas are on the table, the team begins to whittle down the list through the removal of those ideas that do not come close to meeting the goals established. We always start with a grand view and then reduce it to the micro view as we get closer to the solutions.

Gemba Tool – *Again if we are operating from remote locations, we need a way to share our ideas that everyone can see. If we were all in the same location, we could take advantage of flip charts or full-wall white boards. The dilemma can be resolved if we utilize technology and share a tool called a mind map, which can be obtained from Free Mind at no cost.*

The map begins with the circle to the left of Figure 14.3, which represents the system constraint, and then to the right is the child mode or the potential solution. The final level is the sibling mode, or the requirements

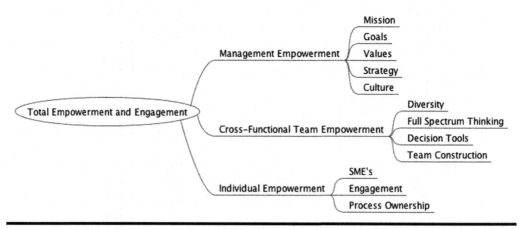

Figure 14.3   Empowered team mind map from Free Mind.[8]

to implement the solution. There is no limit to how many child or sibling nodes you can have. In the end the selection of the solution should be only a matter of following the chains.

The second tool at the disposal of the cross-functional team is benchmarking. The Oxford Directory of Languages tells us that benchmarking is to evaluate or check (something) by comparison with a standard.[7] With the list of potential solutions in place, we need to find a way to narrow down that list. Benchmarking is the way. We take each potential solution and compare it to the available information as to what other organizations are doing in the same situation.

The New City Insurance company tells us that there are four main types of benchmarking in the marketplace. With the recognition that we are not dealing with a universal situation, you can take the situation presented by the system constraints and determine if there has been ever a similar situation and how your organization resolved that one. Take their solutions and insert them into your solution options.

The likelihood that your organizational situation is unique is a rarity. So, in the second form of benchmarking, we take the problem into the marketplace. Who among our competition may have experienced the same issue and how did they resolve it? How does their corporate culture compare to ours? If there are similar components of their culture to ours, can we apply their solutions? Utilize the mind map tool and take the same steps as we did with our own brainstorming situation. Is the competition in the industry experiencing the same issues and why?

Let's put aside our industry for the moment. Is this problem an industry problem or is it a functional problem? Is it caused by the way, say, sales operates within your organization or even outside of your industry? The functionality process can be the root cause of the problem. There is a tendency to follow along with what everyone else does, but what if that is the problem?

The final type of benchmarking opens still another form of problems. We have determined through experimentation whether our problem at hand is an organizational one. We have determined through experimentation whether the problem is one that has been experienced by our competition. We have determined through experimentation whether the problem is created by the functional area of the process. But what if none of these apply? The fourth type of benchmarking is one that is generic in nature. What I mean is that we can take an unrelated business process or function and still create the same issue. This means that as we develop the solutions, we need to explore what other factors are behind the problem.

Step 5: Compare each suggested solution with the effect on the total process

The third stage of the Design4Growth process is to ask the question: What wows. We need to take each solution and in theory apply it to the process at hand. If we choose solution A, what is the effect of the solution on the process performance? The purpose is to make sure we are actually solving the problem, not adding to the problem.

Remember earlier in this chapter I discussed in regard to brainstorming that the intent was to develop a macro view of the potential solutions. This is the point where we begin to narrow down the solution options. A church marquee recently a posted notice that read "attached to choices are consequences, choose wisely." So it is with our problem solutions. Be sure you have clearly in the front of your mind what the impact of a particular solution has on the total organization. Take each solution and ask yourself: If I do this, what will happen? The goal is to have no surprises that are unplanned for.

Gemba Tool – *Take advantage of a number of available tools to assist with the evaluation Use the five whys tool to ask yourself five times why you chose a particular solution. You can also use the Ishikawa fishbone diagram to graphically show the effect of utilizing a certain solution. You can use a SWOT analysis to determine the strength of each of your solutions.*

Step 6: Make solution adoption

You did it. You have gone through the process and determined based on the evidence what the best available solution is and have made the choice to go with one solution. The action requires you to take the next step. The team now has to determine how you are going to implement the plan. What needs to be done to do so? What resources need to be added or subtracted from the organization? Consider the actions you would take to adopt a pet. Lay out a plan very similar to the pet adoption process.

Gemba Tool – *We can return to the fill-kit we discussed earlier. Make careful note of each requirement to introduce the solution to the organizational culture. Do not try and take shortcuts in developing the fill-kit.*

Step 7: Develop the implementation plan

Congratulations, you have arrived at what you believe is the best solution to your customer's needs at the present time. Your goal was to see the problem, feel the problem, and then create the new normal to correct the problem. By finalizing the selection of the recommended solution(s), you met two of the three goals. The next critical task for the cross-functional team is to determine what is necessary to implement the solution selected. Base your answer on the steps every good journalist uses:

Who – Which individual or individuals are going to monitor the solution's implementation to ensure that we are delivering what we promised? Remember the key is are we meeting the customer's needs?

What – Lay out the exact schedule under which the solution is going to be implemented. Include all the allotted time durations of each step. Include the needed resources.

When – Time is of the essence. The implementation process requires that the cross-functional team establish a clear timeline as to when the implementation process will begin and how long it will take.

Where – The solution is not universal in nature to your organization. The problem confronted a specific issue, at a specific time, and in a specific customer. However, it's also critical that we identify whether the solutions are being delivered to the customer, to your organization, or to your suppliers or another stakeholder.

Step 8: Review the entire tree for errors, defects, or misalignment

Before we go on to Chapter 15 and return to reality, the team should review your future reality tree to ensure that nothing is amiss. Every step of the future model needs to be accurate and evidence based. The implementation plan absolutely needs to be aligned with the organization.

It is equally important to review the selection process in order to be sure you did not accidentally include errors in analyzing the data or included defects that will directly affect the end result.

Step 9: Create the new communication plan

The final step in the creation of your future process view is to determine how you will communicate the solution selected. Use all available means to communicate the selection. Post it on a bulletin board (if you still have one of these), physically hand them a copy of the solution documents, and allow them to touch it in some way. All are designed to explain why you chose that solution and what is in it for them if you adopt that solution.

In the next chapter, we will come back to reality, if you will. You know what the current process is and what it is telling you is wrong with the system that is causing the system constraint. You have in your mind what a "perfect" process looks and feels like. Now we have to learn how to deal with the gap between them.

Notes

1 Liedtka, Jeanne and Tim Ogilvie. *Designing for Growth*. New York, NY: Columbia University Press, 2011. E-Book Pages 1564–2003.
2 Dettmer, H. William. *Goldratt's Theory of Constraints: A Systems Approach to Continuous Process Improvement*. Milwaukee, WI: ASQ Quality Press, 1997. Pages 224–229.
3 Goldratt-Ashlag, Efrat. *Goldratt's Rules of Flow*. Great Barrington, MA: North River Press, 2023. Pages 71–80
4 Deming, W. Edwards. The quote is widely written without citing where it came from.
5 Alberta Motor Association. https://ama.ab.ca/ articles/7-things-every-business-needs
6 Standard of work combination worksheet by Christoph Roser at AllAboutLean. com under the Free CC-BY-SA 4.0 License.
7 https://newcityinsurance.com/what-are-the-four-types-of-benchmarking/
8 Bloom, Daniel. *Employee Empowerment: The Prime Component of Sustainable Change Management*. New York, NY: Productivity Press, 2021. Page 69.

Chapter 15

Determining the Gap Analysis

As we reach the end of Part 4 of this book, it is important that we summarize the journey so far. In Chapter 13 we explored the process of determining the state of the system as we find it at the outset of the problem resolution task. Through the use of various Gemba tools we have been able to ascertain how the process works in our organization. It is also possible that we discovered where the problem is found.

In Chapter 14 we let our imagination run wild, and between the members of a fully functional cross-functional team the next step was taken. During this process the cross-functional team explored all the potential solutions to the problem. Beginning with a macro view, we explored the breadth of solutions and their potential effects on our process. Based on this analysis we have been able to narrow down the list of potential solutions to a micro view of the potential lists.

Here in Chapter 15, we come back down to earth, so to speak. We take the findings from Chapter 13 and Chapter 14 and create a comparison of the two to identify the differences and how we are going to eliminate them. Continuous process improvement experts call this a gap analysis.

15.1 Steps to Complete the Gap Analysis

Step 1: Construction of the gap analysis matrix

We begin by constructing the gap analysis matrix. As shown in Figure 15.1, the matrix consists of five columns.

DOI: 10.4324/9780429029196-19

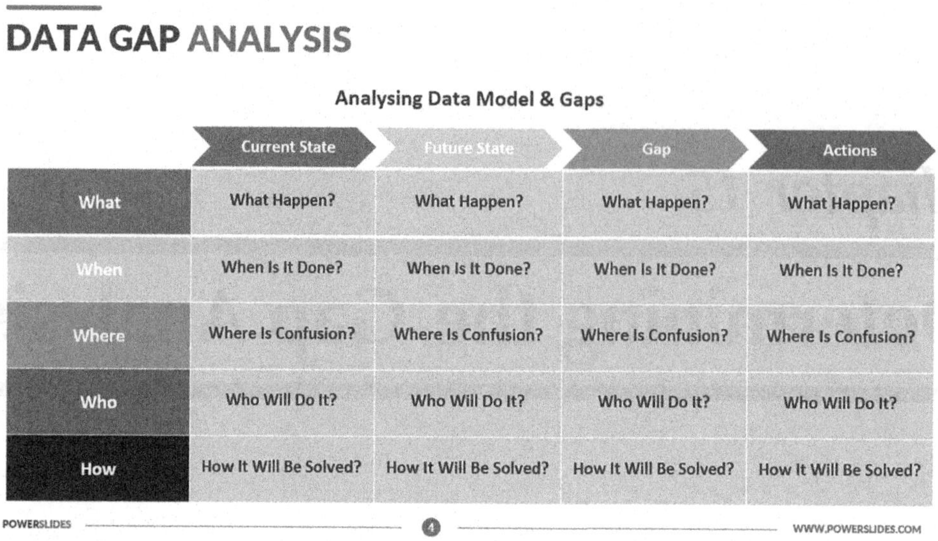

DATA GAP ANALYSIS

Analysing Data Model & Gaps

	Current State	Future State	Gap	Actions
What	What Happen?	What Happen?	What Happen?	What Happen?
When	When Is It Done?	When Is It Done?	When Is It Done?	When Is It Done?
Where	Where Is Confusion?	Where Is Confusion?	Where Is Confusion?	Where Is Confusion?
Who	Who Will Do It?	Who Will Do It?	Who Will Do It?	Who Will Do It?
How	How It Will Be Solved?	How It Will Be Solved?	How It Will Be Solved?	How It Will Be Solved?

POWERSLIDES ————————————————— ④ ——————————————— WWW.POWERSLIDES.COM

Figure 15.1   Gap analysis matrix.[1]

The first column is represented by the necessary factors in the matrix. It defines the scope of the matrix in establishing the necessary factors that assist us in analyzing the gap. So, we begin by determining what we are analyzing. In this case, we are trying to resolve the question of what the system constraint is. The second factor is when does the "what" occur. Is the customer the only one experiencing the problem, or are you having the same issue? Is your supplier having the same issue? Even more extreme, is the problem found only in your customer's customer? By taking the Gemba walk we should have been able to determine the response to this second question. The third factor is looking at the determination in the previous factor and using our Gemba tools and the process maps to determine the location of the system constraint. Is the system constraint appearing at the beginning of the process, in the middle, or in shipment to the next stakeholder? The fourth factor is who is responsible for the issue? Remember if you have a problem with a process, the problem is never the individual. Do not jump to lay blame on the human capital assets. The problem should be rooted in the organizational policies or processes. Do not take this step lightly. Explore in detail what is causing the breakdown and how to resolve it. The final factor delineates how we are going to resolve the issue. What are the proposed solutions to the problem?

The remaining columns look at these factors as they apply to the current state, the future state, the indicated gap, and the recommended solutions to remove the gap.

Step 2: Analyze your current state

Take a moment and go back and review Chapter 13. Step 2 asks us to bring those findings from Chapter 13 and apply them to the matrix.

We begin by asking the question: What is the issue confronting the organization? The problem should be described in detail. From your Gemba walk notes identify what the problem is and place the response in the appropriate space on line 1 in the second column. Proceed to ask yourself the remaining questions from column 1 to complete the analysis of the current state.

Begin with reviewing from the Gemba walk when you find the problem existing. We talk about the TLS Continuum being a continuum because it is an ever-running chain of events running from suppliers, to your organization, to the customer, and to their customers. Be careful to fully explore when the event occurs. For example, do you have a failed new hire every time a certain manager or outside provider gets involved with a candidate? Why?

The third question is: Where is the breakdown in the system? Is it happening at the end of the process, in the middle, or at the beginning of the process? Be exact in your description.

The fourth question is: Who is behind the problem? We are not assigning blame on a human capital asset. Instead, we are concerned about identifying where the problem is occurring within the system flow. This is due to the fact that constraints in one section of the continuum will have a direct response on another section of the continuum.

The fifth and final question is: What is the identified solution that your team arrived at? The team should have been very specific in determining how they planned on resolving the issue confronting the organization. It is also one of the final blocks on the project charter.

Step 3: Identify the ideal future state

Now go back to Chapter 14 and review the results of your exploration of what the ideal process would look like. As we did in step 2 refer back to the questions in step 1 and proceed to fill in the blanks.

The first line of the matrix at this point should be the same as step 2, as it reports the problem at hand. Once again, it should be stated as a complete sentence describing the problem. The remainder of the questions should be the result of the brainstorming sessions described in the previous chapter. The final question as to how you are going to resolve the issue should be the solution statement that the team arrived at during the conclusion of your determination of the process future state.

Step 4: Identify the gaps between the two states

This is the critical stage of the matrix. We know what the process is currently doing. We know what we think the process should look like going forward. Inevitably the two sides do not match.

Bring your cross-functional team back together and provide them with the materials developed in the previous stages of the investigation. Be sure they have all the resources they need and that they begin a brainstorming effort once again.

Once again begin by posting what the issue is. This can be done in one of two fashions. One is to continue to report the problem facing the organization, and the other is to report what the gap is in your matrix. It should be noted that the gaps between the two views will fall under several standard categories.

First, the gap between the two process views may fall into what the organization knows. Is the reason why you are having the problem due to the human capital assets not having the proper training to carry out the process?

Gemba Tool – *The cross-functional team should complete an exercise using the five whys to determine the answer to whether the proper level of knowledge is present in the organization.*

The second area of potential gaps is found in the way communication flows through the organization. Are messages disbursed on a need-to-know basis, or is everyone in the organization included in the message flow? The ideal is to have everyone in on the flow of information regarding the issue at hand.

The third area of potential gaps arises out of the end user. The issue might occur because the customer is using the product or service incorrectly. Additionally, the customer may have changed their needs and forgot to let your organization know they did so. Part of the gap analysis is to determine whether you and the customer are on the same page pertaining to the process.

The fourth gap area is represented by the policies of the organization involved. Remember the primary reason why issues arise is because there is a problem with the organization policies that affect the processes. If the polices hinder human capital asset engagement and empowerment, this can lead to problems. If your human capital assets do not own the processes, an air of complacency is possible. The result is that issues get worse.

The final potential area of gaps between processes deals with how we deliver our products and services. The problems once again can be found in the supplier end, the organizational end, or the customer end.

Gemba Tool – *Taking the view of the current reality tree and the future reality tree, utilize the goal tree tool to determine the gaps. Apply the primary causes of gaps between the two process states, and compare each state in regard to the necessary factors for success for both views of the process. With each solution selected, complete an Ishikawa fishbone diagram to determine the causes of the gap.*

Return to your gap analysis matrix and look at the analysis factors in terms of the gaps. You should have one completed gap analysis matrix for each gap that you identified. Take the gaps, and as we did in the first two steps, determine where to begin. The first order of business is to identify the gap and place that identifier in the section for the "what" of the gap. The statement should be in the form of a full sentence. Once that has been done, proceed down the rest of the steps. Before proceeding, ensure that the gaps are grounded in the process analysis metrics. Any chosen metric should be measurable, meaningful, improvable, and complimentary to the outcome.

Looking at the first criterion, when is the process gap arising based on when the issue is occurring? Utilize the gap criteria and brainstorm the reasoning behind the occurrence. Insert your response in line 2 of step 3. Do the same for each of the criteria.

Now you have done this, move to the question of where. Using the same criteria as we used for the answer to when, evaluate where the problem is coming from. Again, when you have determined the best response to the question, insert your answer in the space on line 3.

We know understand the reasoning behind what, when, and where the issue gaps are coming from; now we need to determine who is going to be responsible for the gap correction. This task should fall on two areas. First is your cross-functional team, and second is that of the stakeholders. Our cross-functional teams accepted the responsibility to correct the issue when the team was formed, and that responsibility is ongoing. The stakeholders have the added task to implement the strategies that the cross-functional team develops.

The final step in the gap analysis matrix is to determine how the organization will resolve the gap. Be specific in your answers. Be inclusive of the entire organization. This brings us to the final step on the matrix form.

Step 5: Create and implement a plan to bridge the gap

Bring the cross-functional team and stakeholders together and look at the matrix as you have completed it to date. The last action that needs to be taken in completing the process is to determine at each stage what actions you are going to take to resolve the gaps between the two views of the process. Be sure to delineate the exact actions at each level of the matrix.

Gemba Tool – *An easy way to accomplish this would be to create a new project charter outlining the steps to erase the gap. It is also important that you complete another fill-kit to ensure that you have identified all the required resources to correct the gap.*

Note

1 Gap analysis matrix. https://powerslides.com/powerpoint-business/business-analysis-templates/data-gap-analysis/

5

ELEVATE THE SYSTEM CONSTRAINTS

If you are reading this, I am appreciative of the fact that you are still with me. This book is designed to take you on a journey, and you have taken the first parts up to this point.

If you read the first four parts of this work, you understand that I established the foundations and the theoretical nature of the TLS Continuum. It is in the conclusion of this work that I bring the journey to the real world if you will.

In Part 1, I introduced you to the TLS Continuum and its associated methodologies. I discussed the need for an open system in taking the journey, one that recognizes the ongoing continuum of the improvement process before, during, and after we deliver the product or service to the customer. We also understand that the continuum continues from our customer to the customer's customer. The final goal of the methodologies is to meet the demands and needs of the customer. I also discussed how the three methodologies come together in the form of the TLS Continuum. It is in this continuum that we continued the journey to this point.

In Part 2, utilizing the methodologies from Part 1, I looked at how to complete the goal statement or problem statement. I defined what a goal is and how to write a powerful goal statement.

In Part 3, I discussed the critical factor of determining the project scope through the eyes of the stakeholders. In order to do this, I demonstrated how to identify the stakeholders and the powerful role of the cross-functional teams in solving our pressing organizational issues. Finally in the conclusion to Part 3, I looked at the individual team members' roles and responsibilities.

DOI: 10.4324/9780429029196-20

In Part 4 I began the process of bringing the problem-solving system down to reality as I looked at how to analyze the process as it is and then let our imaginations run wild as we looked toward what the process could look like. I concluded our examination with the understanding that if we compare the present to the future, there will always be a gap between the two. Therefore, I concluded Part 4 with an understanding of how to conduct a process gap analysis and what is required before we proceed any further.

Now in Part 5 I bring all the information from the previous parts together along with the Gemba tools that have been discussed. The journey now requires us to take two steps. The first step is to review each process within your organization to find those areas where there are unnecessary steps that you are asked to complete. Your goal is to deliver to the customer what they need, when they need it, how they need it, and at what cost they need it at. Don't get me wrong—as we will see, there are steps in the organizational processes that must be there. But many are not. In any case, these extra steps appear as hiccups in our processes. They exist because we have not looked for them. The second step is the actual process of discovering viable solutions to the problem.

My approach in Part 5 is from two perspectives. In Chapter 16, we look at the issue of non-value-added waste within our processes. These are actions that we undertake that don't directly contribute to the customer. The consulting firm Gartner tells us that these non-value-added wastes are activities within a company or supply chain that do not directly contribute to satisfying end consumers' requirements. It is useful to think of these as activities that consumers would not be happy to pay for.[1] We will see that not all non-value-added activities are a bad thing, as some are necessary for the process to take place. As a rule, though, our goal is to eliminate as many of these activities as possible and still meet the needs of the end user. Part of our journey will to be to explore the nine specific kinds of non-value-added activities or wastes found in every organization, no matter the size.

In Chapter 17, we will explore the process of removing the system constraints through the use of a tool called drum-buffer-rope. As mentioned earlier, Goldratt-Ashtag suggests that there is an excellent way to lay this out. Using her control rules of flow, she provides us with a clear explanation on how to achieve this direction for the process. We will look at how to time out the process so we do not waste time in completing the process and delivering the order to the customer.

Note

1 Gartner Glossary. *Non-Value-Adding.* www.gartner.com/en/information-technology/glossary/non-value-adding#:~:text=Non-value-adding%20refers%20to,be%20happy%20to%

Chapter 16

Removing the Non-Value-Added Wastes

Shigeo Shingo told us that "the most dangerous kind of waste is the waste we do not recognize." The business literature tells us someone stated that "removal of waste in our processes makes the organization more sustainable."

Every process in the workplace is destined to have hiccups. Those hiccups are typically due to waste or non-value-added activities of some kind. In many cases, the reason why we don't recognize the wastes in our processes is because we don't look for them even though they are in plain sight. The easiest rule of thumb is that the examples of waste we will see in this chapter are those activities that add nothing to the task of meeting the demands of the customer.

We are confronted with a dilemma. As we begin our exploration of non-value-added waste within our organization, we can do it generically or from a specific function within the organization. My belief is that you as the reader will gain better insight if we do so from a specific function. With that in mind, we will approach our discussions of the non-value-added wastes from the human capital management perspective and the talent acquisition process. Our organizations have been really good at adding steps to the process, whether it is from the suggestion of upper management or someone in the human resource management space who felt that the new step would assist the process. Many of the steps have been added without consultation with their customers, internal or external. I assert that if we

DOI: 10.4324/9780429029196-21

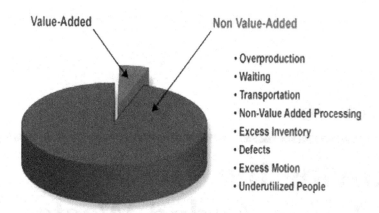

Figure 16.1   Types of MUDA or organizational waste.[1]

were able to look at any organization in existence throughout the global workplace, there would not be a single organization that did not contain waste of some sort. In fact, Jay Arthur of KnowledgeWare suggests that for every $100 of corporate spend in a Three Sigma corporation, $25–$40 of it is wasteful spending.[2]

There is widespread discussion in the continuous process improvement space as to just how many different types of waste exist in our organizations. Toyota looks at seven; others look at eight or nine. For our discussion here, we will look at the latter count and consider nine different types. Whenever you have any form of movement within your process, you are subjected to the potential for non-value-added steps to be introduced. Toyota and the Toyota Production System suggested that every organization actually has present three types of waste. The first is **MUDA**,[3] which refers to those wastes that utilize human activity but do not add value to the customer requirements. MUDA refers to any activity within your organization that to one degree or another requires the involvement of our human capital assets.

The second is **MURI**, which refers to actions by the organization that add unreasonable expectations to it. It means that we have added work requirements that exceed the stakeholder's ability to complete the tasks. It is what occurs when we have out-of-whack takt time or traffic intensity.

The third and final type is **MURA**, which refers to variation and inconsistency within the organization. It is caused when the organization does things one way in a process and when confronted by the same process again does things entirely different.

16.1 Definition of Waste

While it may not meet all our needs, it is simpler to lump all the wastes together under the MUDA umbrella, but we need to clarify a concept before continuing.

By the term waste we are not referring to something that when it is found within the organization that is taken out to the back of the facility and placed in a container for the waste management company to retrieve. We are not talking about wrapping from food or products purchased for the organization.

We are talking about actions by your organization that do not add any value to the earned value proposition. We are talking about those actions that do not directly serve the voice of the customer. This chapter will look at each of the nine non-value-added wastes in more detail with examples of what constitutes waste within your organization.

16.1.1 Non-Value-Added Waste #1: Overproduction

If you are on the manufacturing floor, many organizations operate in a push environment in which the materials needed on the floor are sent through the processes when they come into the building rather when they are needed. Human capital management does the same things with certain transactional actions every day. Part of this is because as human beings we tend to believe that having more is better in the long run even if you have an oversupply on hand. The result is that we get a request for data, and we tend to produce way more than the customer asked for or needs. As I stated earlier, the HR function is just as guilty as the rest of the organization in this regard. As human resource professionals, have you ever experienced these situations:

Example: Excess Job Requisitions

It is normal for your organization at the beginning of each fiscal year to establish a talent management plan in which you determine your manpower needs for the coming year. This plan sets out the number of open jobs, the talent backgrounds needed, and the compensation for each open position. Take a moment and think about your organization and its talent management plan and how many open positions you have. Now consider how many open positions you have. Is the number less than, equal to, or greater than the plan?

If you have more than the plan, then it is a good bet that the conflict with the numbers is the result from a manager who tells HR that they have a critical need for a particular skill set so they ask you to add to the open positions. In reality, they may be real positions, but many managers ask HR to recruit for a particular skill set with no valid opening. The manager gets it into their head that they need to source the marketplace to see what is available just in case someone decides to leave. The collection of talent profiles in case something happens is waste. This tendency makes the talent management effort more difficult. The candidates applying get frustrated with the process and with your organization. The managers get upset because they have this backlog of candidates, and when he or she needs them they are not available. This is equivalent to the push environment on the manufacturing side of the business. This is waste.

If you are like the vast majority of organizations, you are following the compliance requirements and need to enter all the candidates into your applicant tracking system, so you are using valuable time of your HR staff to input them into the system. You are wasting brand capital because more than likely, these candidates are entered and then they never hear from the organization again.

Example: Creation of Too Much Information

If you have ever been at the office water cooler, especially one used by members of management, I am sure you have heard the opinion expressed that they could do HR's job better without the hassles.

As human beings, many of us operate under the premise that more is better. This is equally true when we collect data. There is a simple premise in business, and it says "keep it simple stupid." Here is where the problem is presented. The chief executive officer requests from the head of HR the data on the turnover rate for the past quarter. HR in turn wants to demonstrate to the organization that there is some value in their being a critical part of the organization to dispel the water cooler talk. HR gathers the data requested with a twist. They produce the report for the turnover rate for the past quarter and also present the data for each department and compares it to the previous quarters. The added information is waste. It is not what was requested. Do not get me wrong—the extra data may be valuable, but it is not what the voice of the customer requested (the CEO is the customer).

Example: Creating Excess Reports

In the same venue, some HR departments constantly plan as part of their procedures to routinely create reports on turnover and time to hire and relay the results to the top management of the company. The intention is that HR can justify their existence by demonstrating what it is they do. The problem is that there is no value-added benefit to the extra data reports to the organization, as they do not meet the requirements of any of the function's customers.

A business peer tells the story about when a client of his requested a report, and two years later the report sits on his office bookcase because the client changed their mind about what they need. Albert Einstein said that if you can't explain it simply, you don't understand the problem.

16.1.2 Non-Value-Added Waste #2: Waiting

Put this book down for a minute and think about how you felt the last time you went to the doctor's office. In an earlier chapter I told the story of being referred to a specialist for an 8:30 a.m. appointment, and when I got there the nurse told me that based on the doctor's operating method, I would be lucky if I got into to see him before 3 p.m. in the afternoon.

Our second of the nine MUDA types is that of waiting. Waiting is non-value-added because it is not requested by a customer. It plays no part in fulfilling their demands. We receive many reasons for the delay; however, anytime we delay the delivery of a product or service beyond when the customer requests it, it is waste.

Within human capital management, waste refers to the tendency of both managers and recruiters to put off what they need to do even when there is a deadline in place. Consider these examples:

Example: Undefined Decision-Making

The recruitment process in particular requires a very well-defined outline of how the process is supposed to work. What typically happens is that the hiring manager tells HR that they need the new employee hired and ready to report for work in three weeks. HR sends up the ladder all the sourced, qualified candidates, and the hiring manager sits on them for three weeks or three months. In the meantime, the recruiter has gone out of their way to complete a supposed priority only to find that not everyone is on the same timetable. Consider the fact that for each hour that the critical decision is not reached, it costs the organization a minimum of $42 per hour in salary and benefits for the assigned recruiter.

Example: Fill Times

In congruence with the undefined decision-making, this form of non-value-added waste occurs when the hiring manager tells the HR management that they need this position filled in three weeks due to a critical project. It is now three months, and HR has yet to send up any candidates to the hiring manager. The reverse is also true: HR sends up the qualified candidates and the hiring manager sits on it despite having told HR that it is critical that they find the person immediately. When we experience delays in time to fill, it carries ramifications for the rest of the organization. The holdup of the process creates an obstacle or constraint, which means that the steps that occur later are also held up. The even flow of the hiring process is dictated by certain events happening at precise intervals in the road to new hires, and anything that interferes with that flow creates new obstacles to the rest of the organization.

Example: Unmet Customer Needs

Human capital management is unique in the organization's hierarchy because the vast majority of our customers are internal to the organization. This is compounded by the fact that HR has an image problem. That arises out of HR's persona as existing to hinder the flow of talent through the organization. HR is viewed by many within the organization as a roadblock and your role is the block in the hiring process. Management's solution is to work around you and do the hiring themselves.

Consider what the picture would look like if the rest of the organization could not deliver what was needed when it was needed. In many cases the customer would take their business elsewhere. Internal managers have only two choices: they can deal with HR, which they believe to be lacking the will to get the job done on time, or do it themselves. When this happens, we no longer have a standard of work and thus we have created waste within the organization.

16.1.3 Non-Value-Added Waste #3: Over-Transportation

Whether we are talking about the Hawthorne studies or the original work of Frederick Taylor, every organization at one time or another has been concerned with the flow of materials and resources through the organization. I am sure you have all worked in an organization where it seemed that every time you turned around the organization has rearranged the office. Many times, there is a valid reason for the changes. Other times, it is supposed to be to meet some reported need. The problem is that sometimes the movement creates more problems than believed because the total organization was not reviewed. When this extra movement is present it creates waste.

Example: Unnecessary Movement

Look at how our human capital assets work through the organization. Your goal is to get the right person in the right space at the right time to achieve the goals of the organization. The intent is to have your department be as productive as possible. Consider that one major organization within the mortgage industry hand-carried a mortgage application from beginning of the process to the point of acceptance or rejection. When they were finished, the application had traveled a total of eight miles. Is this a productive use of the human capital's time and efforts?

Example: Office Flow

Consider this scenario: You have a meeting with a hiring manager. How do you get there? I recently sent a fax to a client. After sending it, we called her to see if she got it. The response we got was that she did not know because the fax machine was in the break room on the other side of the floor she was working on. How much time did she lose by walking back and forth to the break room to retrieve a fax? Consider the example of a quality engineer who had her desk moved from the second floor to the first floor, but the organization left all her files on the second floor. Consider how much time came out of her day to walk the entire length of the first floor, get up to the second floor to retrieve the file she needed, and then return the way she came.

Gemba Tool – *One of the tools in the toolbox is a spaghetti diagram. It demonstrates the work floor, and by drawing arrows you can plot out the way things flow through your office. A major mortgage company used the tools to track the flow of a mortgage application and discovered that the application traveled eight miles from beginning to end.*

16.1.4 Non-Value-Added Waste #4: Overprocessing

A member of management attends a conference and hears of a new strategy within the HR arena and comes back to the office and implements it without seeing how it will fit into the total organization. Somewhere back in time a minor crisis occurred, and management decided to avoid it happening again so they implement oversight controls on the HR function. All of these could be great ideas, but if they are not taken in the context of your corporate culture, you are asking for added problems. These added steps were implemented to isolate the organization but do not meet the needs of the customer. Failure to listen to the customer is waste. Consider these examples where good ideas went bad:

Example: Excess Steps in the Hiring Process

Our organizations make changes to our processes on a regular basis every day of the year. Some of these come about due to a member of management hearing about a competitor and the way they handle the hiring process. Or some organizations approach the company with the latest and best tool for creating a seamless process. Often these changes are implemented without consideration as to the effect they might have on the corporate culture. In the course of presenting my seminar, I have come across many examples in this area. A government agency found that in the course of hiring new talent for their agency, the job requisition is reviewed three times—by the same person. Another organization required each and every job requisition be signed off by the HR manager before a recruiter could begin the sourcing process. When I worked in the real estate field handling homes of corporate transfers, if an offer came in outside of a certain price point percentage, the offer was presented to no fewer than seven additional individuals prior to acceptance. Obviously depending on schedules, this would extend the sale of the property.

Let me give you one other blatant example from HR. You have an open job requisition that you have been recruiting for. You had each candidate input their background online; however, when you invite them in for an interview you have them complete a paper application. Why?

It is crucial that in order to eliminate the non-value-added steps that the process be reviewed to see how it fits into the operating culture.

Example: Redundancy

I find in many organizations the tendency to repeat steps in the name of getting it right. The hiring manager informs HR that they need a new IT specialist within three weeks. HR sources and screens the candidates and sends to the hiring manager the candidates that best fit the job requisition requirements, only to have the hiring manager tell HR that they want to see ALL the applications and that he is beginning a search of his own for the right candidate, slowing up the process of selecting and hiring the new talent.

Example: Island Mentality

The key to creating high-performing teams is to look at the organization from the outside looking in. Non-value-added activities get created when we look at our role as an ivory tower. In the current business model, there is no room for organizations confined by thought processes that run through a single part of the organization.

16.1.5 Non-Value-Added Waste #5: Excess Inventory

Wikipedia defines excess inventory as a capital outlay in which there is no return from the customer. We usually consider this from the point of view of a physical item. However, you can also have excess inventory from a service perspective. From the HR perspective, we are talking about the accumulation of too much stuff.

Example: Too Much Work in Progress

Later in this book we will talk more in depth about a concept called traffic intensity. The essence of traffic intensity is that in a given workday, you have only a set amount of time to get done what you need to get done with the resources available.

Traffic time looks at what happens when you add problem requests with the resources unchanged. There is a point at which it is no longer reasonable to expect that you can resolve all the issues on time. It is that point where the number of requests exceeds the available resources that waste occurs.

Example: Physical Pile of Forms

This is the perfect example of the best laid plans. You develop a new form within the HR function, or any department for that matter, so you order what you think is a reasonable supply of the forms. Lo and behold two years later you change the form, and you have two years' worth of the old forms remaining. You have created waste, as the only real choice you have is to dispose of the old forms.

16.1.6 Non-Value-Added Waste #6: Waste of Excess Motion

In virtually every corporate facility in the world, if we utilize the spaghetti diagram tool or the stand in a circle tool created by Taiichi Ohno, we can see that we have designed the workflow not entirely in the most efficient way to move human capital within the system. The added steps required to complete the process based on the workflow creates waste, as we create less productivity. Some real-life examples of this can be found in the following:

Example: Needless Switching of Programs

You are working on a Word document and suddenly the hiring manager calls and wants information out of your applicant tracking system. How many steps do you have to take to switch programs on your screen in front of you? Can you view the other program without losing the first program?

Example: Needless Movement of People

I can walk into an office and see examples of this every day. Consider the organization we mentioned earlier in this chapter, who decided to move an employee's desk from the second floor to the first. No problem—that might be totally reasonable. But the organization left all of the employee's files needed to perform the duties and responsibilities of their position on the second floor. To walk the length of the building, go upstairs, retrieve the required files, and return to their desk ate up 25 minutes of work time. Consider the business analyst who is trying to review an operating procedure and needs some forms to complete the review. To do so means they have to walk to the other end of the floor to the supply room to obtain the forms instead of printing them off their computer.

Example: Needless Movement of Information

Your customer asks for a certain report, and you generate the report only to find out that the manager did not need the report after all. The movement of information that has no importance to the customer is waste.

16.1.7 Non-Value-Added Waste #7: Process Defects

By far, this could be the largest segment of the waste types and includes many easily overlooked examples of non-value-added steps in the HR arena. Many of these defects may be simple slips as part of being human, but they do represent waste in the system. It refers to those opportunities where the wrong information is provided, and the result is a disruption to the customer. A disruption that requires the process be reworked in order to correct the process so the customer requirements can be met. Consider these examples:

Example: Errors in Job Postings

These errors can bring huge ramifications for your organization. You are swamped with trying to market your open positions, and in this rush, you type the wrong compensation, the wrong location, etc. The misinformation can lead to the wrong candidates applying for the position, wrong offers being made to the successful new hire, or the wrong benefit packages being negotiated based on the presented information. The mistake can be totally innocent, or it could cause a major crisis. It doesn't matter because the mistake was made and it is still waste to the organization.

Example: Error in Job Offers

Like the errors in job postings, we are all human and prone to errors. However, this defect example can carry major ramifications for the organization. Consider that you have found the ideal candidate, or your organization and you issue an offer letter with the wrong salary, or the wrong start date. When the candidate reports for work, they are presented with an entirely different set of data regarding the position.

Example: Incomplete Metrics

In order for us to "take our seat at the table," we must be able to produce credible, verifiable data points, as I have discussed earlier. In the rush to create this data from the wide variety of data points that are available to us, it is easy to pull the wrong data points. While the data may be correct, they may not be correct for the question at hand. We need to review all of our metrics to determine that we not only have credible data but valid data for the information requested.

Example: Missed Deadlines

The final example refers to those situations when you are given a precise milestone that you need to meet so that the customer's needs can be met. For whatever reason the deadline comes and goes, and you have failed to deliver on your promises. Think out of HR for a moment. If your organization is routinely late on delivering finished products to your customers, how long do you think they will remain a customer? Same scenario, just within the HR space. Missed deadlines mean we are not meeting the voice of the customer, which results in waste in the system.

16.1.8 Non-Value-Added Waste #8: Underutilized Human Capital Potential

Remember the United Negro College Fund's slogan that "a mind is a terrible thing to waste"? While this was referring to the opportunities for a young African American trying to get through higher education, the same question can be posed to the internal organization and how you treat your human capital. We can waste the contributions of our human capital asset when we place them in a less-than-optimal work environment. Consider the following:

Example: Idle time

Human potential is compromised when you bring on talent and then have nothing for them to do. Take, for example, the hiring manager tells HR that it needs a position filled ASAP but leaves the recruiter twiddling their thumbs when they have to wait for the official requisition to be signed by all parties involved. Consider when your organization has a less-than-ideal onboarding system, and a new employee reports for work and is shown their desk and telephone and asked to get to work.

Example: Understaffing

Linked to the waiting category, when we understaff a function within our organization, we inevitably make the customer wait for delivery. HR has the responsibility to derive the required staffing levels within the organization, and if we use the wrong metrics, we end up with too few headcounts to complete the work at hand.

Example: Overstaffing

Similar to the previous example, if the metrics are wrong, then we could end up hiring too many FTEs, which would leave them sitting at their desks with no work to be delivered.

Example: No Time for Continuing Education

In today's global workplace, knowledge becomes obsolete on a regular basis. This is one of the reasons that most certifications require you to earn continuing education credits. Your human capital is in a constant mode of increasing their career portfolios with added knowledge and skills, but unless you plan for it, there is a scarce amount of time to accomplish this effort. The lack of new kills may hinder the organizational ability to innovate new ideas and products within your industry, leaving your organization less competitive within the marketplace.

16.1.9 Non-Value-Added Waste #9: Material Underutilization

The last of the nine types of wastes is that of material underutilization, and it refers to how we use materials within the organization. Every day we do things within the organizational structure that create waste in the processes and organization such as:

Example: E-Mails

I am as guilty of this as anyone else. We as humans tend to believe that we might lose something. So, an e-mail comes in and we have to rush to make a hard copy of it. I once worked with an individual who posed the question why after he went out and purchased a desktop PC, a laptop, and a PDA he was keeping more paper notes now than he did before. This is an example of the waste that can be created when we underutilize the systems we have in place.

Example: Late Arrivals

Finance tells you it is cheaper to schedule teleconferences than it is to send an employee across the country or the globe for a meeting. So, you schedule a meeting for 8:30 a.m. to last an hour. Many of the teleconference companies will charge you based on that 60-minute block of time. John Smith walks into the meeting 30 minutes late, but you get charged as if he was there for the entire time.

Example: Design Errors

Let's say you are asked to make up a flyer for 500 employees, so you make up the fliers two to the page. What happens to the material surrounding the two fliers? It becomes waste.

In Chapter 17 we now take a trip along the improvement path by traveling through a process. We will look at what elements are required for us to successfully resolve the system constraints so that the process flow is smoother and meets the needs of the stakeholders.

Notes

1 Taken from the Six Sigma Black Belt training materials from St. Petersburg College.
2 Arthur, Jay. *Free, Perfect and Now*. Denver, CO: Knowledge Ware, 2012. Page 18.
3 E-Coach Website. https://www.1000ventures.com/business_guide/lean_7wastes.html

Chapter 17

The Drum-Buffer-Rope

Located approximately 70 miles north of Tampa is the small Citrus County town of Hernando (2020 census population of 8253 residents) and the location of Lake Hernando. Every November the Citrus County Education Foundation hosts the Beast of the Southeast (www.citruseducation.org/dragonboat) dragon boat races, one of the largest dragon boat festivals in the Southeast United States. The dragon boat races draw 5000 participants comprising both corporate and community teams from all across the country. Each team that registers will race a minimum of three times on race day. Corporate and community teams will be racing on a 300-m racecourse, and there will be an optional 2000-m race for those top five fastest big boat teams and the top five fastest small boat teams, as time allows. The boats are similar to canoes. They're large and ornately decorated with carved dragon heads and tails. The crews of about 16 sit in pairs and use paddles to race.

The strategy for winning the race is that you establish the length of the race and then the drummer beats out the pace at which everyone needs to row to maintain the beat. If one rower "slacks" off, it affects the entire effort.

Some of you reading this may be asking yourself what does a dragon boat race have to do with the application of the TLS Continuum? The purpose of Chapter 17 is to look at the TLS Continuum tool called drum-buffer-rope. Here is a clarification. I would suggest that the correlation is as follows. The rope is the length of the continuum and represents the time required to complete the project. The drum is the amount of time required for each step. The buffer is how we plan out the project.

DOI: 10.4324/9780429029196-22

Figure 17.1   Chinese dragon race boats.[1]

Before we can discuss the drum-buffer-rope tool, there is one other issue that we have to tackle first. This issue is how do we plan out our projects and resources? The workplace presents us with two different alternatives: the critical path method (CPM) and the critical chain project management method.

17.1 Critical Path Method

You might not have known what to call it, but we have all used it. Think back to your days as a student, and at the beginning of the semester the instructor presented you with a course syllabus which contained the dates when reports or projects were due. When did you start them? If you are like most students, I would hazard a guess you started to earnestly work on it the night before and probably asked the instructor for more time because you did not finish on time.

This typical action can be explained by a humorous article that appeared in the publication *The Economist* in 1955. In this article Cyril Northcote Parkinson, who was a British naval historian, coined the term Parkinson's Law. In a series of principles, Parkinson suggested that work expands to fill the time allotted for its completion. Like your term paper, in

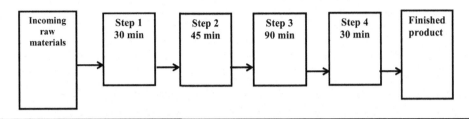

Figure 17.2   Bob Sproull sample timeline.[2]

actuality it may take longer than necessary to complete or even though you had enough time to complete the paper, you made the decision to burn the midnight oil to try and get it done the night before it was due. His fifth law stated that "if there is a way to delay an important decision most people will try and find it especially if we are talking about a governmental operation."[3]

Think about the last time you planned out a project. How did you determine how long it would take? If you are a typical manager, you made a guestimate as how long the task would take and then just so you did not get surprised in the end, you padded the time estimate a tad. But here is the problem. When you do this, you end up extending the time of the project in the long run.

Bob Sproull, in his book *The Focus and Leverage Improvement Book*, provides us with some good examples.

In Figure 17.2, Bob lays out a typical project chain in the CPM model. Each step establishes a set time frame for each task. Taking a walk through the project chain, we can see that the continuum is represented by the two ends of the process—receiving the materials and sending them to the customer. If we look carefully at Figure 17.2, we find that the reason why the process is having problems is that Step 3 is taking longer than the rest of the process chain. The purpose of the TLS Continuum is to eliminate the system constraint.

Gemba Tool – *In order to predict the timing of the various steps, go back and look at Figure 8.1 where we produced a process map more accurately. We can create a process map on steroids. If you remember during your discussion of the Gemba walk, a part of that is with a stopwatch you should time each step of the process. With that evidence-based metric, you can insert the accurate times at each task and the in-between times.*

As I stated earlier, the best guess is that each of these has been padded to cover for unintended consequences. They in essence are protecting themselves regarding the success of the project. The problem comes when you have the consequences.

If the timeline is inaccurate, the direct result is the buildup of inventory and work in the process, which are both waste. In Figure 17.4 and Figure 17.5, we can see the effect of this error after one day and after three days.

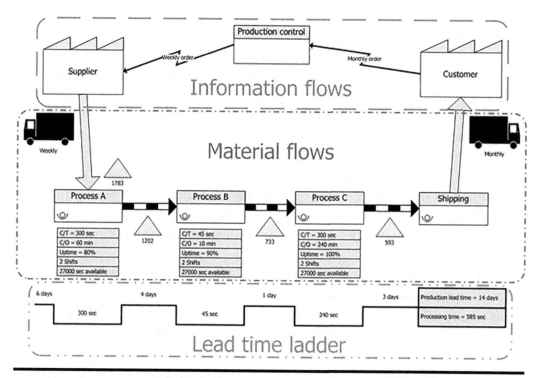

Figure 17.3 Value stream map.[4]

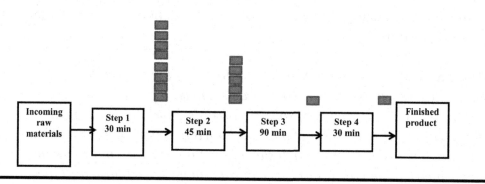

Figure 17.4 Bob Sproull's process timeline after an eight-hour shift.[5]

Stop for a moment. If this were an ideal world, everything potentially could be great. Every organization has a single customer that they handle at a time. Unfortunately, we do not live in an ideal world. To survive, most organizations need multiple clients. This means the front of the process is started multiple times. If they each submit a demand, as shown in Figure 17.4, problems begin to arise. After the first eight hours of work time, the work in progress begins to back up. Why? Because as the process begins to flow, they hit this brick wall called Step 3. If we return to our dragon boat example, if the rowers are not in unison, the boat slows down and can't make its goal in the way of the target time to complete the race. The problem is that without correcting the system constraint, things only get worse. More and more product or service flow enters the process flow, and we begin to accumulate a backup behind Step 3.

As we continue on with the process flow for not hours but days, the problem becomes more intense. If we look at the same process after three days, we can see that the work in process continues to accumulate, making the process even slower. If we were to run either a takt time calculation or a traffic intensity calculator on the process, we would find that we were in an overload state. If we are in an overload state, it means we are not meeting the needs of our customers. This leads to unhappy customers and the likelihood they might take their business elsewhere.

There are several recourses to this state that we can explore. First, we can turn away business, telling the excess business to return when the load

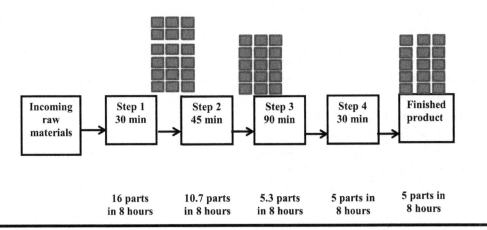

Figure 17.5 Bob Sproull's timeline after three days.[6]

decreases. This would most likely look at turning away customers on a permanent basis. The second option is to analyze the workload and take steps to correct it. We can analyze the workload using the traffic intensity calculator tool as shown in Figure 17.6.

Gemba Tool – *As you review the traffic intensity calculator, it asks us to notate the number of days we have to resolve the goal/problem statement and add in the number of new problems that hit our table (i.e., the buildup of work in process as shown in Figures 17.4. and 17.5). The calculator then asks how many people are available to solve the issue. Once you have entered your data points, the calculator determines the level of problem traffic flowing through the organization. If the result is under 80%, your problem-solving process is working well. If it is over 100%, it is time for you to cry uncle because you are overloaded.*

The traffic intensity calculator can show us the path to correct the overload by either changing the number of requests in the flow or increasing the number of human capital assets working to resolve the problem, which can lead to additional issues (manpower staffing, manpower load assignments, etc.) However, there may be still another route for the organization to pursue.

Traffic Intensity Calculation	
Days to Solve	0
# of New Problems per Day	0
Number of Problem Solvers	1
Traffic Intensity	0.00%
Created by Roger Bohn in the article "Stop Fighting Fires," *Harvest Business Review,* July-August 2000	
When traffic intensity nears 100% — Problems sit in the queue for a while	
When traffic intensity is greater than 100% — More problems than can be solved	
When traffic intensity is <80% — System works well	

Figure 17.6   Traffic intensity calculator.[7]

17.2 Critical Chain Project Management

We need take the method in which we base the time allotment of our processes out of the critical path management that the vast majority of us follow because that is the way we always have done it. This new method is called critical chain project management (CCPM), and it considers a different path to allot time to a project. The remainder of Chapter 17 will look at this dynamic method in depth.

CCPM was created by Dr. Eliyahu Goldratt in his book *The Goal.* It stressed that we were not interested in balancing process capacity. but rather in the concept of balancing the process flow.

At first look that is the problem with the traffic intensity tool because it seems to look at the idea of work overload or work capacity. My contention, as I will discuss further in this chapter, is it is also a guide to workflow.

Goldratt discussed this in his creation of the drum-buffer-rope concept. If we return to Figure 17.4, Step 3 is the segment of the project that takes the longest. In practical terms that means that the process flows up to Step 3 and comes to a grinding halt. It means that the customer's demand will not be met. The drum tells us that the steps before the weakest link should not move any faster than the constraint moves. The rope is the timeline from the front of the process to the point where the system tells us "not so fast." The essence of the problem thus becomes how do we balance the process flow?

If we analyze the chain presented, we know that from the initiation of an order to delivery to the customer takes 204 minutes, or 3 hours and 40 minutes, with an hour and a half taken up by Step 3. In reality Steps 1 and 2 may not take the full allotted time. One solution is any unused time in a step is reallotted to the system constraint. For, example if Step 1 is supposed to take 30 minutes but only takes 15 minutes, then do we wait around for the full 30 minutes to accomplish what we said we would? We saw the dangers of that in Figure 17.5. What we can do instead is increase the time allotted to Step 3 so that instead of 90 minutes it now is allowed to take 105 minutes. This will allow the entire chain to end on the target established by the customer.

This is a good spot to return to our discussion of the traffic intensity calculator we introduced on page 176. The original intent of the traffic intensity concept created by Roger Bohn was to determine at what point do you have too much work for the resources assigned to the problem. In other words, what is your capacity for the work to be completed? I contend that the traffic intensity calculator can also be used to balance the flow through the chain.

If we change the focus on how much work is flowing through the system and determine the takt time focus on the traffic intensity calculations, we can utilize this dynamic tool.

Gemba Tool – *The traffic intensity tool begins with asking you for the number of new requests per day. Change the question to ask how many orders are in the system. Then determine, based on the human capital assets involved, what their capacity to clear up the customer orders is. The final step is to analyze the results and determine how many FTEs are necessary to achieve that goal. Use the goal statement to take the level of increased manpower and determine where the extra bodies can come from. They should come from a realignment of manpower from under-utilized segments of the organization.*

The drum-buffer-rope concept is an easy method to overcome our tendency to procrastinate to the very end to achieve that term paper that was due and we did not get done because we were burning the midnight oil trying to get it done before it was due.

As we reach the conclusion of Part 5 of this work, it is appropriate at this juncture to review where we have been and what is still left to explore. The purpose of this work was to demonstrate how the TLS Continuum and its aligned methodologies can transform your organization. To this point I have worked diligently to show you the path of that transformation, along with tools from the TLS Continuum toolbox to help you on the way. I hope that the path is clearly set out enough so that it can be of benefit.

Before I begin the discussion of how to implement all this material, let me reference where we have come from. In Part 1, I established the nature of the TLS Continuum, including a breakdown of the individual components (the Theory of Constraints, Lean, and Six Sigma). As we moved to Part 2, I established that in order to resolve a problem/system constraint, you need to have a direction in which to travel. I also discussed the criteria for setting that goal in Part 3. The key to successful implementation of the TLS Continuum is a working group of individuals dedicated to finding the solution. We do that through our stakeholders, subject matter experts, and management. At the same time the team is not an island, so we looked at the collection of duties and responsibilities of the team members.

In Part 4, I defined the crux of our continuous process improvement efforts—finding the system constraint. We accomplished that through comparing the nature of the current process, what we think the process is going to look like in the future, and how to resolve the gap between the two.

In Part 5, I addressed one other major stumbling block in the process improvement effort—the presence of the nine kinds of non-value-added waste that exist in every organization. With the process refined to delivering value-added benefit to the customer, it was time to talk about how to plan out our efforts.

This leaves us with one other issue that we need to confront. This issue is when you are left with the impression that while the information so far is of value to you, you know that in many cases management will put up its own system constraint and stop the process in its tracks. In Part 6, and the final section of this work, I will discuss how to take the information so far and implement it in your organization.

Notes

1 www.xinhuanet.com/english/2018-06/18/c_137262816.htm
2 Sproull, Bob. *Focus and Leverage Improvement Book*. New York, NY: Productivity Press, 2019. Page 71.
3 www.creativesafetysupply.com/glossary/parkinsons-law/
4 Value Stream Map. https://tallyfy.com/value-stream-mapping/
5 Sproull, Bob. *Focus and Leverage Improvement Book*. New York, NY: Productivity Press, 2019. Page 72.
6 Sproull, Bob. *Focus and Leverage Improvement Book*. New York, NY: Productivity Press, 2019. Page 72.
7 The traffic intensity calculator was developed by Roger Bohn in an article for *Harvard Business Review* in the July-August 2000 issue titled "Stop Fighting Fires."

6

TLS CONTINUUM IMPLEMENTATION

With the publication of *Achieving HR Excellence through Six Sigma* in 2013, I introduced the concept of the TLS Continuum.[1] At the time, it was my belief that referring to the continuous improvement process as a cycle was delimiting the process because it suggested that every continuous process improvement effort was narrow in its approach. The TLS Continuum is anything but narrow in its view of the world. It is truly grounded in the idea that, as Shirley MacLaine said, "We are not victims of the world we see; we are victims of the way we see the world." For the purposes of this part of the book, I need to change the statement slightly. The change means that we as organizations are not having problems as we see them, but rather we are having problems because of the way our customers see the problems. So, the last part of this book looks at what we must do to see the problems from the eyes of our customers.

In Chapter 18 I introduce the TLS Continuum manifesto. For going on nearly six years I have discussed in various media the workings of the continuum but I have never really talked about the reasoning behind it. In Chapter 18 I will do so.

The remaining question is how you as an organization implement what we discussed in the proceeding pages. Like the Toyota Production System. We do so by walking through the TLS Continuum implementation system. The system consists of three pillars, and over three chapters, I will delve into each of the pillars.

In Chapter 19, we look at the implementation purpose and why we strive to implement the changes in the first place. In Chapter 20, we will look at

DOI: 10.4324/9780429029196-23

Figure Part 6.1   The TLS Continuum.

the continuum from the view of the customer and what they are telling your organization. In Chapter 21, we will look at the dedication to constantly work to improve the organizational processes. In Chapter 22, we will look at the requirement for our efforts to be the walk the walk and talk the talk message of the organization. Finally in Chapter 23 I will present a mock TLS Continuum process reviewing all the steps involved in your organization to introduce the changes discussed heretofore.

Note

1 Bloom, Daniel T. *Achieving HR Excellence through Six Sigma*. 1st Edition. New York, NY: Productivity Press, 2013. Page 143.

Chapter 18

TLS Continuum Manifesto

18.1 Introduction

If you read the works of Jeffrey Liker et al., you will stumble on an ongoing debate. Some will tell you that they don't do Six Sigma, they only do Lean. Others will tell you the opposite. Peter Pande, in his book *The Six Sigma Way*, tells us that when looking at process improvement, there is always a better way.

While Lean, Six Sigma, or even Lean Six Sigma, which tries to resolve the debate by merging the two methodologies, do have their benefits, my belief is that there is still another methodology which is the better way for continuous process improvement to occur, and it is found in the TLS Continuum.

So why now? This work is devoted to showing how the TLS Continuum can assist in the process flow within your organization. Thus, this manifesto. I am fully cognizant that in today's highly charged atmosphere the term manifesto has some detrimental aspects. It seems these days when we hear the term manifesto, it is usually in relationship with a domestic terrorism event. But that is not the frame of reference I am coming from. There is a brighter side to the term. The Dictionary of Oxford Languages defines a manifesto as a written statement declaring publicly the intentions, motives, or views of its issuer. The field of agile management had its agile manifesto.

While over the past several years I have written in my books and on my blogs about the TLS Continuum in broad terms, I have not to date provided a clear picture of the TLS Continuum.

DOI: 10.4324/9780429029196-24

The issuance of this manifesto, then, is to provide a clear picture of my beliefs. In the case of the TLS Continuum, in the past I have provided a superficial overview of what it is, and so this manifesto is a way for me to more precisely state what it is and how it affects your organization.

18.2 Purpose

The TLS Continuum manifesto finds its basis in ten separate but interrelated principles that provide a clear picture of the TLS Continuum and continuous process improvement playing field. Each one builds on the one before it to establish a continuous improvement process that is grounded in the combination of all the methodologies heretofore implemented.

Principle #1: The TLS Continuum is focused on the system constraint

Like Lean, the TLS Continuum is centered on the flow of our processes as we improve our organizations. However, its focus is on what is causing the process to slow down in the first place. The TLS Continuum is focused on following the chain and its elements to discover what is holding up the system. We saw in the previous chapter what happens when the system slows down for any reason, whether it is underestimating the time required or not taking into consideration the effects of Parkinson's Law.

Principle #2: The TLS Continuum is focused on the enduring chain

Many continuous process improvement professionals like to talk in terms of cycles (DMAIC cycle). These cycles are based on a series of actions ending in a supposed final step. Following that, we get to choose whether we move the continuous process effort until we decide we need it again, possibly sometime next year, or start the process over again. I believe that the effort of continuous process improvement is not a closed system such as a cycle, but rather an open-ended one. As a result, my view of any process is a continuous chain of events. If we place our organization at the center of the chain, it runs from us, to our customers, to their customers, and to their customers enduring no end. At the same time, we can go in the other direction. Our chain runs from us, to our suppliers, to their suppliers, and to their suppliers. The goal of the TLS Continuum is to maximize the power of the enduring chain at all times and to create an even process flow in all directions and remove the system constraints wherever they may exist.

Principle #3: The TLS Continuum is oriented toward increasing revenue rather than cost reduction

Goldratt showed us the folly in relying strictly on cost reduction in the improvement of our organization. Rather than being guided by how much overhead we can eliminate in order to increase the bottom line, we should shift our attention to the increased throughput and increase the bottom line by raising the amount of revenue. I further believe that unless our organization is going to file for Chapter 11 bankruptcy, there is never a reason to eliminate headcount. Rather, we reallocate our resources where they are needed within the organization.

This requires us to shift from a primarily cost accounting view of the world in the direction of a throughput accounting view. We end up in the same position with an increased bottom line—we just do it with a different perspective.

Principle #4: The TLS Continuum's highest priority is meeting stakeholder needs

We understand that the value in our organization is found in the entities who purchase our products and services. It is through their voice that we establish our values, goals, strategies, and missions. We also recognize that it is critical that we understand and comprehend the "true north" definition of what a stakeholder is for our organization. Dr. R. Edward Freeman tells us through his stakeholder theory that a stakeholder definition stresses the interconnected relationships between a business, its customers, suppliers, employees, investors, communities, and others who have a stake in the organization.[1] The value is determined based on the degree that we involve the stakeholders as vital members of the cross-functional team apparatus.

We understand that we provide value to the stakeholders when, as Jack Welch said,

> [The] best Six Sigma projects begin not inside the business but outside of it, focused on answering the question—how can we make the customer more competitive? What is critical to the customer's success One thing we have discovered with certainty is that

anything we do that makes the customer more successful inevitably results in financial return to us.[2]

Hence, our purpose is to provide the stakeholders what they need, when they want it, how they want it, and at what financial investment they want it.

Principle #5: The TLS Continuum is focused on empowerment of our human capital assets

Listen to your corporate message and what it is really telling you. Most organizations will tell you that their people are their greatest asset. The TLS Continuum does not believe in platitudes. We recognize that our human capital assets represent a nonowned, leased corporate asset who is seeking a valued and meaningful place to thrive. We believe that everything we do must provide a learning environment that will create the opportunities for our human capital assets to grow and learn new skills for their career portfolios. We do this by supporting and recognizing the new knowledge gained by the human capital assets and put it to use to benefit all parties involved in the process. We recognize today's human capital asset is striving to learn more everyday across a wide spectrum of areas.

When we moved from the industrial age to the knowledge age, or even to the collaboration age, our perspective changed from one of what do we produce to one of what do we dream. It is ideas that bring critical importance to our organizations. It is job number one for our organizations to empower the human capital assets through the provision of tools and resources that enhance that learning effort.

Principle #6: The TLS Continuum is focused on the development of cross-functional teams and centers of excellence

We recognize that, as Deming said, we need to eliminate silos. We further understand the meaning behind what Steve Jobs said: Great things in business are never done by one person, they're done by a team of people. The power of the TLS Continuum is grounded in the belief that we are only as strong as our collaborated efforts that come out of our cross-functional teams. Each team shall have a stated purpose and have at its disposal all the required resources to complete their tasks as the system requires. Further, management understands and accepts the power of our teams come from the cross-functional teams taking ownership of the processes, resulting in empowerment to meet the needs of the customers. By ownership we mean that our cross-functional teams have not only the responsibility but the power to institute changes to our processes if it improves the stakeholder experience. With that knowledge and mandate, the cross-functional team will develop centers of excellence or competencies throughout the organization.

Principle #7: The TLS Continuum is centered on the development of a maximum flow through the system

The TLS Continuum believes our strength comes from controlling the flow of the individual processes and the entirety of the processes within the organization. It is my belief that on a daily basis, our goal is to remove those constraints that are causing the existence of non-value-added aspects of our processes. We find and eliminate organizational inefficiencies when we ask each and every day: How does this [process, procedure, action, initiative, project, policy] help the organization achieve its business objective? If we can't answer this in a clear way that is measurable and where there is evidence that the answer is true, then we must stop doing it. As an organization, our management and our cross-functional teams must get out of the office and go to the Gemba and see what is going on. We must be consistently on the frontline of the action in order to observe where the processes are slowing down and why.

Principle #8: The TLS Continuum provides the proper training to the entire organization and its stakeholders

The TLS Continuum imposes on the organization the need to follow the Toyota Production System model and implement our own version of shu ha ri. In Toyota's shu ha ri, we repeat the forms and discipline ourselves so that our bodies absorb the forms that our forebearers created. We remain faithful to the forms with no deviation. Next, in the stage of ha, once we have disciplined ourselves to acquire the forms and movements, we make innovations. In this process, the forms may be broken and discarded. Finally, in ri, we completely depart from the forms, open the door to creative technique, and arrive in a place where we act in accordance with what our heart/mind desires, unhindered while not overstepping laws.[3]

We need to ensure that everyone involved in the process (meaning along the entire continuum) learns what is necessary to complete the task, takes ownership of the process, and then begins to seek and implement improvements to the system. It means that the only acceptable path to reach this goal is learning by doing. Both the organizational human capital assets and the stakeholders must learn what is necessary to bring out improvements by personally getting their hands dirty in the process.

Principle #9: The TLS Continuum is focused on the development of a process improvement roadmap

I believe that the path to continuous process improvement is accomplished by the development of a logic-based toolkit that can utilize a variety of tools to develop a clear path to process improvement success. Process maps provide us with a grand overview of the process involved, and value stream maps get us down to the micro view of the same process, and the combination of the two helps to establish a standard method for controlling process flow. While not mandating a process, since I recognize that not too many problems will be resolved in the same fashion, I also recognize that there are certain steps that should be common to all continuous process improvement efforts. It is incumbent on the organization to provide a roadmap of these steps, including the use of visual management tools.

Principle #10: Through the use of logical thinking tools, the TLS Continuum will establish a universal problem-solving process

Beginning with the identification of the system constraint, the organization should establish the format for the development of any problem-solving process. We recognize that this process is an evidence-based scientific experiment toward resolving organizational issues. We believe that there exists a proven method for how we go about resolving the issues at hand, starting with the current state and finishing with the future state. From there we understand that we establish the goal/problem statement along with the establishment of the critical success factors, along with the factors necessary to reach those goals. To reach this ultimate state, the use of the Gemba walk becomes a critical essence of any problem-solving effort in any organization, no matter the size or industry that you are involved with.

Notes

1 Definition of a stakeholder derived from R. Richard Freeman's Stakeholder Theory website. http://stakeholdertheory.org/
2 Taken from a presentation to the General Electric shareholders meeting.
3 Definition of shu ha ri. https://www.accenture.com/us-en/blogs/software-engineering-blog/shuhari-agile-adoption-pattern

Chapter 19

Implementation Purpose

In order to understand how the TLS Continuum will transform your organization and the various process flows, we needed to understand the basics of the TLS Continuum process. I accomplished that by taking you, the reader, through the various steps to get to this point. In Part 1, we looked at the various methodologies available to you to reach this point, stressing that the best of all worlds was the combination of the Theory of Constraints, Lean, and Six Sigma. In Part 2, we looked at how to determine what your goal/ problem statement is to resolve an issue. In Part 3, we explored the project boundaries through the eyes of our stakeholders and cross-functional teams. In Part 4, we explored the identification of the system constraints in your processes. In Part 5, we looked at organizational waste and project timelines. Now in Part 6, we reach the culmination of the journey.

The Toyota Production System stresses to us that the only way to see our successful continuous process improvement efforts is to learn by doing. This means that gaining the knowledge is fine, but if it is knowledge for knowledge's sake, we will never achieve our goals. The next step, then, is to look at how we implement all that knowledge into working processes.

In Figure 19.1, I have created what I call the TLS Continuum implementation plan structure. It is a structure constructed around three primary concepts that are absolute requirements for success. It also stresses that the structure's foundation is grounded in two actions on your part. The first is your organization needs to be proactive. The time to take steps to resolve organizational issues is before they become a problem. The second critical foundation is that of being organization-wide. You will only be successful when the improvement process is extended to all aspects of the organization.

DOI: 10.4324/9780429029196-25

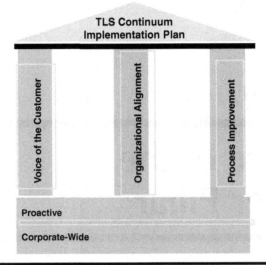

Figure 19.1   TLS implementation plan.

To reach this point, the roof of the structure is supported by three pillars which represent the goals of the organization. The first pillar is that of the voice of the customer. In the TV show *Mission Impossible*, the opening dialogue states "if you accept this assignment." Well, in our continuous process improvement efforts, in order to accept the assignment, we have to listen to those who know the problem best—the customer. We can't make the assumption that they don't know what they are talking about, because they do. The second pillar represents the area of organizational alignment, and the final pillar represents the successful inclusion of these concepts across the entire organization.

Chapters 20, 21, and 22 will take a deep dive into each of the pillars. Finally, in Chapter 23, I will take you on a hypothetical journey through the continuous process improvement journey implementing what you have learned in the earlier material in this book.

Chapter 20

The Voice of the Customer Pillar

I have stressed since the opening pages of this book that one of the crucial factors in any continuous process improvement effort and in the TLS Continuum is the voice of the customer.

Dr. Tony Alessandra, in his book *The Platinum Rule*, tells us that the reason organizations exist is to acquire and maintain customers. Joseph Juran tells us that quality planning consists of developing the products and processes required to meet customers' needs. Jack Welch, in a presentation to GE stockholders, said,

> The best Six Sigma projects begin not inside the business but outside it, focused on answering the question—how can we make the customer more competitive? What is critical to the customer's success? . . . One thing we have discovered with certainty is that anything we do that makes the customer more successful inevitably results in financial return to us.

Kathy Schissler of Destination Breakthrough LLC tells us that in order to play in the game, we need to choose to play, stop and think, seek to appreciate your customers, and learn to execute by hearing the voices of the customer.

The impact of these views can be found in the voice of the customer paradigm, which was inspired by Kathy Shissler's "In the Game" presentation, as shown in Figure 20.2.

DOI: 10.4324/9780429029196-26

20.1 Core Services

To begin our discussion of the voice of the customer, we need to establish a theorem about why our organizations exist. Understand that a theorem is a general set of principles that we believe to be true. In the case of the voice of the customer, that theorem is that my company and your organization each exist to contribute something to the global marketplace. Your organization does not exist in a bubble. Your clients do not exist in a bubble. In

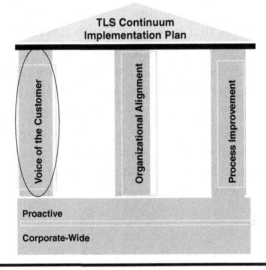

Figure 20.1   Voice of the customer pillar.

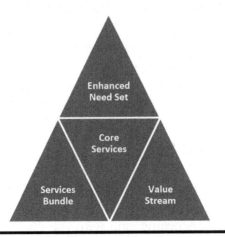

Figure 20.2   Voice of the customer paradigm.

order for us to acquire the customers, we need to have something to contribute to the marketplace. Typically, this is in the form of products and services. Thus, the first part of the voice of the customer paradigm is our core
services.

The voice of the customer tells us what products and services they need.
It makes no difference whether these clients are internal to the organization
or out in the marketplace. They will not be the same with every customer,
so as an organization, we need to strive to have a wide variety of core services. It is also a necessity that you understand that these core services may
be offered on an interim basis. As the client needs change, so must your
core service package. That voice of the customer tells us what it is about
those products or services that brought them to us rather than one of our
competitors. Our message tells the customers that we are able meet their
basic demands: Can they get our products when they need them? Can they
get our products where they need them? Can they get our products how
they want them? Can they get our products at the price they want them at?
Failure to meet these voices means that we will not acquire and maintain
customers. It means that they can look at the marketplace and see who
else may also fit their needs. There is no such thing as customer loyalty in
today's marketplace. The way we maintain them is to listen genuinely to the
voice of the customer.

20.2 Services Bundle

The second component of the paradigm is that of the services bundle. Based
on the customer needs, what other services can you offer that complement
their needs?

The service bundle allows you to answer the voice of the customer more
completely as to what they need at that moment. This allows the voice of
the customer to help you further understand the value to their needs.

20.3 Enhanced Need Set

The third component of the voice of the customer paradigm is that of
enhanced need set. You know how you get a handle on the needs of the
customer—you do it by becoming one with the customer. You do it by
knowing your customer so well that you can anticipate their needs before

they know they need them. Remember in Chapter 19 we talked about being proactive—here it is. Once you do that, you need to be ready with the product and services that answer those needs with the customer contacting your organization.

20.4 Value Stream

The Merriam Webster Dictionary tells us that value is defined as the monetary worth of something, the fair return or equivalent in goods, services, or money for something exchanged or the relative worth, utility, or importance.[1] Everything we do must be value-added in nature. This means that the value flows throughout the supply chain. This true whether we are talking about the lifetime value of a client (LTV = total sales/tenure as a client) to your organization or the benefit the client receives from the product or services they obtain.

It is imperative in our listening to the voice of the customer that we ascertain the value stream of our products and services. It is imperative in our listening to the voice of the customer that we ascertain just what the customer is seeking to gain from our services. The easiest way to determine the value stream is to follow the supply chain and seek to remove the non-value-added parts of the process.

20.4.1 Stakeholder vs. Shareholder?

That may seem like a crazy question, but it is mandatory that we understand the answer to that question. Pick up any organizational annual report. Open any corporate website. I am not a betting man, but I am willing to bet that almost all of them will refer in some fashion to serving their shareholders. They will make some reference about returning the shareholders' financial investment in the organization through a larger bottom line.

But is that really who you need to be servicing? Is that the only people you need to be listening to? This brings us to that other factor that needs to be explored. What is the difference between a shareholder and a stakeholder? The place to begin is to look at the definition of the terms.

Many corporations contend that their purpose is to meet the needs of their shareholders. First let me make it abundantly clear that all shareholders are in themselves stakeholders. The difference is that their involvement in the organization is purely financial in nature. Your shareholders are those individuals and entities who own shares of stock in your organization. They come and go based on how well your organization is making money. The opposite side of the coin is the stakeholders.

The Pearse Trust[2] tells us that shareholders are the owners of the company and provide financial backing in return for potential dividends over the lifetime of the company. A person or corporation can become a shareholder of a company in three ways: by subscribing to the memorandum of the company during incorporation; by investing in return for new shares in the company; and by obtaining shares from an existing shareholder by purchase, by gift, or by will. Their involvement is not the same as stakeholders, as we will see next.

The stakeholders play an active role in your organizational processes. It considers the active role that the various stakeholders play in the organizational processes. This includes both the external and internal stakeholders. It is worth our time to stop for a moment and define what we mean by stakeholders.

In 1984, Dr. Edward Freeman suggested that stakeholders are any entity that is either affected by or can affect the business processes.[3] Dr. Freeman's concept suggests that we take a broader view of the organization and take into consideration how our actions and processes affect the entire global perspective of the outputs of our organizations.

Dr. Edward Freeman created the stakeholder theory which is a view of capitalism that stresses the interconnected relationships between a business and its customers, suppliers, employees, investors, communities, and others who have a stake in the organization. The theory argues that a firm should create value for all stakeholders, not just shareholders.

With the definition of stakeholder in plain view, the next task is to determine who they are in our organization. One of the easiest ways to do that is through the use of a tool out of the TLS Continuum toolbox in the form of a SIPOC.

20.4.2 SIPOC

In order to better understand the voice of the customer, it is imperative that we understand the roles each of the stakeholders play in the process improvement efforts. The easiest way to achieve this is through the usage of a tool called the SIPOC diagram. Created during the push for total quality management, the SIPOC is a tool that can be used to identify the stakeholders and their roles. It is a chain of a series of actions resulting in process

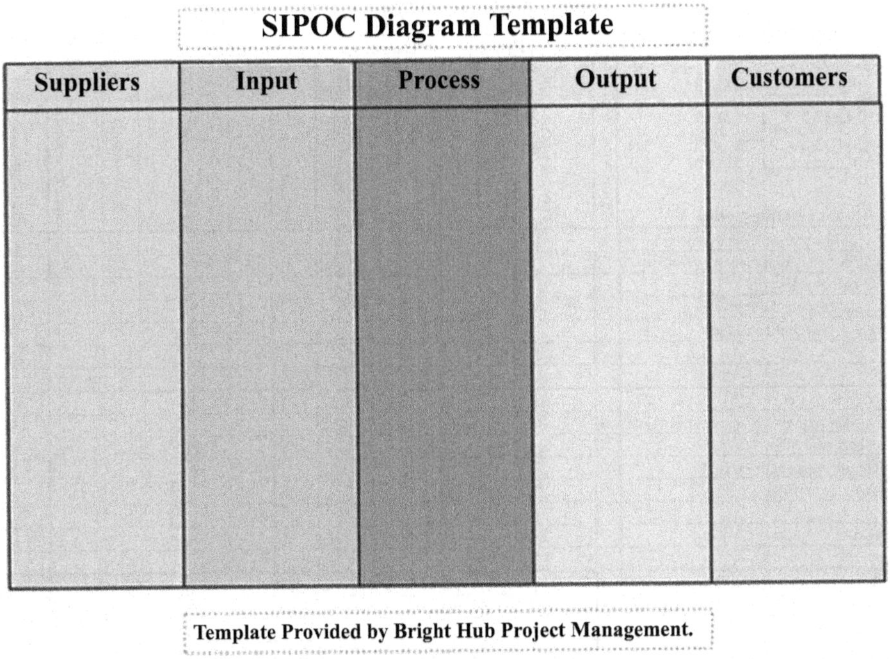

SIPOC Diagram Template				
Suppliers	**Input**	**Process**	**Output**	**Customers**

Template Provided by Bright Hub Project Management.

Figure 20.3   SIPOC diagram.[4]

improvement. In order to begin implementation of process improvement within your organization, you need to gain an eagle's-eye view of the processes and the performance gaps from the customer's point of view. The first step is to conduct a stakeholder analysis of the organizational processes.

The first step in the journey is to look at the organization from above and identify the players in the mix. The SIPOC can be used as a stakeholder analysis process.

Using the form seen in Figure 20.3, the process begins with the construction of a SIPOC analysis of your operation. In order to achieve this analysis, the SIPOC is divided into five segments or columns which lay out the steps in the process chain. While we eventually will be concerned with the critical few, at this macro viewpoint, we want to include all that are applicable to the process in each column.

The S in SIPOC refers to the suppliers to the system. They are represented in the first column of the diagram. They represent those entities that contribute the materials that are used to produce our products and services. These materials are delivered to the organization in the form of an input of some kind.

The I in the SIPOC refers to the inputs. As an organization you seek out suppliers to provide you with something. Whether it is materials or software,

Customer Requirements	Importance (1-5)	Plan			Develop			Market			Deliver			Support		
Voice of the Customer		Internal Consultant	Customer Surveys	X functional Team	Internal controls	Talent Screening	Dept partnerships	Policies	Procedures	Process	Sourcing vehicles	Talent search	Employmnt offers	Pre-Interview steps	Pre-hire steps	Onboarding
Better — Treat me like you want my business	5	1	2	2	4	2	4	4	2	2	2	2	2	1	1	2
Deliver services that meet my needs	5	2	2	2	2	2	2	2	2	2	2	2	2	2	2	2
services that work right	3	2	2	2	1	2	2	2	2	2	2	2	2	2	2	2
Be accurate, right the first time	4	2	2	2	1	2	2	2	2	2	2	2	2	2	2	2
Source us the right candidate	5	2	2	2	1	2	2	2	2	2	2	2	2	2	2	2
Faster — I want it when I want it	3	2	2	2	1	2	2	2	2	2	1	2	2	4	2	2
Make commitments that meet my needs	4	2	2	2	1	2	2	2	2	2	2	2	2	4	2	2
Meet your commitments	4	2	2	2	1	2	2	2	2	2	2	2	2	4	2	2
I want fast, easy access to help	4	2	2	2	1	2	2	2	2	2	2	2	2	2	2	2
Don't waste my time	5	2	2	2	1	2	2	2	2	2	2	2	2	2	2	2
if it breaks, fix it fast	4	2	2	2	1	2	2	2	2	2	2	2	2	2	2	2
Cheaper — Deliver irresistable value	4	2	2	2	1	4	2	2	2	2	2	2	1	2	2	2
Help me save money	5	4	2	2	1	4	2	2	2	2	2	2	1	2	2	2
Help me save time	5	4	2	2	1	4	2	2	2	2	2	2	1	2	2	1
Total Weight		135	120	120	80	148	130	130	120	120	117	120	106	137	115	115

Legend: ● 4 Strong ○ 2 Medium △ 1 Weak · Business Functions

Figure 20.4 Voice of the customer matrix.[5]

you still seek out their inputs. Inputs come from sources both within and outside our organizations. They are designed to furnish or provide us with what is lacking or requisite or to make up, compensate for, or satisfy something missing from a process. These inputs ultimately feed into one or more of your organizational processes.

The P in SIPOC and the third column represents the processes that flow through your organization. The system is designed in such a manner where the suppliers and their inputs feed the processes by which your organization functions. You need to have a precise path of how the supplier's inputs are utilized in making the product or delivering the service to meet the client needs. Your definition of the process involved must be clearly noted.

We do not conduct a process without expecting it to result in some sort of product or service. The O in SIPOC refers to those outputs. When we complete a process, it needs to present something tangible. The process is undertaken because it is creating something. This thing is the output. It is the product or service that you deliver to the end user.

The C in SIPOC refers to the last stage of the stakeholder analysis. It stands for the customer or end user. Understand that both the supplier and the end user are able to complete SIPOCs at their individual ends of the chain, going back in time or forward in time, respectively.

20.4.3 How Do We Measure the Voice of the Customer?

Remember that we can't take steps to implement the TLS Continuum and continuous process improvement without some credible data. So where do we get those data points? The easiest way is to ask our customers directly. The difficulty here is that their immediate answers may not be the full story.

The TLS Continuum toolbox contains a tool called the quality function deployment (QFD) tool as shown in Figure 20.4. The QFD is actually a process within a bigger process and is designed to define more effectively what is the all-important voice of the customer. The end goal is that with the customer telling us what is critical to them, your organization is better able to establish those products and services that meet those voices. It is the completion of the voice of the customer matrix that completes that goal.

Gemba Tool – *To get a better understanding of how the matrix works, turn back to Figure 20.4 and I will take you through the various components and their interactions with the rest of the form. Running horizontally across the top of the matrix is the delineation of the phases of the process in question. In this case, the phases are laid out as plan, develop, market, deliver, and support. Under each of these are three options that might be undertaken for each phase. For instance, in the planning stage the options shown are internal consultant, customer surveys, and the cross-functional team. On the far left is a vertical column denoted by the three goals of the TLS Continuum. We want to strive to get your product or service to the end user better (fewer defects), faster, and cheaper (not in total cost, but in the outlay of funds to produce the end product).*

By entering this data into an Excel-type spreadsheet you construct a grid between the components. The next step is to ask the customer what would characterize a "perfect product for them." Your final task is to then to identify the customer priorities in their response on a scale of 1–5, with 5 being the strongest want. When you enter the priority ranking into the column, the matrix is preloaded with weighting formulas for each square. The last horizontal row is the calculation of the totals of each column, giving you the ability to identify what is most important, thus giving you the critical few items that must be worked on immediately.

When we are considering the impact of the voice of the customer, there are several strategic steps we can take to utilize the voice of the customer in our organizations.

Strategy #1: Walk the walk, talk the talk, and do the Gemba walk

As managers we can sit in our wood-paneled conference room around the big table and brainstorm all day long about the existence of problems, their potential causes, and potential solutions. But all of that is anecdotal in nature. That is based on someone's thoughts, not on evidence-based data. The solution is to get out of the office.

As mentioned earlier, the Gemba walk originated with the work of Taiichi Ohno at Toyota. He liked to take his managers and have them stand in a circle on the factory floor (Gemba) and observe the processes in action. He would stand there for a half an hour at a time and watch. At the end of the period, Ohno would ask them what they saw, and if they could not find process constraints, he would send them back to the floor again. In essence, a Gemba walk means go and see.

In order to gain a clear picture, I suggest that you anticipate three separate Gemba walks. The first walk is to choose any of your products and start at your receiving deck and follow a part, from the back door to the front door. Watch how each part moves through the process and, like Ohno's managers, look for what may be holding up the process. At the same time, you need to recognize you are only looking at a third of the pie.

The second Gemba walk is a backward one. Take that part that you followed through your process and track it back through your supplier's processes. See how that part came in their back door and follow it to your back door.

The final Gemba walk is forward in nature. Follow your product or service from your shipping desk to the back door of the customer and follow the product through their processes. This will provide you with some insight about why the customer is finding issues with your organization.

The goal here is to see the problem, feel the problem, and then take whatever steps are needed to create a new normal, removing the system constraint so that the process flows smoother until you find the next system constraint.

Strategy #2: Focus on the process

I guess it is human nature to discover a problem and assume it is some-body's fault it happened. When your organization has a process system constraint, it is never about a person. It is always something wrong with the system. It is the process flow that does not meet the needs of the customer. It is the process design that throws up system constraints to the timely response to the customer demands.

Part of the TLS Continuum tells us that we need to focus our efforts on five areas within your organization. Eliyahu Goldratt, in his book *The Goal*, tells us that the five focusing steps to resolve the issue are 1) to identify the system constraint, which we did as we walked through the TLS part of the process; 2) decide how to exploit the constraint; 3) subordinate everything to the constraint; 4) if necessary, elevate the constraint; and then 5) return to step 1. The overall goal is to identify the system constraint and take specific actions to remove it. You can't undertake that effort unless you understand the process. You can't undertake that effort unless you walk the walk, talk the talk, and do the Gemba walk.

Strategy #3: Do it now

Human beings are known for their tendency to procrastinate. Just think back to when you were in high school and college as to when you tended to try and work on assignments. At the last minute, right?

Corporate America is also known for its methods of arriving at a decision, usually by committee mentality. The direct result is that any attempt to reach a conclusion regarding process system constraints is to postpone indefinitely. The only way to resolve the tendency is to do it yesterday.

In the real estate field, we have a clause in the contract that states that time is of the essence. The idea behind the clause is that the contract requires prompt and timely fulfillment of the obligations under the contract. Continuous process improvement is no different. Your customer has a prob-lem, and they want it resolved yesterday. It is your responsibility to attend to the problem now rather than yesterday.

Strategy #4: Gain knowledge

I am totally cognizant that much of what I have presented to you so far is almost like trying to speak a foreign language for the first time. But there is a solution. Take whatever steps are necessary to better understand the concepts.

This knowledge comes in two facets. The first is knowledge of your organization. Learn how your processes work by taking the Gemba walk. Talk to the front-line workers and ask them about the processes they work on. Understand why and how you do things in the way you do. Spend some actual time working the floor.

The second facet is gaining a better knowledge about the TLS Continuum tools. Learn how to use them and when. Further utilize the Internet and locate courses, seminars, and webinars that can enhance your knowledge of the TLS Continuum. Go to Amazon or Barnes and Noble and research books on process improvement and order and read some of the available titles. Enhance the knowledge level by seeking out employers who are utilizing the tools and ask permission to spend a day or two working side by side with their organization so you can see how it is done.

Notes

1 Merriam Webster Dictionary. *Definition of Value.* www.merriam-webster.com/dictionary/value
2 Investopedia. https://www.investopedia.com/terms/s/stakeholder.asp
3 Freeman, R. Edward. *The Stakeholder Theory.* http://stakeholdertheory.org/about
4 SIPOC Diagram. https://drive.google.com/file/d/17gj65PNuqIuZ5EeWVn3EAwRNSV5Ao8Xr/view
5 Voice of the customer matrix. Taken from the Black Belt Training Program at St. Petersburg College, Florida.

Chapter 21

The Organizational Alignment Pillar

The second support pillar to the infrastructure is that of organizational alignment. Every organization has its unique set of mission statements, values, and strategies. They are all fed by the unique corporate culture. In order for the implementation plan to be successful, the organization as a whole must buy in to the plan. The organization must walk the walk and talk the talk.

Lawrence Miller of Management Mediations stresses that both the social (people) side of the organization and the technical (process) side of the organization must be aligned. The goal of this alignment, as I mentioned in the previous chapter, is to bring value to the customer. This alignment should include your processes, your human capital assets' skills, your organizational motivation to get things done, and how you go about making decisions on solving problems.

Like the voice of the customer pillar, the organizational alignment pillar consists of a series of strategies that help the process on its journey.

Strategy #5: Change managers to leaders

Dr. Jeffrey Liker,[1] in his discussions regarding the Toyota Production System, has represented a different focus for corporate management. In this new corporate culture, the role of management is not to occupy that corner office. It is not to turn to the organizational assets and say "this is the way we going to do it and there is no room for further discussions." It is time for

DOI: 10.4324/9780429029196-27

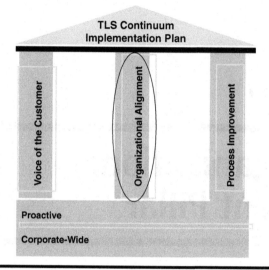

Figure 21.1 Organizational alignment pillar.

management to take on a new focus. We are no longer managers, but rather leaders of the organization.

I, however, emphasize that the new role as the corporate leader is grounded in the idea that your role is to be both a problem solver and a guide toward professional development. Your role now is one of leading the cultural change in such a way as to maximize the results of the changes. It is not to be a slave driver of those who report to you. As I stated earlier, the command-and-control method is basically obsolete in today's workplace. Your Gen X and Gen Y human capital assets will not tolerate it to begin with. I am not suggesting that managers have to become buddies of their co-workers, but they must learn how to work as part of an overall team within the organization. They must understand that in the role of the leader, they are guides to the improvement process and do not control the ultimate outcomes. The outcomes are determined by the team, and the leader has the responsibility to assist the team in the implementation of those outputs.

The other side of the coin is that our leaders must strive to transform their organizations. This effort is critical to the successful process improvement. It does not serve the organization well to just becoming leaders; you must transform the organization.

The vast majority of leaders I have encountered during my consulting practice have been **_transactional leaders_**[2] in nature. By this I mean that their efforts are centered on the concept of what they do. There was a time and place when being a transactional leader was the proper and realistic role for the HR professional. It was a time when the reason we were there was to handle the administrative duties of the professional. Our daily lives were centered around the actions we took every day to resolve employee issues. When the employee had a problem with a paycheck or a policy question, we were to the go-to person for the resolution. This was what we did.

When we transition to ***transformational leadership***, our views of the workplace change. The response becomes one of how what we deliver as human capital management professionals fits within the new corporate cultural perspective.

Today's global workplace calls for a renewed focus on our roles. As the organizational strategic initiatives become more critical in the economic market, the HR profession is likewise required to show how what we deliver to the organization is part of those initiatives. We need to be heavily involved in the development of our human capital assets by providing programs to enhance their skills. If we are, in fact, planning our operations based on perpetuity, we need to develop succession plans for the management roles within the organization to ensure that future leaders are where we need them, when we need them, and how we need them.

Much has been written over the last couple of years regarding the transformational leader, with a good chance that I would be duplicating good work. I suggest you go to Amazon or Barnes and Noble and ask about book titles regarding the term. Barnes and Noble alone brings up 1294 entries of titles on the topic.

Strategy #6: Educate and train

While I recognize that in the scientific method and the DMAIC process, the solution is arrived at by a series of trial-and-error efforts upon the part of the team members, I will also contend that this change in corporate cultural can't be obtained by a sink-or-swim attitude. We need to begin the process by ensuring that the entire organization understands what is in it for them (WITFM) from the earliest point in the implementation process. This will come about from a vigorous range of educational programs, which in the end compare the current state of the organization and the future state of the organization with a concentration on why the change is being made and how it will affect the rank and file of the organization. The education must come from direct communication to all segments of the organization, from the corner office to the person in the maintenance department. The communications must be continuous and with a clear message as to the direction we are headed in. One of the direct results of this effort will be the identification of those individuals who can't or won't make the required alterations in the way they perform their responsibilities. I fully understand that both members of management and the rank and file are going to feel totally out of place in the new environment of a changed corporate culture. This new workspace is not how they were trained to believe organizations functioned. But this is a different worldview than what they grew up in. It is not a bad thing if they feel they need to move on.

On the flip side of the coin, you may have undertaken the steps of the DMAIC process to resolve a particular problem within your organization. You have looked at the problem and measured how the process is operating. You then analyzed the results for credible, verifiable data, which led you to make changes within the process and establish a standard of work going forward. The standard of work will quite likely lay out new methods for performing the process within the organization. You are left with two choices: the first is to undertake a management edict, as I discussed earlier, and let the organization continue to try and reach the goal based on how they have always done things. The other option is to design an employee development program that takes the new process steps and trains the organization on how the new process looks and behaves. The training program must put the employee base in the position of understanding how the cultural changes and process changes in the long run should make their jobs easier.

Strategy #7: Break down silos

Silos are the bane of our existence. As the global marketplace has evolved, everything we do affects the total organization. As a result, when we start acting from the perspective that it is not our job or that it is someone else's responsibility, then we find ourselves falling into the silo mentality. It is when we fully realize that, as John Donne said, "no man is an island," that we understand that the reason we implement cross-functional teams is because what we decide to do will affect HR, finance, purchasing etc. Every part of the organization is directly affected by the continuous process improvement efforts. In turn, we need to act like we understand that. Don't misunderstand me; I am not saying that functional areas do not have a place in the organization—they definitely do. However, the functional areas are part of a much bigger picture, and in order to implement this we need to encompass the improvement suggestions from across the spectrum of the ides from employees.

The purpose of the cross-functional team is to take into consideration all the available views regarding organizational issues. When we allow office politics to enter into the picture, we are asking for trouble. When we allow a function or an individual to claim their department or job as sacred ground, our improvement efforts fail.

Strategy #8: Avoid quotas

Many of our organizations tend to quantify their operations based on some hypothetical numbers. Ask your salespeople whether their sales quota is reasonable. Most will tell you they're not. The establishment of arbitrary goals helps nobody within the organization. Instead, let the TLS Continuum methodology set the targets for improvement. The people within the organization who will recognize if the numerical goals are reasonable are the rank and file, not the managers per se.

Quotas do not set the data points for problem resolution. Credible, verifiable data does. The cross-functional teams will determine what the appropriate outputs are for the organization. These should be the basis for the organizational goals and strategic initiatives.

Strategy #9: Coach

In Strategy #6, I discussed that the role of management was to educate and train the organization on the new processes. Not everything is going to work the way you plan it—that is just human nature. It is imperative that your leaders are there to help the organization through the valleys. The leaders need to assist with the exploration of alternatives that will resolve those issues. The coaching has to be from a beneficial point of view rather than a punishment. Remember a coach does not create solutions; they assist in finding the solutions by the questions they ask and observations they make. It is not the role to be the single source of solutions, nor is it the leader's responsibility to solve the issue by inserting their knowledge or effort.

As a coach, the transformational leader needs to work with the human capital asset to reinforce what is expected and where they are falling short. From there the leader is tasked with helping the employee to understand what needs to be done to get the them up to where they need to be. If there are still problems, then the leader should consider coaching the employee in the direction of a different career.

Notes

1 Beginning with the *Toyota Way* (2003) and followed with seven subsequent titles, Dr. Liker has laid out the benefits of the Toyota Leadership System, which differs greatly from the Western management model. See the Further Reading section for a full list of the titles.
2 Transactional Leadership. http://en.wikipedia.org/wiki/Transactional_leadership

Chapter 22

Continuous Process Improvement Pillar

The final pillar in the TLS Continuum implementation plan is that of continuous process improvement. It is the essence of what we do. Peter Pane tells us that there is always a better way. The TLS Continuum tells us that once we identify the system constraint and eliminate it, another constraint will appear, requiring us to start the process once more. Upon the review of our process improvement efforts, we find that there are some strategies that will enhance the potential for a successful improvement effort.

Strategy #10: Conduct long-term planning to optimize your service offerings

If we return to the Introduction, I mentioned that we were commencing a journey. And while I said that this journey had no end, we still can't begin to embark on the journey without some initial planning. Whether it is your vacation or the road to continuous improvement, we have to begin by planning what we are going to do.

A business colleague told me recently that the goal of every organization is to plan, based on the idea that your organization will survive until the end of time. In this day and age that might seem to be unrealistic, but consider the alternative. Are you going to tell your human assets that "we really appreciate the service you have given to this organization, but we only expect to be around for say three months?" Are you going to tell your customers that "we can meet your voice of the customer demands but for only three months which is when we expect to be out of business"? I have to believe that is most likely not your method of operations.

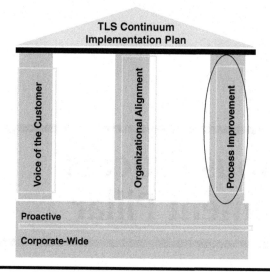

Figure 22.1   Continuous process improvement pillar.

This initial journey planning contains multiple facets in order to achieve successful implementation of TLS Continuum into your organization. These factors include understanding the corporate culture, the value of human capital assets to the organization, decision-making process, and in the long term knowing what you want the organization to look like.

Your corporate culture is what tells the world who and what your organization is. This corporate culture is the basis for everything we do or say in the name of the organization. The problem is that it is easy to define in its original state, but it is highly difficult to change it once you have established it. In order to implement a TLS Continuum process within the organization it is a necessity. It is not a wish. It is not "we will get to it when we can." The change is the very first step in that implementation path.

Corporate culture determines how we approach both our internal assets and our ultimate end users. As we begin the process, we have to start with the understanding that this process will turn the organization on its head. The new corporate culture will have a dramatic effect on the very essence of the organization. The cultural change is required because we are changing the way we approach the organizational policies and procedures. In discussions with Kent Linder of Systems Thinking, this change of culture can have both a positive and a negative impact on the organization. In the field of mergers and acquisitions, it tends to have a negative impact as elements of the corporate culture are lost. It can have a positive effect if the change is created with a participatory direction. By this we mean that the changes are brought about by the involvement of the entire organization.

The new corporate culture reorients the organization from an internal focus to one based in the wants and needs of the customer who purchases our product or services. The change causes us to take a deep review of how we operate and the activities that we undertake which provide no value to the customer. That is not what they pay us to deliver. The impetus therefore falls on your organization. This cultural change also means that we have to look internally to see how our current values, mission, and policies relate to the rest of the internal organization.

In Chapter 2, I defined HR excellence in part by stating that HR excellence means dreaming more than others think practical about the potential for your organization. What is the role of the human capital assets in that definition? It may on the face of it sound like a stupid question, but in reality, it is at the heart of the cultural change we are implementing. Another aspect of this question is how do you categorize your human capital—as an expense or asset? Your answer will dictate how effective the corporate cultural implementation will be.

In my breakout session entitled *Who Am I: The Role of Human Capital Within the Global Workplace*, I challenge the participants to look at the evolution of these assets from the agriculture period to the knowledge period. Many organizations still function from the belief that we are still in the industrial age. In this period our human capital assets were just a number and as such treated as an item on the balance sheet from the expense column. The direct results are that when we enter difficult economic times, the immediate action is to cut headcount. The human capital assets are disregarded in the long run for their contribution to the organization. Management needs to understand in the global marketplace our employees are nonowned, leased corporate assets which are critical to the success of the organization. While the impetus for the change has to come from top management, it also involves the active role of the entire organization. The best ideas for the critical aspects of this change come not from the top, but the front line of the organization. They are the ones who recognize the changes that will make the organization operate more effectively.

Strategy #11: There is always a better way

In the beginning of this work, I asked you to consider that you were taking a journey. It was a journey, but was like none you ever have taken in your lifetime. This journey has a beginning but does not have a set ending. The reason for this is as we implement the TLS process, we uncover system constraints, which impose non-value-added aspects to your processes, which slow down the organization. As the process continues, we remove those system constraints and establish a standard of work going forward. We have removed any variations from the process following the roadblock elimination.

The result of the implementation of the TLS process within your organization is that we have found a new method for uncovering the detriments to a well-oiled organization. We have done very well in meeting the demands of the customer based on the voice of the customer surveys we have conducted. But the irony of the process is that once we remove one of the system constraints, another one shows up. We then need to recommit to the process once again. The rule of thumb is described by Jeffrey Liker in his recent book *Toyota Way to Lean Leadership: Achieving and Sustaining Excellence Through Leadership Development*. I talked earlier in the books about the TLS Continuum toolbox and that our ultimate goal was to create a standard work for each of our processes. The key to discovering problems is that anything that varies from the standard of work is the problem. The result is that as we identify these variations from the standard of work, we find new system constraints that must be removed. Once we identify the new system constraint, we need to start the process over in its entirety, including new project charters. The usual time frame is approximately every three to six months. The proponents of the ultimate improvement cycle will tell you that the discovery of the new system constraint happens almost instantaneously.

It is critical that we realize that nothing is forever. It means that we need to be ready to change on a heartbeat. That means that we are improving the total organization going forward.

Strategy #12: Drive for zero defects

Allow me to step back in time a little bit and reconsider the improvement and control part of the DMAIC process. I discussed earlier that once we had defined the problem, measured the results, and analyzed the credible and verifiable data, we then turned to establishing how we removed the variations in the processes.

Once we established the standard of work for the process at hand, we put in place a system to ensure that there was a smaller opportunity for making errors in the processes. On the factory floor this included such things as a peg board containing the outlines of all the tools. Thus, the factory workers knew that when they were finished with a tool, they placed it back in its appropriate space. The service end of the spectrum, and HR in particular, can introduce steps to eliminate or drastically reduce the chance for mistakes. Through the use of such tools as kanban, we can ensure that the chance for errors within the HR process is diminished. In the kanban environment in those instances where you have a supply of parts, the card is placed in the supply bin to alert you when you need to order new ones so there is never the circumstance where you do not have them when needed.

Remember that I stated earlier that one of our responsibilities is to get the service delivery to the customer when they want it, where they what it, and how they want it. It does not mean going back to the customer and stating that you know they needed delivery by next Tuesday; however, we made some mistakes in following the orders and the service will be ready for delivery a week later. Rework is a variation from the customer's point of view. Our goal is not to do rework. So, to achieve that goal requires us to ensure that we make as few errors as possible.

I discussed earlier the importance of letting the organization continue to try and reach the goal based on how they have always done things. The other option is to design an employee development program that takes the new process steps and trains the organization on how the new process looks and behaves. The training program must put the employee base in the position of understanding how the cultural changes and process changes in the long run should make their jobs easier.

Strategy #13: Drive out fear

How many of you have seen the television commercial in which the speaker is suggesting that the company consider starting a new television channel with VJs, and the response is laughter from the executives in the room with one of them scoffing, what next a weather channel?

Suggestion boxes were started in order to get a handle on the pulse of the employees. It was an attempt to enhance employee engagement through the use of collecting suggestions from employees on how to improve the workplace. The drawback was that the retribution for suggesting something contrary to management policy could and did result in terminations and in some cases even death. This brings us to the problem present in many of our modern organizations.

In an unscientific poll of some of my fellow HR professionals, the consensus was that while all suggestions are considered, many are shot down for a wide range of reasons. Any of this sound familiar? That is not the way we do things around here. We tried that; it did not work. Our shareholders would not like it. That is not the way management wants it done.

The change in corporate culture brought about by the introduction of the Six Sigma methodology relies on the premise that every employee's input has merit. I fully recognize that not everything will work every time and in every place. The difference here is that if we try something and it does not work, the recourse is not to tell the employee, "you made your suggestion, and it didn't work." It is not to tell the employee that you tried something that never should have been done and it will affect your career. We go back to the define stage and review our plans and see if there is another route we can take to tackle the problem.

The implementation of the TLS Continuum into your organization is not difficult. With the use of a few logical thinking–based tools any organization can do so. I would recommend that you order any of Bob Sproull's books, especially his latest *The Secret of Maximum Profitability* in which Bob walks you through the entire process from start to finish.

Chapter 23

TLS Continuum Roadmap

As we reach the conclusion of this journey, you are confronted with two very distinct choices as to where you take this journey next. The first path is "okay, I have read this book to explore the ways the TLS Continuum can contribute to my organization." That is all well and good but it does not bring you or your organization the maximum benefit from the material presented in the previous chapters. Taking the message from Jeffrey Liker, the key to maximizing the benefit of what we have discussed so far is to learn by doing.

Chapter 23 will provide you the roadmap to achieve just that. Let's dive into that process. As a model of the path, consider our friend the process map as shown in Figure 23.1. Consider each block of the map as another way for you to learn by doing.

To do that let's review the stages of the Toyota shu ha ri again. In the Japanese process of shu ha ri, each stage brings about further development of the human capital assets involved and thus the organization. In the shu stage, you are provided the training as to how the process is supposed to flow. We are not guided through the process; rather, we are shown the path and then we are turned loose under supervision to implement the process. If we step out of bounds a mentor is there to guide us back on track. In the ha stage, it is understood that you have the path down pat enough that you can begin to make changes to what you have been taught as you continue the journey. You are still under the guidance of the mentor if you run into problems. Finally, at the ri stage you are ready to reach out on your journey. As long as we stay within the project scope, you are ready to make changes to the system as you find appropriate. With that in mind, let's jump into the heart of the roadmap. You might find it helpful to have an editable version

DOI: 10.4324/9780429029196-29

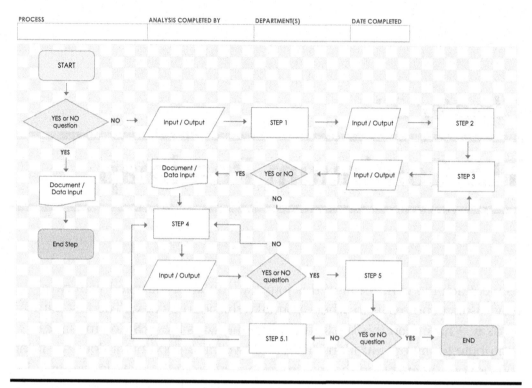

Figure 23.1   Process map.

of a process map in front of you. There is a free downloadable copy of the process map on our Google Drive.[1]

23.1 TLS Continuum Roadmap

Step 1: Gain Knowledge

Slightly different from our discussion earlier, there are three phases to this first step in the TLS Continuum roadmap. The first process is to gain knowledge of how the methodology performs in practice and how it applies to your organization. Reach out to your local institutions of higher learning or many of the online resources and consider earning certification as a Six Sigma at least at the Yellow Belt level. Word of warning: do not expect that you can get the full benefit of belt training over a weekend, especially at the Black Belt level.

The second phase is gain knowledge by taking the Gemba walk through each of your organizational processes and mapping the process via the process map template.[2] You can't be expected to understand fully the processes from the comfort of your corner office.

The final phase is get out of the office. Via the chamber of commerce or other business organizations, locate an organization that is currently conducting continuous process improvement efforts. It does not have to be within your industry. Contact them and arrange the possibility of spending one or two days at their facility observing and where you can become involved in the operational flow of the process.

Step 2: Process Gate

Taken from the book *Goldratt's Rules of Flow*,[3] create a mechanism where, as we do in Plan-Do-Check-Act process, we stop to ensure that we have adequately completed the necessary actions from the previous step before we continue. The gate provides a vehicle to monitor the process and whether we are on track to reach our end goal.

The purpose of this particular gate (you will see more gates as we continue the journey) is to ascertain whether you have a basic understanding of how to deliver the methodology to your organization.

In this gate, the project champion should seek answers to the following questions:

1) Have we achieved a basic understanding of the TLS Continuum and its effects on our organization?
2) Do we understand the improvement process for each of our organizational processes?

Step 3: Build Your Cross-Functional Team

The rule of thumb is that if someone or some function touches the process in any shape or fashion, they need to be a member of the team. The initial question is how is your organization is going to utilize the cross-functional team once they are in place. John Ricketts, formerly of IBM, suggested looking at the cross-functional team as a skill bench.[4] When the skill is needed, the human capital asset is transferred to the project. When the skill is no longer needed, the human capital asset is returned to the skill bench until they need to be redeployed again.

The secondary question is who should make up the team and how many people do you need. As for the size of the team, that is up to your discretion. Some say, as I said earlier in Chapter 11, the team can as few as 5 or as, Safi Bahcall suggests, it can be as large as 150. I fully recognize that a collaborative effort with 150 in one room could be difficult, but if we are operating under the skills bench model, the individual skills can be alternated in and out as needed.

That leaves us with the question of who should be included. Jeffrey Liker, in his book *Toyota Way to Continuous Improvement: Linking Strategy and Operational Excellence to Achieve Superior Performance,*[5] suggests, at a minimum, one selected to serve on a cross-functional team should possess the following criteria:

1) Each team member should demonstrate they have the basic ability to understand how processes and tools work in a continuous process improvement effort.

2) It is critical that each member of the team understands that they are now a human capital management scientist, and as such they should have a natural curiosity and be willing to question everything.

3) Each team member should have the goal to constantly be in the mode to expand their learning and as a result their personal growth.

4) Each member is going to be expected to be involved as an active participant, so they should have a sense of basic presentation skills.

5) Your team is going to be composed of members of management as well as subject matter experts and external customers. Each team member should be able to interact at all levels with the team members on an equal basis.

6) Each team member should be able to undertake active listening with everyone involved.

7) Critically, every member of the team should realize and understand that they are there for an important role within the organization. As a result, they must respect the positions and the roles of each participant. No one is better than anyone else.

8) Lastly but not least, you want team members who can look at a process and see problems and have a passion to assist the organization in getting it right.

Step 4: Complete a Fill-Kit Form for Your Cross-Functional Team

Once again taken from *Goldratt's Rules of Flow*[6] the project champion should compile a project fill-kit. It needs to be completed in fine detail. In its simplest form, it is a list of all the elements you need to utilize in building your team. Be precise. For example, if you were going fishing, besides the rod you would need the fishing line, the lure, the bait, the car to get there, and the container to put your catch in. You will see this action as we go through the process.

Step 5: Process Gate

In this second process gate, the project champion is trying to ascertain whether or not the correct resources are in place. The champion should be asking these questions:

1) Have we defined who all of our stakeholders are?
2) Does the assembled cross-functional team represent all the affected parties to the process?
3) Do each of the cross-functional team members understand their roles and responsibilities?
4) Have we asked the right people to be part of the cross-functional team?
5) Does the team have all the required resources at their disposal?

Step 6: Problem Selection

In step 6, we begin the work of the team in earnest. From the Gemba walk of your organizational processes, identify the current state of the processes. Consider the design thinking question as to what is? Be specific as to what is happening. Consider converting your process map to a value stream map by inserting the time intervals for each step of the process. Don't just guesstimate the timing—clock it with a stopwatch that you should be able to find on your smartphone. This will enable you to locate and define the system constraint.

Part of this effort is the examination of what the current process looks like and then comparing it to what we think the process will look like later. Inevitably this will bring up a gap between the views of the world, and so the final task at this juncture is to build a gap analysis and brainstorm the potential solutions to get us from the current state to the future state.

Step 7: Process Gate

The process champion must once again review the progress in resolving the critical issue by checking what has been accomplished to date. Once again this must be done through a series of questions:

1) Have we explored all the potential cause-and-effect relationships influencing the problem?
2) Have we explored the alternatives in how we conduct the process steps?
3) For each potential problem, have we completed a Ishikawa fishbone diagram?
4) Does the cross-functional team understand how all the process stakeholders affect the process?
5) Does the cross-functional team understand the roles and responsibilities of the stakeholders at each phase of the process?

Step 8: Remove the Constraint

In step 8, the cross-functional team has identified the constraint, acknowledged that it is hurting the organization, and taken steps to remove it. In doing so we realign the process timings so that we can avoid Parkinson's law. The cross-functional team understands the natural tendency to fill all the available time, even if that is with an item that does not meet the needs of the customer. It means that the team, by walking through the process, must be able to spot where there are variations in the process that are holding it up. Consider this example from one of my training programs. A government agency had a hiring policy which called for the job requisition to be reviewed and approved three times. In this case in completing the policy, the job description was reviewed and approved by the *same person.*

Once we find these variations, the team must take steps to remove them. Utilize the drum-buffer-rope tool to even out the flow of the process in order to avoid a backup in the work in progress.

Step 9: Progress Completion Gate

As we reach the final aspects of the TLS Continuum implementation, the project champion must combine two actions. The first is to complete a second fill-kit form. In this version the champion needs to ensure that we have in place everything we need to deliver the final product/service to the end user. Are all the elements in place and ready to go?

The second action is to complete the final process gate. It is time to ensure that we have in place what is needed to bring the process improvements to a close. The champion should be asking the cross-functional team and the organization the following questions:

1) Has the cross-functional team put in place a communication plan to present the new normal to all parties involved?

2) Have the cross-functional team and management put in place a method for monitoring the new process going forward?

3) Have the cross-functional team and management begun the process of seeking out the new system constraint that is before their eyes and begun the process once again?

4) Has the project champion put in place a system to reward the cross-functional team for their successes, failures, and involvement?

The roadmap presented in this chapter is a generic one at heart. It provides a view of the basic steps of an implementation plan. Your organization, your processes, and your customer's needs may call for different steps or different content. Be willing to experiment with the process. Be willing to take yourselves from shu and ha to ri. Now that you have a basic understanding of why we do things the way we do, use your skills and knowledge to find ways to do it even better. And by the way, when you do find a better way, be open to share those improvements with the improvement community at large.

Notes

1 The downloadable free template for the process flow chart can be found on my Google Drive publicly. https://netorg5223078-my.sharepoint.com/:u:/g/personal/dan_dbaiconsulting_com/EZThOA9dbIJNtzbAJwvfNT0BhWwwf7Tbl0a2-dawHjHytw?e=6gWFxV

2 Editable Process Map Template. https://docs.google.com/spreadsheets/d/1FGqc_tjOL4-n1PC3jDvSORHuaxK8uoHN/edit?usp=share_link&ouid=107195385541289798559&rtpof=true&sd=true

3 Goldratt-Ashlag, Efrat. *Goldratt's Rules of Flow.* Great Barrington, MA: North River Press, 2023. Pages 103–108.

4 Ricketts, John. *Reaching the Goal: How Managers Improve a Service Business Using Goldratt's Theory of Constraints.* New York, NY: IBM Press, 2008. Pages 75–76.

5 Liker, Jeffrey K. *The Toyota Way to Continuous Improvement: Linking Strategy and Operational Excellence to Achieve Superior Performance.* New York, NY: McGraw-Hill, 2011. Page 258.

6 Goldratt-Ashlag, Efrat. *Goldratt's Rules of Flow.* Great Barrington, MA: North River Press, 2023. Pages 71–80.

Further Reading

The TLS Continuum

Bloom, Daniel T.

Achieving HR Excellence through Six Sigma. New York, NY: CRC Press, 2014

The Field Guide to Achieving HR Excellence through Six Sigma. New York, NY: CRC Press, 2016

The Excellent Education System: Using Six Sigma to Transform Schools. New York, NY: Routledge, 2018

Reality, Perception, and Your Company's Workplace Culture. New York, NY: Routledge, 2019

Employee Empowerment: The Prime Component of Sustainable Change Management. New York, NY: Routledge, 2021

Achieving HR Excellence through Six Sigma. 2nd Edition. New York, NY: Routledge, 2022

Sproull, Bob et al.

The Ultimate Improvement Cycle: Maximizing Profits through the Integration of Lean, Six Sigma and the Theory of Constraints. New York, NY: CRC Press, 2009

Epiphanized: Integrating Lean and Six Sigma. Great Barrington, MA: North River Press, 2012

Epiphanized: Integrating Lean and Six Sigma. 2nd Edition. Great Barrington, MA: North River Press, 2015

Focus and Leverage. New York, NY: CRC Press, 2016

The Problem-Solving, Problem-Prevention, and Decision-Making Guide. New York, NY: Routledge Press, 2018

The Focus and Leverage Improvement Book. New York, NY: Routledge Press, 2019

Theory of Constraints Lean and Six Sigma Improvement Methodology. New York, NY: Routledge Press, 2019

The Secret to Maximizing Profitability. New York, NY: Routledge Press, 2020

The New Beginning. New York, NY: Routledge, 2021

Bibliography

Part 1: The Foundation

Junewick, Mary A. *LeanSpeak*. New York, NY: Productivity Press, 2002

Miller, Lawrence. *Whole System Architecture: A Model for Building the Lean Organization*. New York, NY: Columbia University Press, 2011

Liedtka, Jeanne and Tim Ogilvie. *Designing for Growth: A Design Thinking Tool Kit for Managers*. New York, NY: Columbia Business School, 2011

Part 2: Continuous Process Improvement Journey

Alessandra, Tony. *The Platinum Rule*. New York, NY: Warner Books, 1996

Bloom, Daniel T. *Achieving HR Excellence through Six Sigma*. 2nd Edition. New York, NY: Routledge, 2022

Fishbach, Ayelet. *Get It Done: Surprising Lessons from the Science of Motivation*. New York, NY: Little, Brown Spark, 2022

George, Michael. *The Lean Six-Sigma Pocket Toolbox*. New York, NY: McGraw-Hill, 2005

Goldratt, Eliyahu. *The Goal*. 2nd Revised Edition. Great Barrington, MA: North River Press, 1992

Handy, Charles. *The Age of Unreason*. Boston, MA: Harvard Business School Press, 1989

Harry, Mikel. *Six Sigma: The Breakthrough Management Strategy Revolutionizing the World's Top Corporations*. New York, NY: Currency Random House, 2005

Miller, Ken. *We Don't Make Widgets*. Washington, DC: Governing Books, 2010

Miller, Lawrence. *Lean Culture: The Leader's Guide*. Annapolis, MD: Lawrence Miller, 2011

Miller, Lawrence. *Whole System Architecture: A Model for Building the Lean Organization*. New York, NY: Columbia University Press, 2013

Sproull, Bob. *The Ultimate Improvement Cycle*. New York, NY: CRC Press, 2009

Sproull, Bob. *Epiphanized*. 2nd Edition. New York, NY: CRC Press, 2015

Womack, James et al. *Lean Thinking: Banish Waste and Create Wealth in Your Organization*. New York, NY: Free Press, 2003

Part 3: Defining Boundaries

Bahcall, Safi. *Loonshots*. New York, NY: St Martin's Press, 2019
Bloom, Daniel T. *Achieving HR Excellence Through Six Sigma . . .* New York, NY: Routledge, 2014
Dettmer, H. William. *The Logical Thinking Process: A Systems Approach to Complex Problem Solving*. Milwaukee, WI: ASQ Press, 2007
Hayden, Michael. *The Assault on Intelligence*. New York, NY: Penguin Press, 2018
Johnson, Steven. *Farsighted*. New York, NY: Riverhead Books, 2018
Kahneman, Daniel. *Thinking, Fast and Slow*. New York, NY: Farrar, Straus, and Giroux, 2011
Ricketts, John. *Reaching the Goal: How Managers Improve a Services Business Using Goldratt's Theory of Constraints*. New York, NY: IBM Press, 2008
Sproull, Bob. *The Focus and Leverage Improvement Book*. New York, NY: Routledge, 2019

Part 4: Identification of System Constraints

Alessandra, Tony. *Non-Manipulative Selling*. New York, NY: Prentice Hall, 1987
Bloom, Daniel. *Employee Empowerment: The Prime Component of Sustainable Change Management*. New York, NY: Productivity Press, 2021
Goldratt-Ashlag, Efrat. *Goldratt's Rules of Flow*. Great Barrington, MA: North River Press, 2023
Harry, Mikel. *Six Sigma: The Breakthrough Management Strategy Revolutionizing the World's Top Corporations*. New York, NY: Currency Random House, 2005
Imai, Masaaki. *Gemba Kaizen: A Commonsense Approach to a Continuous Improvement Strategy*. 2nd Edition. New York, NY: McGraw Hill, 2012

Part 5: Elevating the Constraints

Arthur, Jay. *Free, Perfect and Now*. Denver, CO: Know Ware International, 2012
Goldratt, Eliyahu. *The Goal*. 2nd Revised Edition. Great Barrington, MA: North River Press, 1992
Sproull, Bob. *The Focus and Leverage Improvement Book*. New York, NY: Routledge, 2019

Part 6: Organizational Implementation of the TLS Continuum

Bloom, Daniel T. *Achieving HR Excellence through Six Sigma*. New York, NY: Routledge, 2014

Goldratt, Eliyahu. *The Goal*. 2nd Revised Edition. Great Barrington, MA: North River Press, 1992

Liker, Jeffrey. *The Toyota Way to Continuous Process Improvement: Linking Strategy and Operational Excellence to Achieve Superior Performance*. New York, NY: McGraw-Hill, 2011

Index

Note: Page numbers in *italics* indicate figures, and references following "n" refer notes.

Printed in the United States
by Baker & Taylor Publisher Services